IMAGES
of America

RIM OF THE WORLD DRIVE

I0800467

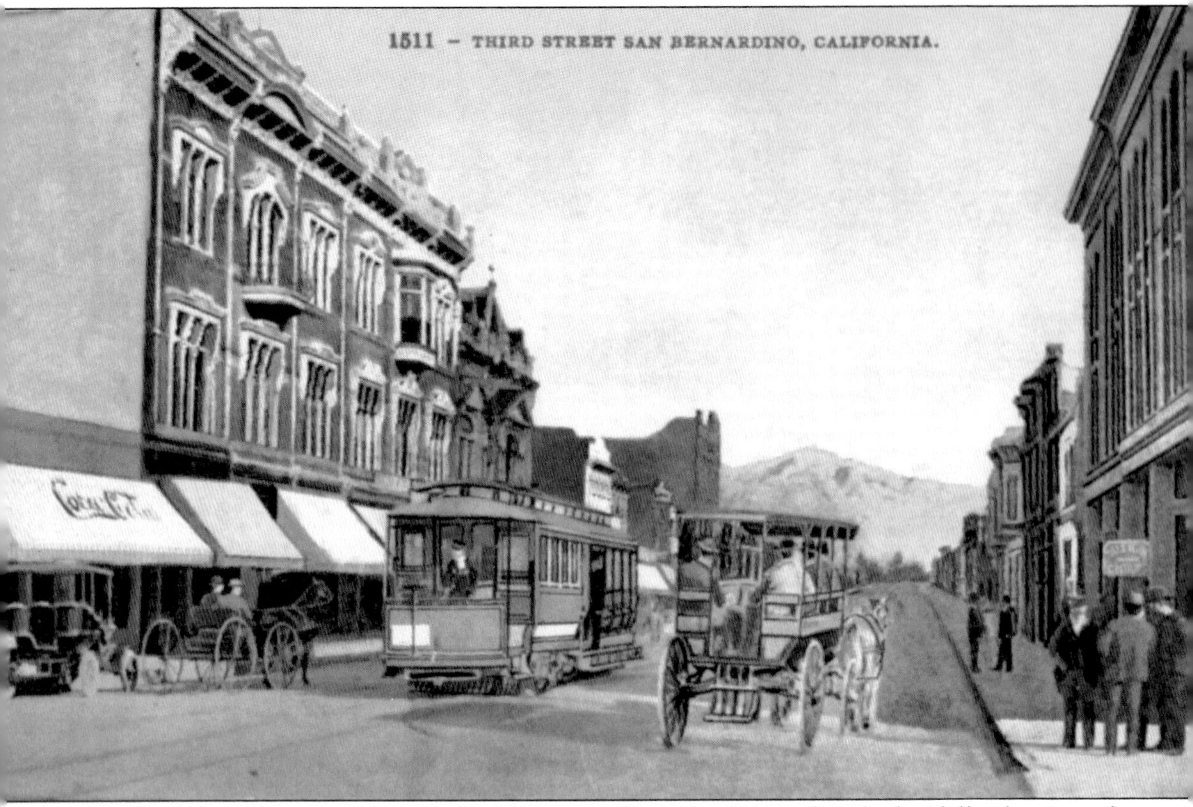

WHY HEAD FOR THE MOUNTAINS? This view from San Bernardino looks idyllic, but in reality it was unbearably hot pre-air-conditioning in the valley for much of the year. From prehistoric times to the present, man has sought to reach the cool pine-scented mountains by trails, roads, and highways. This book tells the story of the best-known road to the mountains, the Rim of the World Drive. (EHM.)

ON THE COVER: Taken *c.* 1912, this studio-quality photograph depicts two White trucks converted to Bear Valley Transportation Company stages. Clearly, this is an elite group of men and women on a thoroughly modern tour through an unspoiled wilderness. (Photograph courtesy of Russell L. Keller.)

IMAGES
of America

RIM OF THE WORLD DRIVE

Roger G. Hatheway

ARCADIA
PUBLISHING

ISBN 978-0-7385-4770-1

Published by Arcadia Publishing
Charleston, South Carolina

Printed in the United States of America

Library of Congress Catalog Card Number: 2007923087

For all general information contact Arcadia Publishing at:
Telephone 843-853-2070
Fax 843-853-0044
E-mail sales@arcadiapublishing.com
For customer service and orders:
Toll-Free 1-888-313-2665

Visit us on the Internet at www.arcadiapublishing.com

Contents

Acknowledgments 6

Introduction 7

1. Prehistoric Trails to Wagon Roads 9
2. Automobiles Conquer the Heights 27
3. Historical Tour around the Rim 59
4. Then and Now on the Rim 93
5. Up Here on Top of the World 111

Select Bibliography 127

Acknowledgments

I thank my friend Russ Keller, as nearly all of the images used herein are from his massive collection of ephemera dedicated to the preservation of San Bernardino Mountain history. Carol Keller gets a vote of thanks for her perusal of thousands of postcards to find those mentioning mountain roads. Several years ago, I made the Rim of the World Historical Society a promise to write a book on the Rim of the World Drive, and although it took longer than anticipated, the delay has borne unexpected fruit with Russ Keller's recent acquisition of a remarkable collection of photographs. The John Andreson Jr. photographs present a stunning portrait of family life in the early years of the 20th century, and they record a pivotal period in history by documenting the critical transition from horse-drawn vehicles to the modern age of the automobile.

One newspaper, the *Sun*, has allowed me to reprint and quote portions of historic newspaper articles, whereby the reader is instantaneously transported back in time, bringing history alive in a very personal manner.

My interest in history grew from seeds planted in childhood. My father was an academic historian, and I tended to regard my grandparents and their Colonial farmhouse in Connecticut as a form of living history. I thank these three individuals: Russell (grandfather), Ruth (grandmother), and Glover Hatheway (father) for much of what my sense of history is all about. My two children, Samantha and Benjamin, and I have a special connection to the Rim of the World Drive, for I sat in the passenger seat of the family car while they learned how to drive on the "Rim." Finally, as in all matters, I especially thank my wife, Lora, for her editorial skills, advice, historical sensibility, and never ending patience.

INTRODUCTION

Today the historic Rim of the World Drive threads its way through the most urbanized mountains in America. Assembled from many component parts and continuously realigned and rebuilt from 1915 to the late-1960s, it is the very "backbone" of the San Bernardino Mountains, connecting all towns, resorts, and recreation areas. Portions of the Rim of the World Drive have been determined to qualify as eligible for the National Register of Historic Places, and preservation of this significant historical resource is an idea promoted by local, county, and state organizations.

This book details the history and development of this utterly unique transportation alignment from prehistoric trail to state highway. Each chapter tells a stand-alone story. Chapter one documents mountain travel from Native American trails to horse-drawn stages and wagons. Chapter two describes the introduction of the automobile in the early years of the 20th century and the development of various segments of the Rim of the World Drive from narrow rock-strewn track to four-lane highway. Chapter three is a "historical" tour across time on the Rim of the World Drive, targeting specific landmarks and communities along the way. Chapter four compares a few select "then and now" images, recording locations that are either virtually unchanged now or were radically different then, with each telling an interesting story about the history of the Rim of the World Drive. Chapter five brings to life a powerful sense of what the Rim of the World Drive meant to those who were actually there, quoting from interesting handwritten text on the back of postcards dating from 1908 to the 1960s.

The Rim of the World Drive is a thoroughly American story. Dedicated on July 18, 1915, and first officially known as the San Bernardino Mountain Crest Highway, the road was soon touted as being the longest and highest mountain highway in America. Some even called it world famous. How did it get the name Rim of the World Drive? Dr. John N. Baylis, owner of the now historic Pinecrest Resort, is generally credited with first using this moniker, but newspapermen may well be the real culprits. The official name, San Bernardino Mountain Crest Highway, appears to have been too long for the space allotted to a column headline, and long before the road was dedicated, reporters were using the name Rim-of-the-World Drive.

A 1915 *Touring Topics* article places the importance of the road in contemporary historical perspective, noting "there is one long distance motor highway in this part of the state that attracts the automobile traveler beyond all rival roads and that is the same 'Rim of the World' drive through the heart of the San Bernardino Mountains." The salient point here is that the Rim of the World Drive was built as an automobile alignment first and foremost. The Rim of the World Drive permanently brought the rustic and comparatively backward mountains into the 20th century, ushering in a new and modern generation of automobile tourists, campers, and holiday seekers. Advertised as a true wonder of engineering and beauty, where rugged canyons and mountain peaks were conquered and nature's wonder was miraculously revealed at every turn, for a period in time, the Rim of the World Drive truly defined the very identity of the San Bernardino Mountains.

Roads are curious things. In fact, not much would get done anywhere on earth without them, and yet most are driven without thought or care. Yet similar to countries, people, or famous homes and estates, they develop fascinating histories or biographies of their own. Herein is the pictorial biography of one of the best-known mountain roads in California—the Rim of the World Drive.

Photo Credits

Virtually all of the images contained herein are from Russell L. Keller's private collection of San Bernardino Mountain ephemera. Some images are from family scrapbooks and private collections. These have been credited where a provenance is known. Other images were originally produced by a wide variety of sources including clubs, book publishers, businesses (hotels, restaurants, camps, gas stations, and so forth), land developers, postcard companies, real estate offices, and tourist information bureaus. Those published by companies or business enterprises with registered trademarks or with indications of copyright are credited by specific identification letter codes at the end of each caption. The following "publishers" are referenced: Andreson family collection (AFC); Automobile Club of Southern California (ACSC); Arrowhead Lake Company (ALC); Bledsoe Photo Company, Los Angeles, California (BP); B. R. Montgomery, Riverside, California (BRM); Barry's Studio (BS); the Bear Valley Photographer (BVP); Colorpicture, Boston, Massachusetts (CB); Curteich-Chicago "C. T. Art-Colortone" (CC); Columbia Wholesale Supply, Hollywood, California (CW); Desert Souvenir Supply, Boulder City, Nevada (DS); Edw. H. Mitchell, San Francisco, California (EHM); Ferris H. Scott, Santa Ana, California (FHS); Frashers, Inc., Pomona, California (FI); General Land Office (GLO); Johnson Photo (JF); *Los Angeles Times* (LAT); Luring Development Company, Los Angeles, California (LD); Lewis Murray (LM); Mountain Auto Line, San Bernardino, California (MAL); Motor Transit Company, Los Angeles, California (MTC); Neuner Corporation, Los Angeles, California (NC); Newman Post Card Company, Los Angeles, California (NPC); Putnam Studios, Los Angeles, California (PS); Pacific Stereoptican Company, Los Angeles, California (PSC); Putnam and Valentine Photo, Los Angeles, California (PV); Rosecraft, Crestline-Inyokern, California (R); *Rim O'World Guide*, Santa Ana, California (ROW); Royal Pictures, Colton, California (RP); Rim O' the World League, Big Bear, California (RWL); San Bernardino Chamber of Commerce (SBC); Steele Photo Service, San Bernardino, California (SPS); Santa's Village, Skyforest, California (SV); the Cadmus Press, Los Angeles, California (TCP); the *Sun*, San Bernardino, California (TS); Wright M. Pierce Photos (WMP); Western Publishing and Novelty Company, Los Angeles, California (WPN); and Western Resort Publications, Santa Ana, California (WRP).

One

Prehistoric Trails to Wagon Roads

This chapter tells the story of a bygone age where time simply moved more slowly than today. In this distant and rustic time past, the basic Rim of the World Drive alignment slowly evolved as various trails, wagon roads, and toll roads that would be assembled in 1915 as an automobile road.

For thousands of years, abundant natural resources attracted prehistoric Native Americans to the San Bernardino Mountains on a seasonal basis, and their well-worn trails literally covered the mountains. In 1776, Father Garces, a Franciscan missionary, walked these trails as the first known nonnative mountain traveler, but it was not until 1845 that mountain trails were first explored with official accounts reported.

Early mountain roadways developed separately on the east leading to Big Bear Valley and on the west to Little Bear Valley. On the east end, the initial route of choice led up Santa Ana Canyon, a steep and treacherous trail used sporadically from the mid-1850s until the first wagon road was built to Bear Valley in 1888. On the west end, the Mormon Road was built by settlers from San Bernardino to the crest in 1852. Beginning in the 1870s, lumber toll roads were built leading up Devil and Daley Canyons, and in 1892, the Arrowhead Toll Road was completed as the first general-use west-end roadway.

Also in 1892, the Bear Valley Wagon Road Company Toll Road was completed connecting the east to the west by way of Green Valley and Fawnskin, and in 1899, the Bear Valley and Redlands Toll Road leading up the Santa Ana River and Clark's Grade was built. Beginning in 1905, the County of San Bernardino began buying toll and lumber road alignments to create free county public highways. In 1913, the last link in what would become the Rim of the World Drive was purchased. Horse-drawn stages still ran as late as 1912, but by 1910, it was abundantly clear to most that the age of mules, buggies, and wagons was at a close.

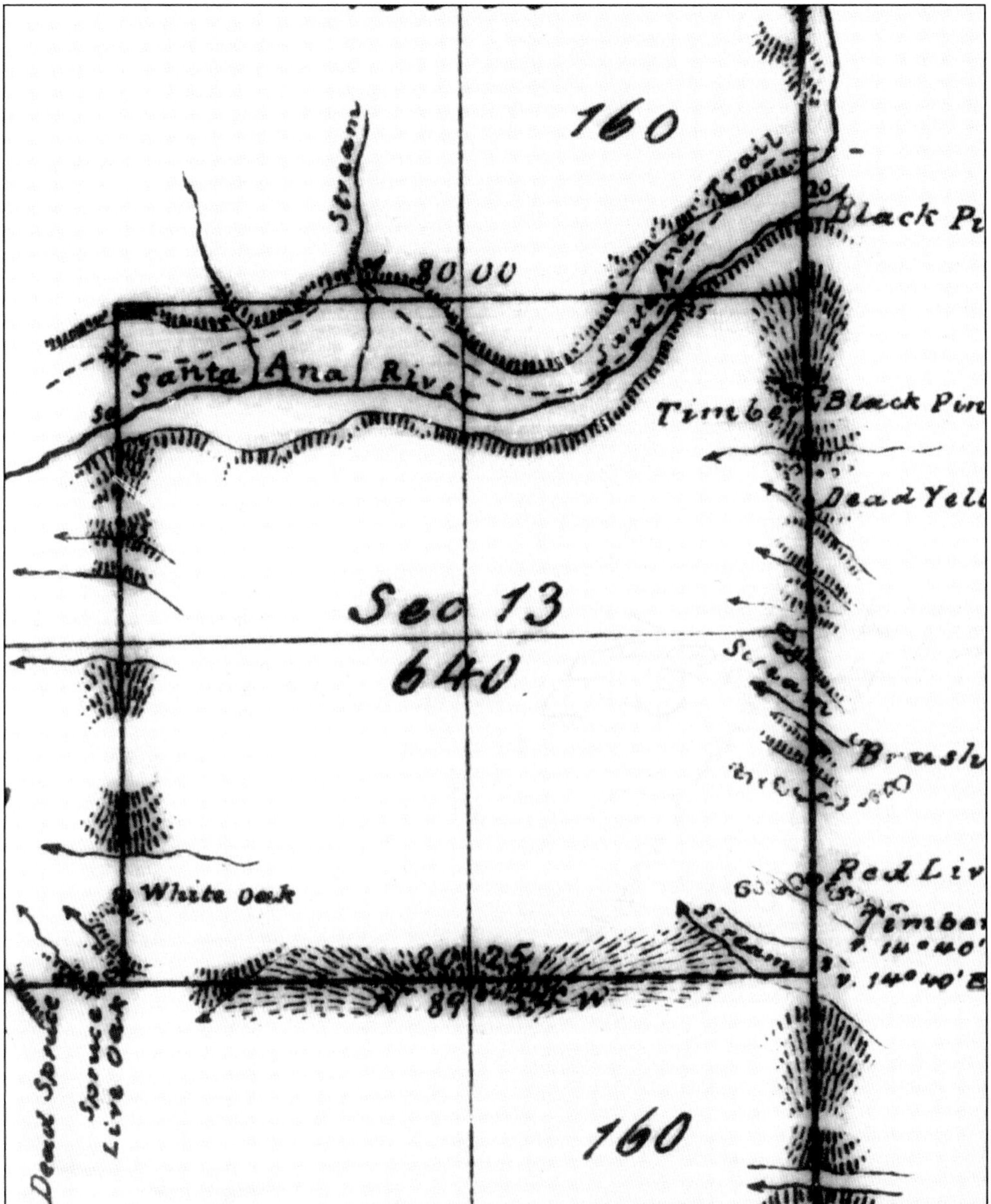

The Santa Ana Trail. Native Americans traveled to the mountains on a seasonal basis by a well-established system of trails following rivers and streambeds, leading up and down steep canyons, and connecting to ridgelines. Prior to 1845, the trail up Santa Ana Canyon was used almost exclusively by Native Americans, with occasional incursions by fur traders and trappers. In 1845, this situation would change almost overnight when Benjamin Wilson made his way to Bear Valley. This historic 1877 General Land Office survey map depicts the Santa Ana Trail as it follows the bed of the Santa Ana River north to Bear Valley. At this time, the route was used only sporadically, but it is the same trail used for thousands of years by Native Americans and by miners in the 1860s seeking the fastest route to gold in Holcomb Valley. Segments of the early Santa Ana Trail eventually became key components of the original 1915 Rim of the World Drive alignment. (GLO.)

UTE CHIEF WALKARA. In the mid-1830s, Native American raids on San Bernardino Valley ranchos slowly increased, and in 1840, Walkara (left), a legendary adversary, led the most successful horse stealing foray ever. Walkara and others frequently fled to the mountains on narrow, unmapped trails to escape pursuit, but this tactic would first fail in 1845, following California governor Pio Pico's order to end the raids forever.

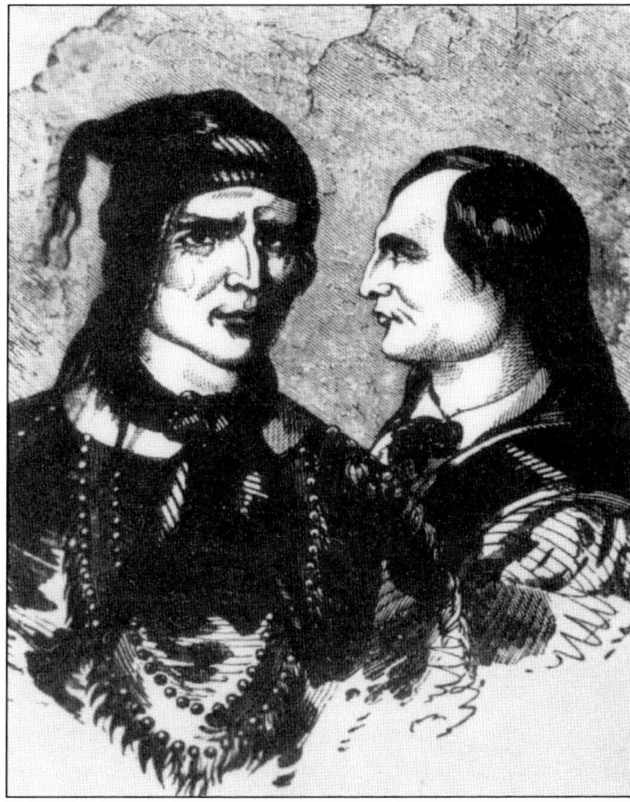

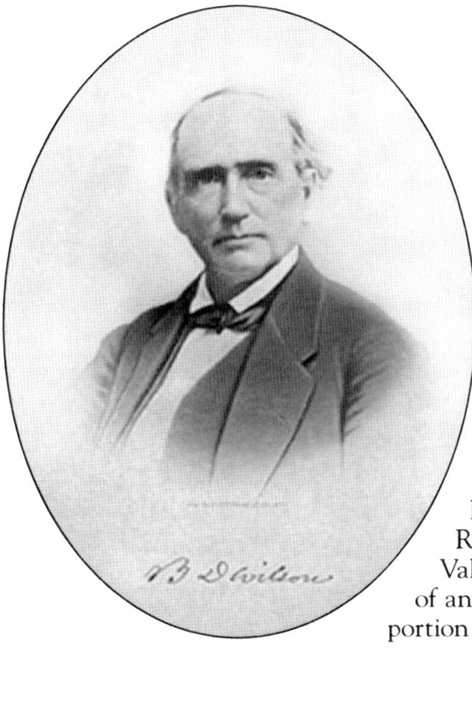

BENJAMIN D. WILSON. In 1845, Wilson led an armed party pursuing Native Americans who had raided San Bernardino Valley horse herds. Wilson later related that he traveled up the San Bernardino River (Santa Ana River) by mountain trails to Bear Valley. His account is the first detailed historic record of any trip being made over what would later become a portion of the Rim of the World Drive.

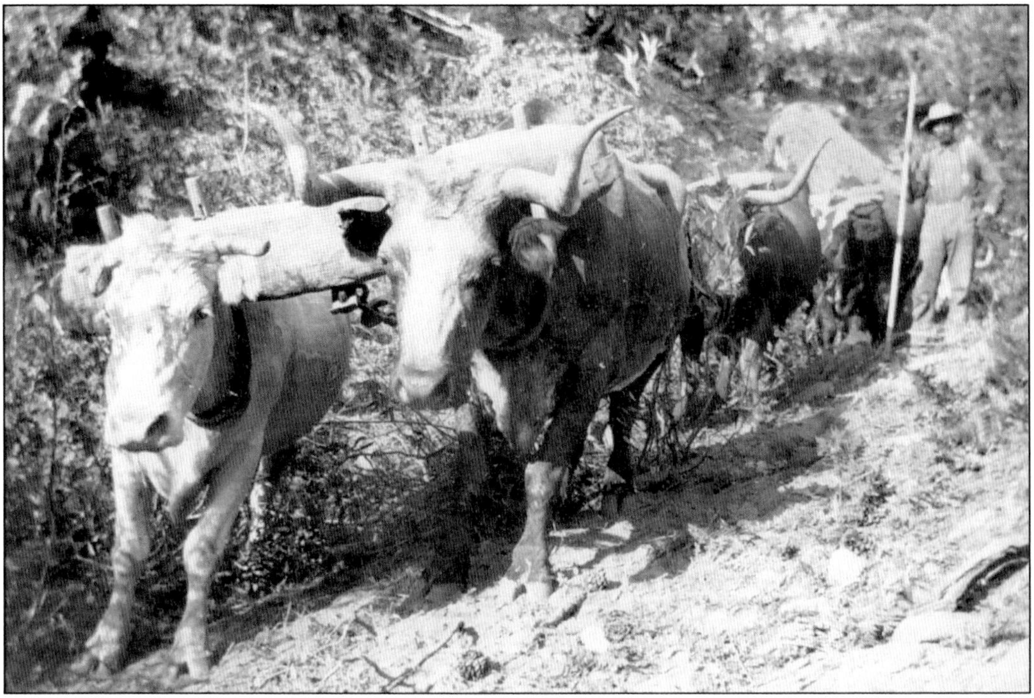

OXEN DRAGGING LOG. In 1852, Mormon volunteers constructed a road to the mountain crest near Seeley Flat to tap rich stands of timber. Known as the Mormon Road, it was really more of a widened trail fit for oxen. Portions were later utilized in 1892 as the Arrowhead Toll Road and even later as the original Rim of the World Drive. (AFC.)

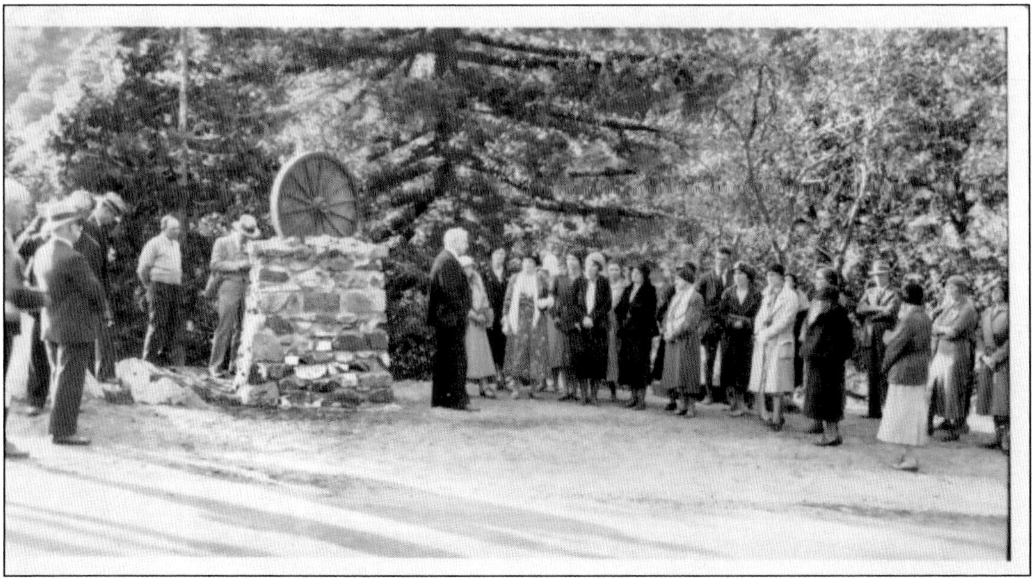

MORMON TRAIL DEDICATION. The original route of the Mormon Road was surveyed in April 1852, and by July, the road had reached the Crisman lumber mill site near Seeley Flat. This was primitive but extremely fast road building. By way of comparison, the engineered Rim of the World Drive high-gear road, allowing a car to reach the crest in high gear, was surveyed beginning in April 1925, but the last section wasn't completed until October 1933.

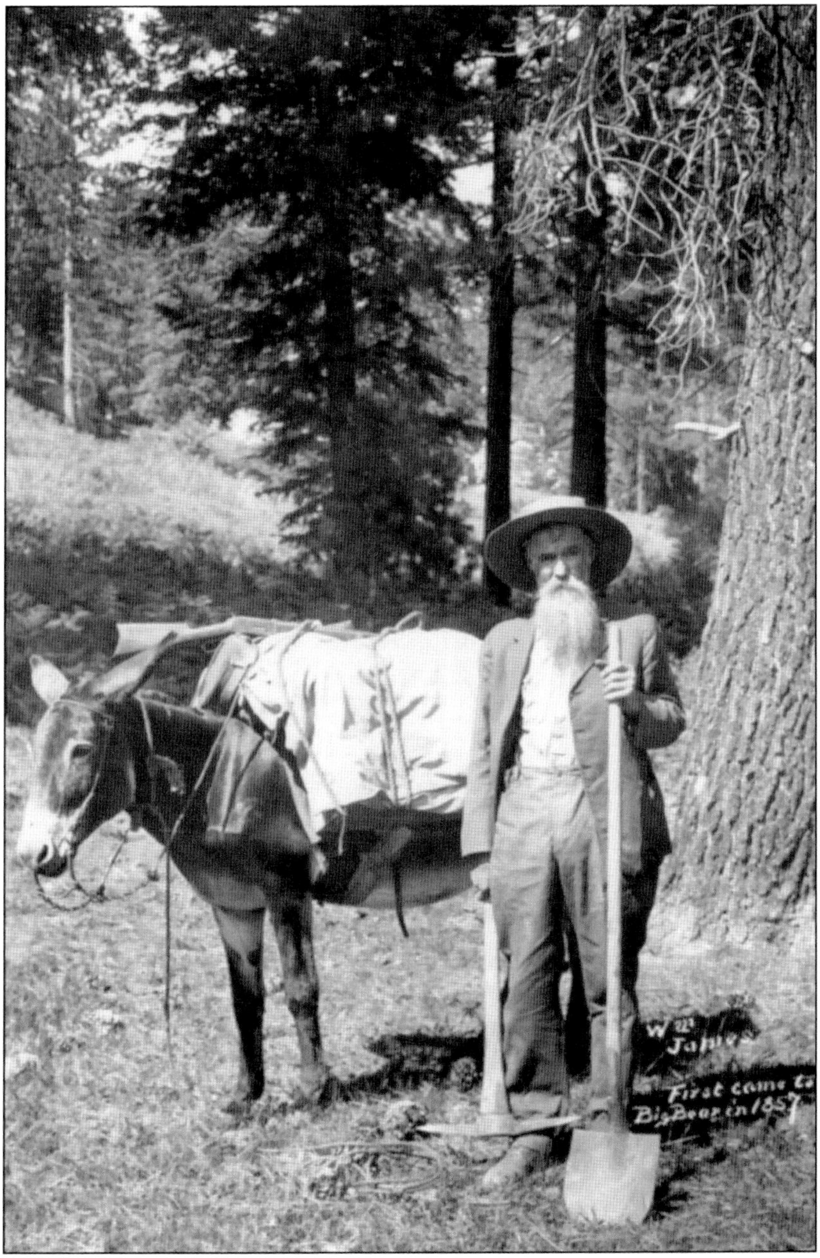

MINING AND MOUNTAIN ROADS. As early as 1855, limited mining operations near Bear Lake were underway, but it wasn't until 1860 that William "Billy" Holcomb made his historic gold discovery in Holcomb Valley and the rush to the mountains was on. This 1920s postcard of William James is somewhat misleading, for although he poses here as a miner, he was only eight years old in 1857. Although he likely traveled to Big Bear with his lawyer father, he certainly didn't go as a miner. Interestingly, in 1910, William James does list his occupation as a gold miner in the U.S. Census. In the 1860s, burros and pack trains used the Santa Ana Trail as the primary route to Bear and Holcomb Valleys. Thousands of hopeful miners struggled upwards along the same general route that would become the original 1915 Rim of the World Drive automobile alignment to Bear Valley.

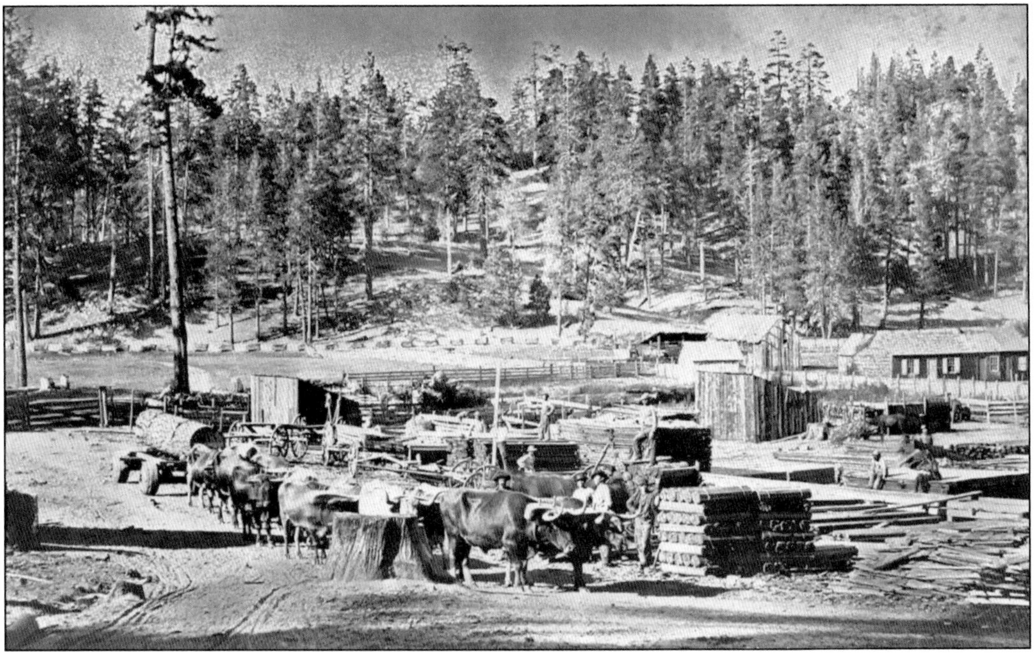

TALMADGE MILL AT LITTLE BEAR. Photographed in 1874, this historic mill site is now beneath the waters of Lake Arrowhead. From Little Bear to Big Bear, the name Talmadge was synonymous with the lumber and cattle industries. By this time, the first of many toll roads had been built to address the increased demands of the lumber industry. (SPS.)

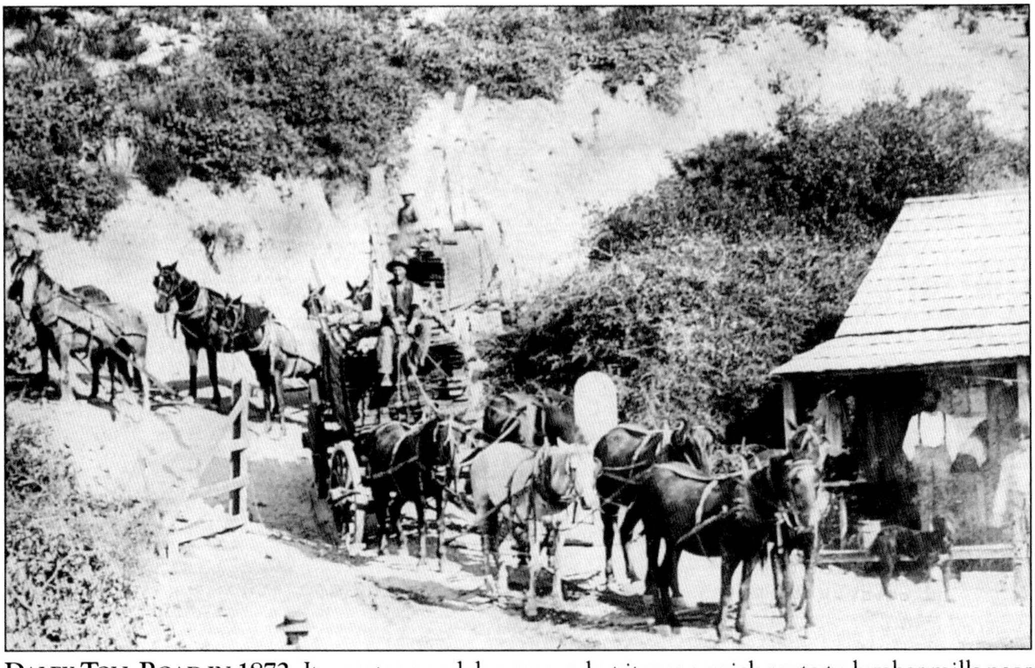

DALEY TOLL ROAD IN 1872. It was steep and dangerous, but it was a quick route to lumber mills near Little Bear Valley. Opened in July 1870, Daley Toll Road was used primarily by lumber wagons (few private citizens dared) until the mid-1890s. Like the 1879 Devil Canyon Toll Road, this alignment was considered but rejected by county supervisors for purchase as a free county road.

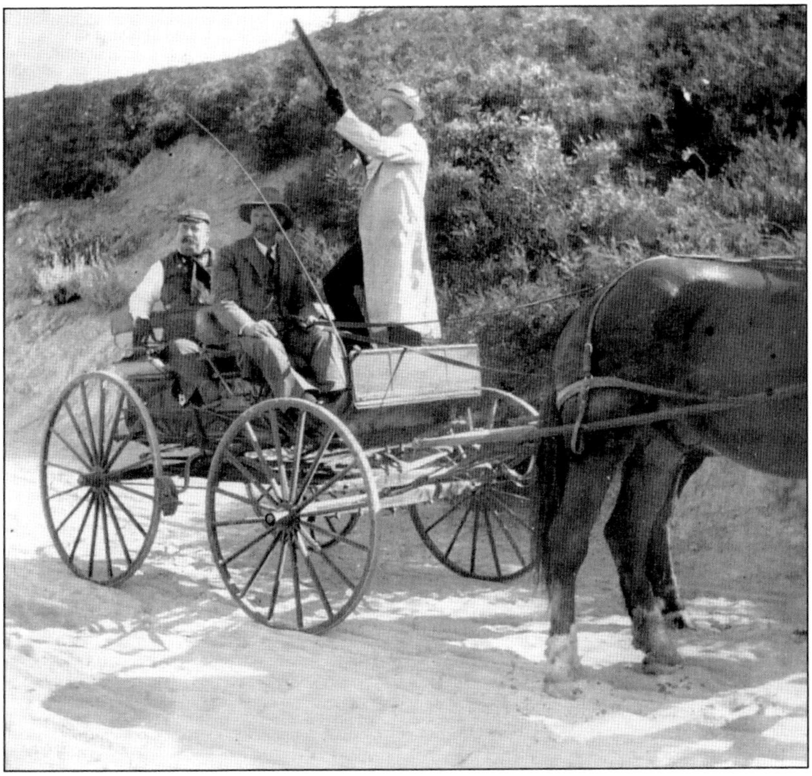

The Historic Clarke Rim Jaunt. About 1900, Alywin C. Clarke and friends took a toll-road buggy vacation up the hill to the Squirrel Inn, across the mountains through Green Valley to Big Bear, and down the hill to San Bernardino. This early trip was recorded by photographs, from beginning to end, on what would later become the Rim of the World Drive. (LM.)

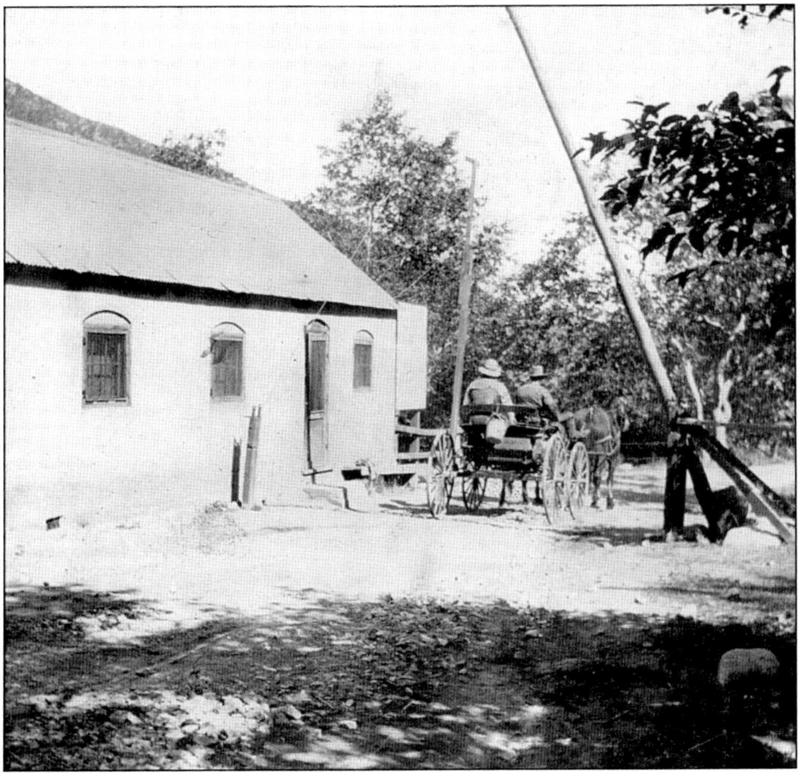

Arrowhead Toll Road Lower Tollhouse. Clarke and company began their journey heading up Waterman Canyon on the Arrowhead Toll Road. When the road was completed in the spring of 1892, an outraged public protested the cost, but it wasn't until 1905 that the toll road became a free county road. From 1915 to 1930, Waterman Canyon was part of the Rim of the World Drive. (LM.)

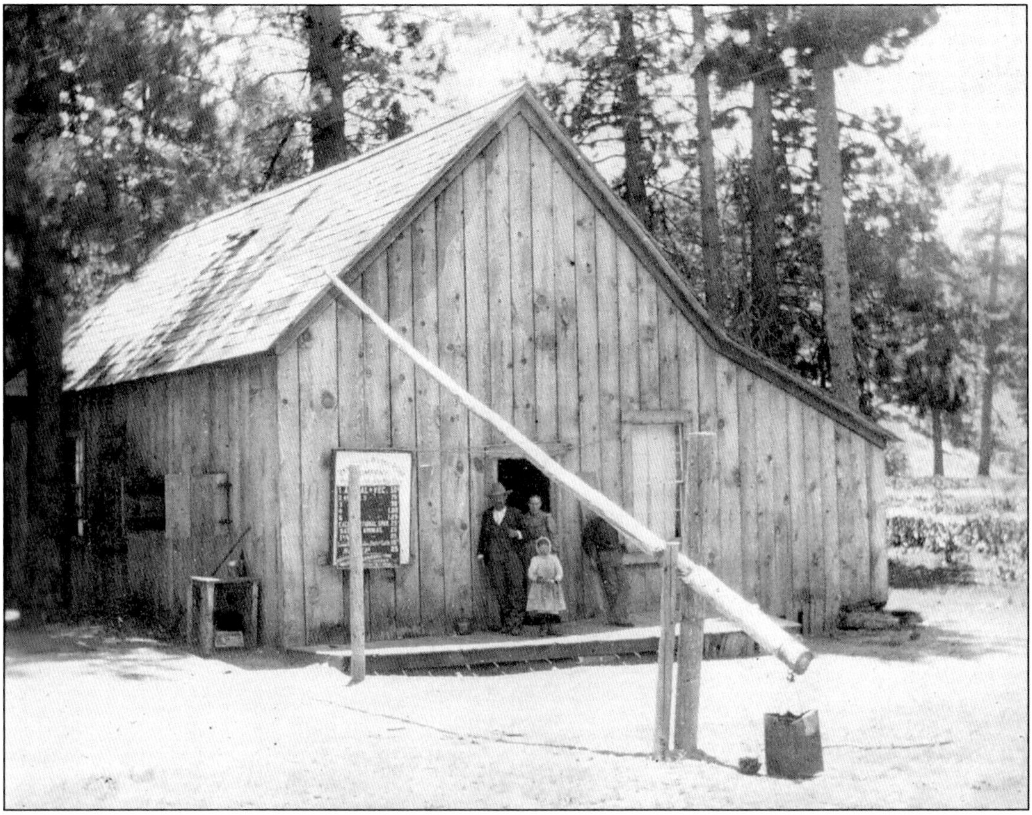

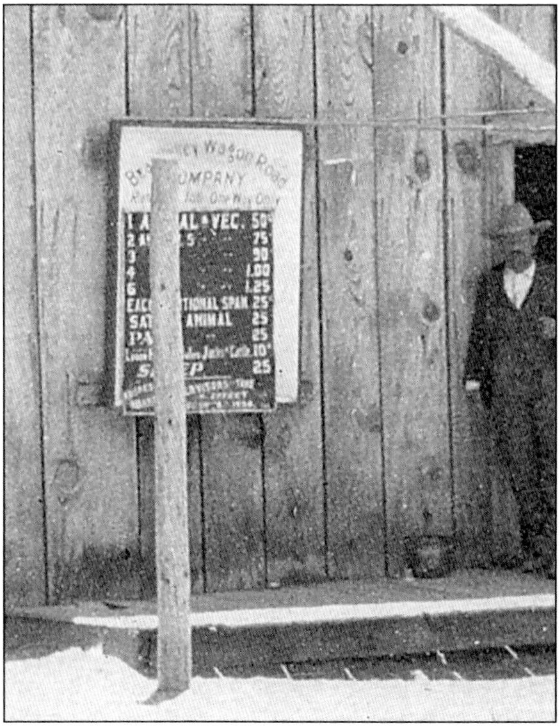

BEAR VALLEY WAGON ROAD COMPANY. In 1892, Gus Knight Jr. and John Metcalf opened a toll road from Bear Valley to Green Valley, connecting with the 1892 Highland Lumber Company Toll Road up City Creek. The Clarke outfit passed through the Green Valley Toll Gate on their way to Bear Valley. They had a "2 Animal + VEC" rig, so they must have paid a toll of 75¢ for a one-way passage in a two-animal vehicle. Toll roads were privately constructed, especially in mountain areas across California, as cash-strapped counties simply didn't have enough money to build public highways.

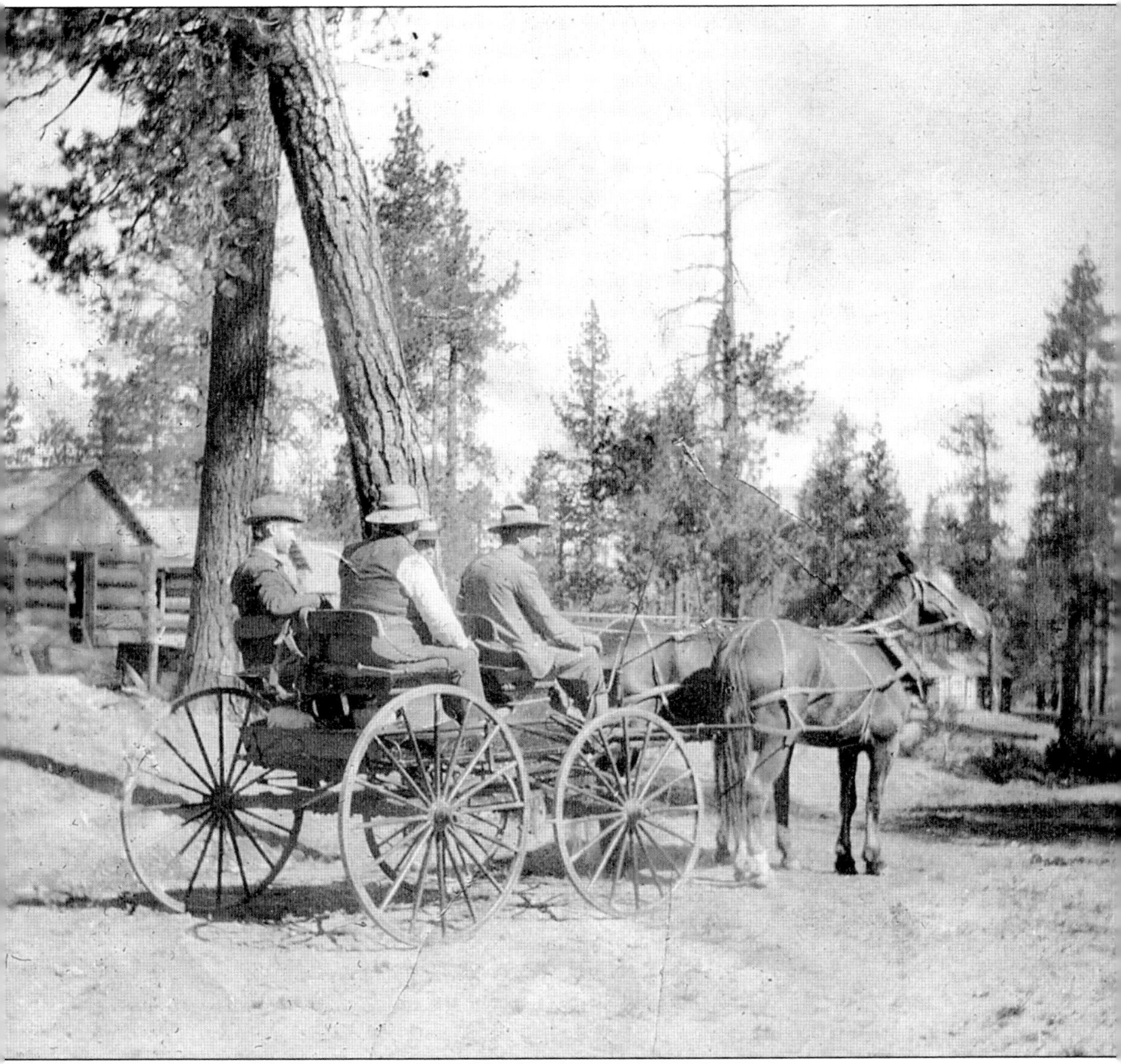

LEAVING BEAR VALLEY. Here the Clarke boys leave Bear Valley on their way to San Bernardino. They almost certainly took the Bear Valley and Redlands Toll Road, which was incorporated in July 1899 and completed in August 1899. Leading down the hill by way of Clark's Grade (no relation) and the Santa Ana River, this later became an essential link on the Rim of the World Drive. Clarke was a prominent citizen of the county of San Bernardino, last employed as secretary of the Southern California Asylum for the Insane at Patton. His "time capsule" photograph recordation of his horse-and-buggy adventure along wagon and toll roads that would become, in only a few short years, the original Rim of the World Drive is a genuine historical treasure. (LM.)

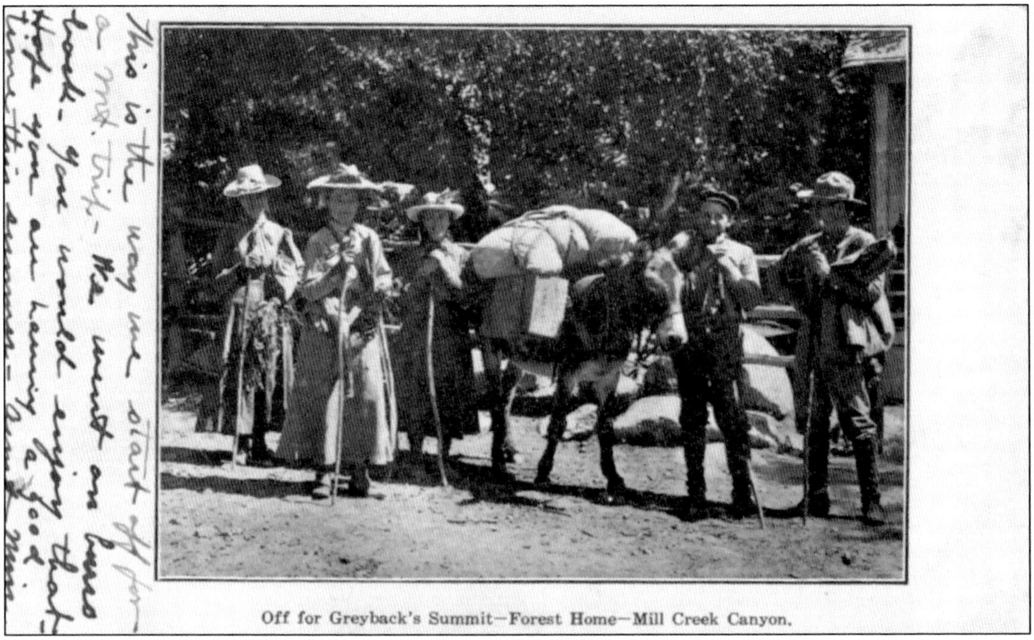

BURROS AND STAGES. A popular pastime from the late 1880s to *c.* 1915 was to take a mule (above) to the summit of "old Greyback." Much as mule rides in Arizona's Grand Canyon fascinate tourists today, burro trips in the San Bernardino Mountains were recorded in newspaper articles as breathtaking adventures. In 1907, the Bear Valley stage (below) left early in the morning from Redlands, stopped in Highland at the train station, and then continued up the mountain to Bear Valley. The daylong trip (one way) departed on Tuesday and Wednesday mornings and returned every Monday and Friday. By 1915, auto stages on the Rim of the World Drive made the same trip in five hours from San Bernardino.

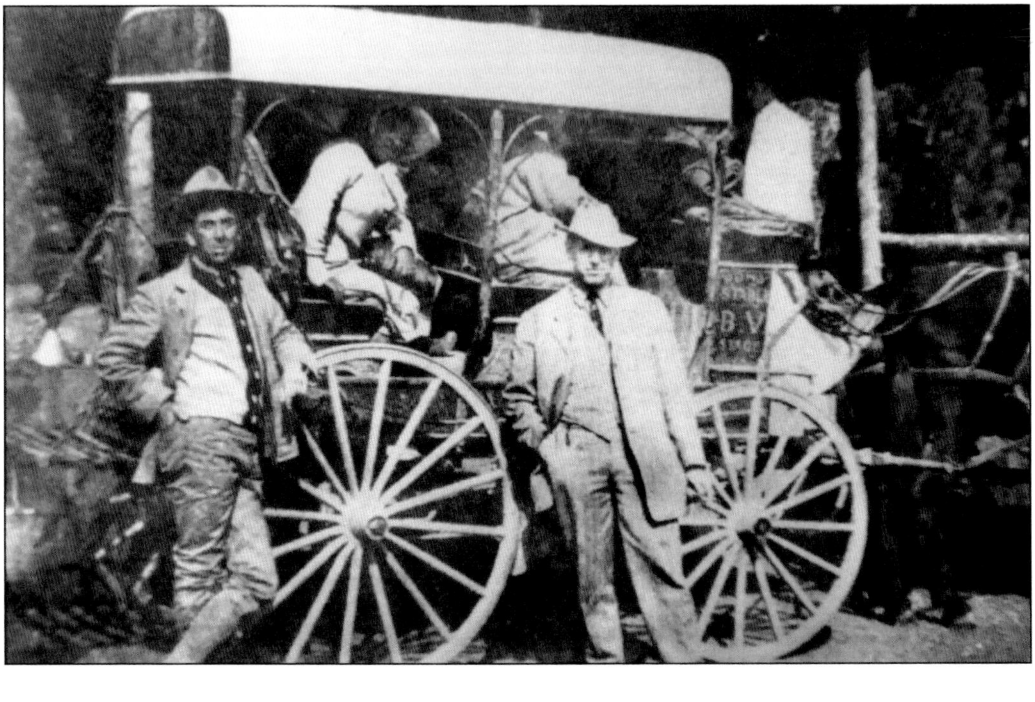

Where and How
To the Mountains

IDYLLWILD—In the beautiful Strawberry Valley of the San Jacinto Mts. Altitude 5250 feet. Reached by stage from Hemet on the Santa Fe. Stage fare from Hemet $5.00 round trip.
SEVEN OAKS AND BEAR VALLEY—Under same management. Located in San Bernardino Mountains. Elevation 5000 feet and 6800 feet, respectively. Reached by stage from Redlands on the Santa Fe. Stage fare to Seven Oaks $5.00 round trip. To Bear Valley via Seven Oaks $9.00 round trip.
FOREST HOME—Located at the head of Mill Creek in the San Bernardino Mountains. Altitude 5200 feet. Reached by stage from Mentone on the Santa Fe. Stage fare from Mentone $3 round trip.
PINE CREST—Located on south face of San Bernardino Mountains. Reached by tri-weekly stage from San Bernardino or from end of trolley car line at Arrowhead Hot Springs. Stage fare $3.50 round trip. Stage leaves Tuesdays, Thursdays and Saturdays.
ARROWHEAD HOT SPRINGS—Located just north of San Bernardino at the foot of the famous Arrowhead Mountain. Noted for its hot springs. Elevation 2000 feet. Reached by trolley car from San Bernardino on the Santa Fe. Trolley fare fifty cents round trip.
FOLLOWS CAMP—Located in the beautiful San Gabriel Canyon. Reached by stage from Azusa on the Santa Fe. Stage fare $1.50 each way.
GLENN RANCH—Located in Lytle Creek Canyon a short stage ride from Keenbrook on the Santa Fe. Altitude 3256 feet. Stage fare fifty cents each way.
COLD BROOK CAMP—Located in the North Fork of the San Gabriel Canyon in the heart of the Forest Reserve. Altitude 3500 feet. Reached by stage from Azusa on the Santa Fe. Stage fare from Azusa $2.50 each way.
CAMP RINCON—Located in the picturesque San Gabriel Canyon a short stage ride from Azusa on the Santa Fe. Stage fare $1.50 each way.
FREDALBA PARK—Located on the south slope of San Bernardino Mountains, at an altitude of 5600 feet. Reached by stage from Highland on the Santa Fe. Stage fare from Highland $3 round trip.
WILLIAMS, ARIZ.—Located at the foot of Bill Williams Mt., and not far from the San Francisco Peaks. Altitude 6768 feet. Excellent camping grounds among the pines. Reached by Santa Fe transcontinental trains—three times a day each way.
FLAGSTAFF, ARIZ.—Located at the base of the beautiful San Francisco Peaks. Altitude 6885 feet. Fine camping grounds near by. The most important Cliff Dwellings of this continent lie within a radius of eight miles.
GRAND CANYON OF ARIZONA—Earth's wonder. A mile deep, 13 miles wide, 217 miles long. All glorified by a rainbow beauty of color. Altitude 7000 feet. Hotel El Tovar on brink of Canyon under Fred Harvey management.

For detail information phone or call on

E. W. McGee, Gen. Agt., 334 S. Spring St.

Santa Fe

RAILROAD RECOMMENDED MOUNTAIN ADVENTURES. This July 1909 newspaper advertisement has it all. Much like fly-drive "package" vacations to exotic locations advertised by airlines today, trips to rugged and naturally beautiful mountain resorts were historically offered by the Santa Fe Railroad across Southern California and the American Southwest. One simply took the train to a conveniently located station, connected to any number of horse-drawn stage lines, and then continued on to the Santa Fe recommended resort of choice. At this time, the Santa Fe Railroad was one of the largest passenger carrying entities in the world. The truly remarkable thing about this advertised mountain vacation package is that in 1909 the San Bernardino Mountains (Seven Oaks, Forest Home, Pine Crest, Arrowhead Hot Springs, and Fredalba) were placed on the same footing as the Grand Canyon for vacation excitement and value. (LAT.)

Arrowhead Hot Springs

Special Summer Rates

Special Low Rates on Trolley Saturday and Sunday.

STAGE to Crestline and Skyland

Will leave Lyman & Son's Stables at 7 a. m. on Tuesday, Thursday and Saturday for the above mountain resorts.

FARE: Round trip, $3.00. Up, $2.00. Down $1.00.

25 lbs of baggage allowed to each passenger.

Packages carried for 1 cent a pound.

Specialty of moving campers.

LYMAN & SON. 265 D Street, San Bernardino

Phones: Home 558, Sunset, Main 105.

BRAZELTON BROS.'

MOUNTAIN STAGE LINE

To Skyland, Squirrel Inn and Pine Crest

Going Up Tuesday, Thursday and Saturday.

Coming Down Monday, Wednesday and Friday.

Stage meets street car leaving San Bernardino at 6:15 a. m. on "going up" days and returning leaves Pine Crest at 10 a. m. and Skyland at 11:30, connecting with Traction car at 1:00 p. m.

Mountain traffic and freight of all kinds handled from end of car line at Reasonable Rates at any time.

Further information at Traction office or Phone Brazelton, Arrowhead.

STAGE LINE ADVERTISEMENT. Horse-drawn stages regularly operated from San Bernardino to west-end mountain resorts beginning with the 1905 county purchase of the old Arrowhead Company Toll Road and the opening of a free public highway to the crest. This July 1907 advertisement in the *San Bernardino Daily Sun* newspaper notes that two lines, the Brazelton Brothers and Lyman and Son, were operating thrice-weekly service up and down the hill. Take note of the fact that the trip up the hill cost twice as much as the trip down the hill. Passengers had a luggage weight limit, and packages were delivered for a penny a pound. Like scenes from movies of the Wild West, historic newspaper articles record San Bernardino mountain stage wrecks and robberies. Slow-moving wagons and stages didn't guarantee that traveling mountain roads was an entirely sedate affair. (SBS.)

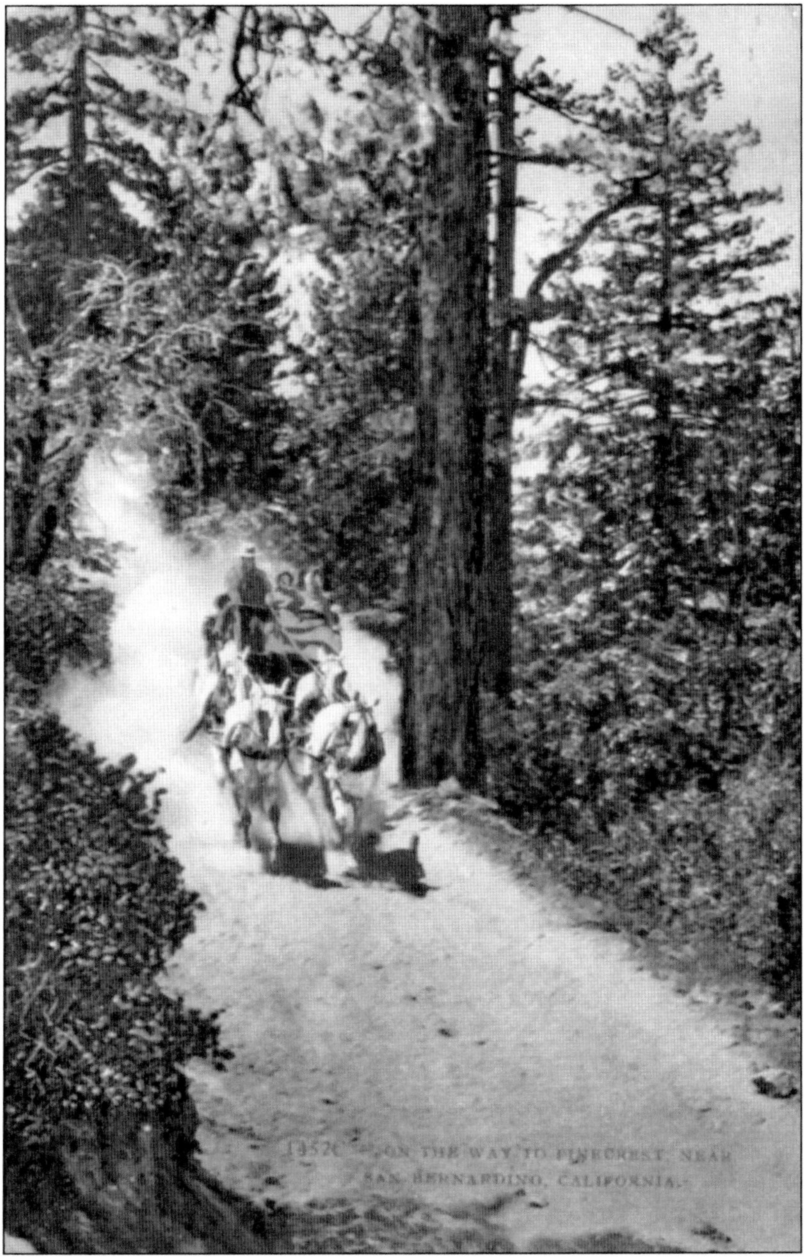

STAGE ON THE WAY TO PINECREST. The front of this card reads, "On the way to Pinecrest, near San Bernardino, California." In 1906, John N. Baylis, a San Bernardino doctor, began construction of his rustic but luxurious Pinecrest mountain vacation retreat for the masses. Pinecrest would become one of the most popular and widely known resorts in the San Bernardino Mountains. Seasonal stage service was already available to the Squirrel Inn and other west-end mountain resorts, and Baylis had clearly conceived of using transportation as a shrewd marketing tool. Like many other prominent local businessmen, he saw better roads as the essential key to the profitable development of mountain resorts and resources. He would ultimately become one of the principal promoters of the Rim of the World Drive, and Baylis Park on the high-gear road is named after him. (EHM.)

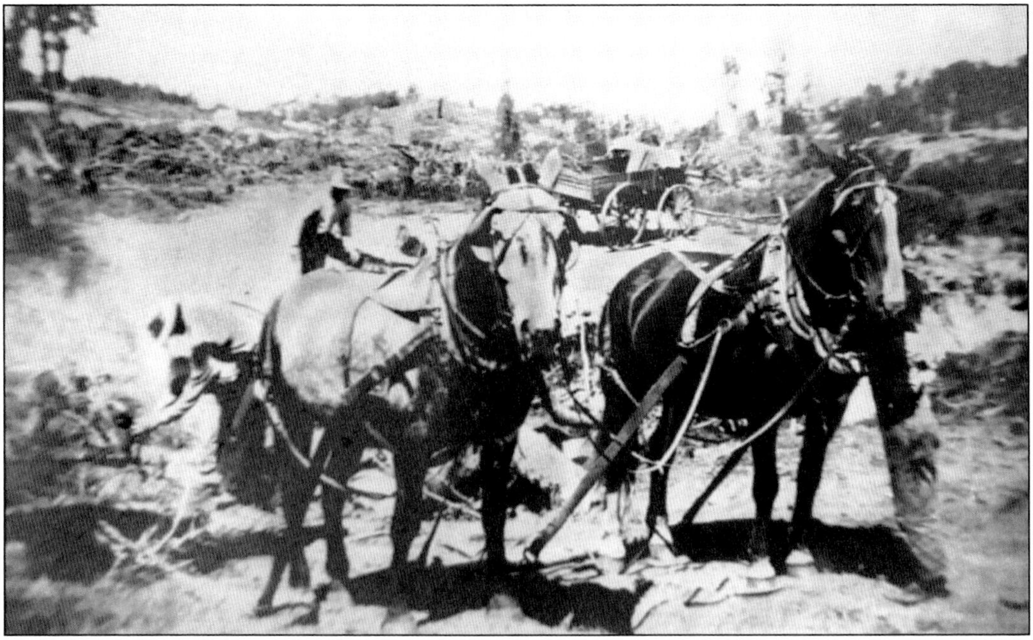

PRIMITIVE ROAD MAINTENANCE. The Bear Valley Wagon Road Company Toll Road through Green Valley would eventually become a part of the original Rim of the World Drive. This Tillitt family snapshot, taken immediately prior to county acquisition of the alignment in 1910, records what road maintenance was like when everything was done by horses, mules, and the limited muscle power of man.

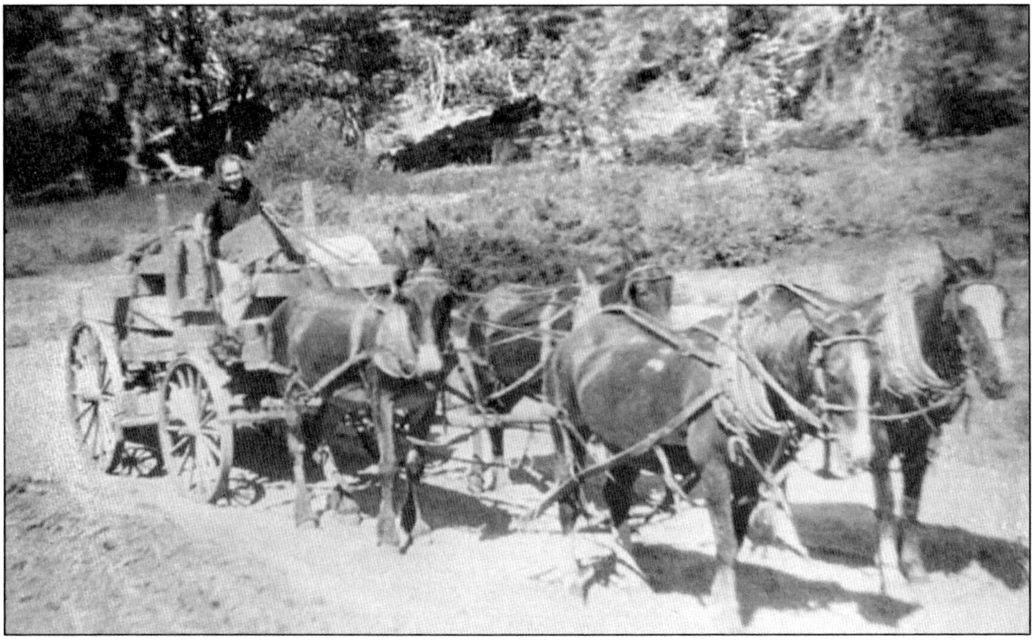

A TRIP TO TOWN IN 1910. When the wife of tollhouse operator George Tillitt went to town (San Bernardino) by wagon for supplies in 1910, it was a two-day trip. When this picture was taken, automobiles had already navigated the loop that would become the Rim of the World Drive, but wagons were the still the standard means of travel.

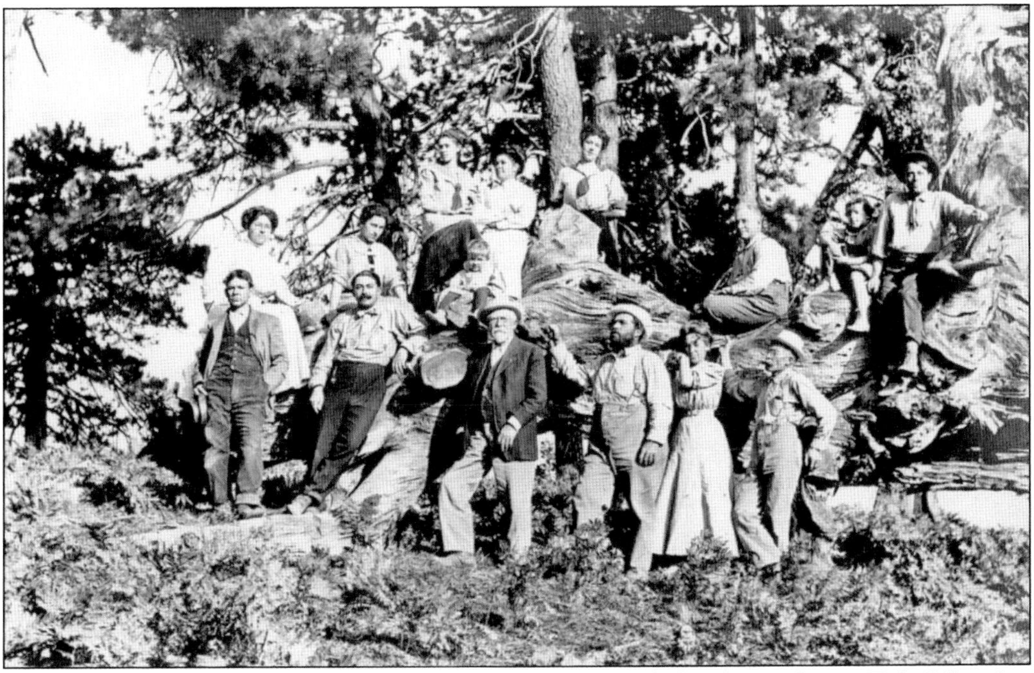

The Andreson Tribe. The 1908 photograph above is labeled "The Andreson Tribe" (brother and sister-in-laws only). The family patriarch was John Andreson Sr. (center), a Schleswig-Holstein immigrant sailor, grocer, and brewer who settled in San Bernardino in 1871. Here he prospered, ultimately becoming an organizer of the prosperous Farmer's Exchange Bank. He married and had five children, the most senior son being named John Andreson Jr. (right of center). The younger Andreson was an award-winning amateur photographer, and the following images document family vacations that were casual, lengthy, leisurely, and large. The 1909 photograph (below) was taken on the way to Skyland. Unlike early automobiles, wagons could be heavily loaded, and it was not uncommon to see 10–12 people and their luggage in one wagon. (AFC.)

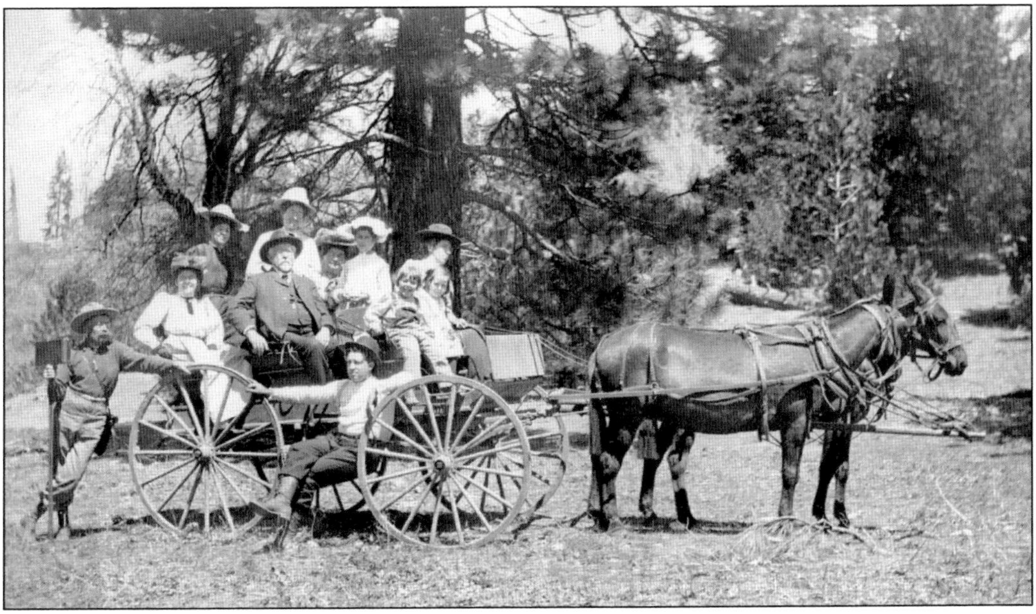

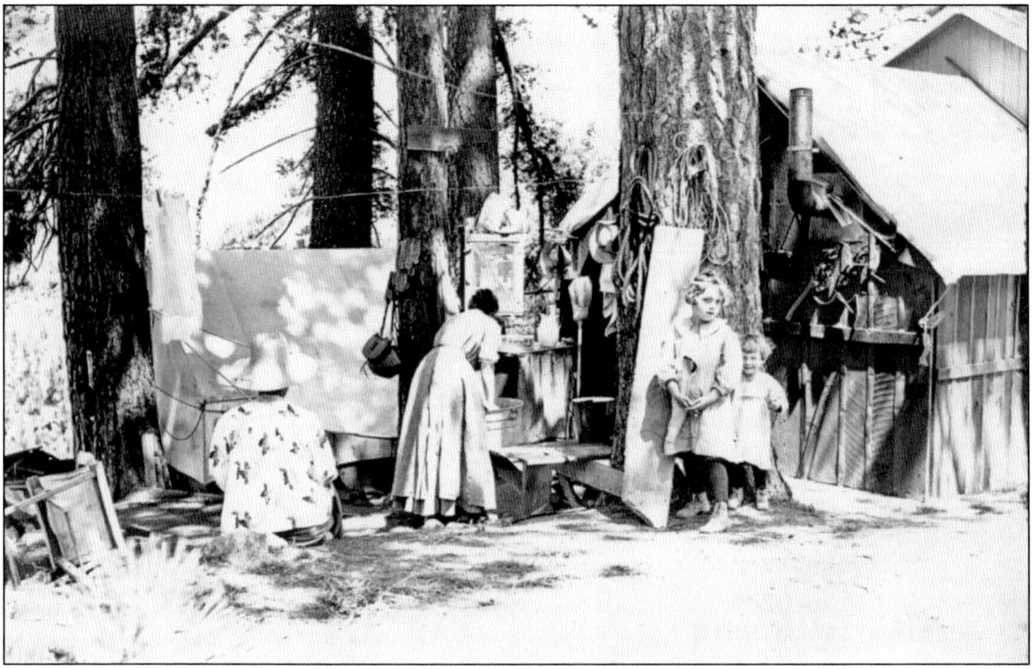

CAMPING AND FISHING IN 1910. At Skyland, wagons were unloaded, gear was stowed, and children played. Initially, the women worked (above) and the men assaulted nature en masse in search of dinner (below). Family vacations during the age of horse- or mule-drawn wagons were clearly much different than those in the age of the automobile. By wagon, it took the better part of a day to reach Skyland by way of Waterman Canyon, many stops were made along the way, and one must have felt much closer to nature. The world turned at a much more leisurely pace, especially for prosperous Andreson family members and friends. (AFC.)

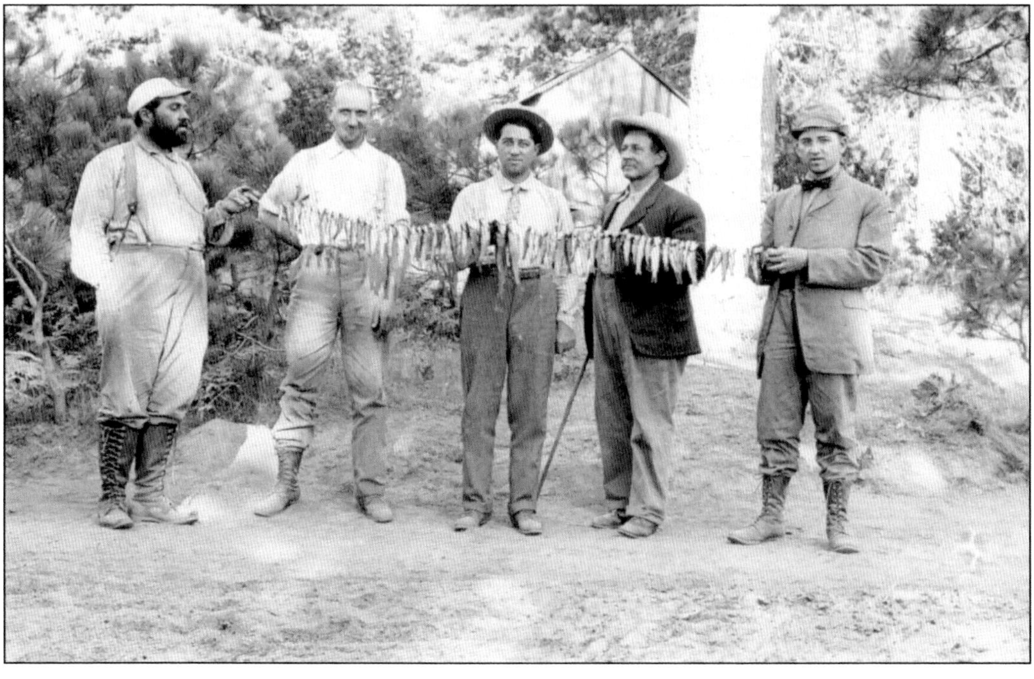

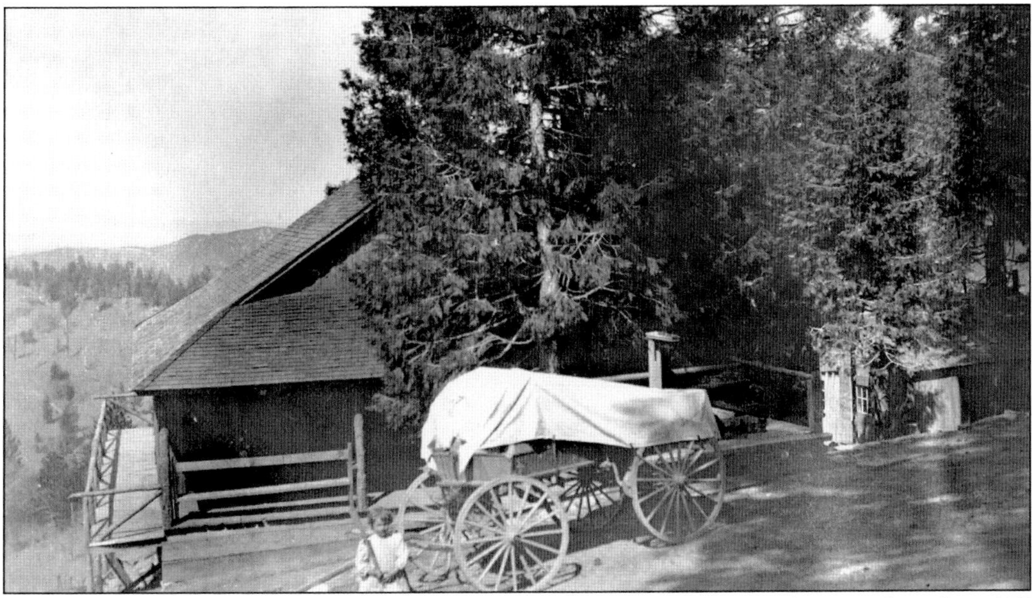

WAGON PARKED "CURBSIDE." One particularly interesting Andreson photograph is this 1907 image of a wagon parked in front of the Skyland Inn. The idea that wagons were parked "curbside" in exactly the same manner as automobiles are today is astonishing, as Hollywood generally puts together a more exciting movie set, and few historic photographers wasted their film on such a prosaic subject. (AFC.)

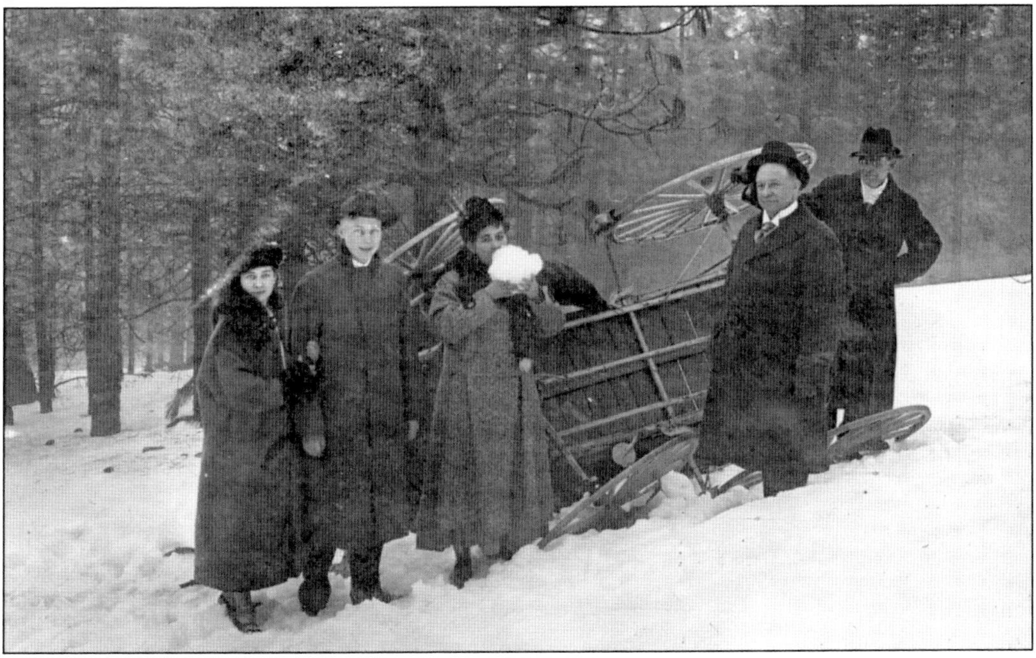

A BUGGY WRECK. As many accidents occurred historically in buggies and wagons as there are in automobiles today—especially on mountain roads where grades were steep, guardrails were unheard of, roads were particularly narrow, and horses were distracted by an unfamiliar environment. Fatalities occurred, but many wrecks were just inconvenient accidents, like this 1908 Andreson buggy wreck. At this time, automobiles were prohibited by law on mountain roads. (AFC.)

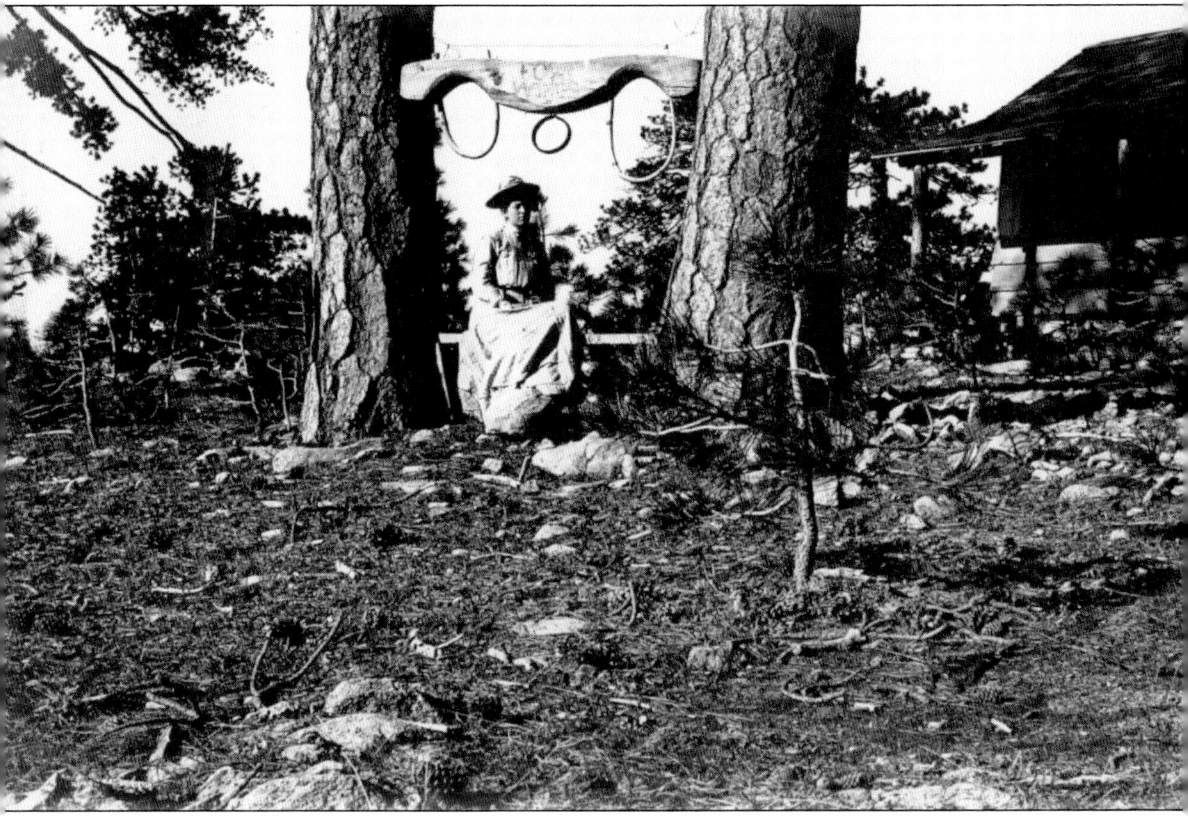

ON THE CUSP OF CHANGE. This 1909 image of a member of the Andreson family is particularly poignant. First, it was taken in the San Bernardino Mountains at Skyland, a favorite Andreson vacation destination. Second, the woman arrived here on a free county road (old Arrowhead Toll Road) by a mule-drawn wagon, the traditional means of mountain travel by the Andreson family. Family photographs show as many as 12 family members sitting in a single wagon, a number that certainly guaranteed a daylong trip to the crest. Third, by 1908, an automobile had already scaled the heights, and change was definitely in the wind as she sat perched on a bench. Finally, she probably felt rather modern sitting under an ox yoke, a historic relic of an era that time had truly passed by. Yet within only a single year, everything would change, for in 1910, automobiles would not only scale but assault the heights. The age of wagons and buggies would end in a heartbeat. (AFC.)

Two

Automobiles Conquer the Heights

Rim of the World Drive automobile history begins in 1902 when the Arrowhead Reservoir Company asked county supervisors to prohibit their use by astronomically raising tolls. Supervisors complied as it was thought "horseless carriages" would frighten draft animals and cause accidents. A statewide automobile–mountain road debate soon raged. The legislature ultimately acted in March 1905 to legalize automobile traffic on all California mountain roads. County supervisors responded in May 1905 by allowing automobiles limited access in Waterman Canyon but not to the summit.

In 1903, the California legislature authorized counties to build roads from general funds, freeing huge sums of money to create free roads out of tolls roads. In 1905, the county acquired the Arrowhead Toll Road as the first of many purchases of toll and lumber roads, beginning the slow process of assembling the component parts of the future Rim of the World Drive. The last such link was purchased by the county in 1913.

Automobile restrictions still in place on San Bernardino mountain roads were put to the test in May 1908 by W. C. Vaughan. Leaving Los Angeles, he and several other enthusiasts ascended the Arrowhead Grade in two automobiles pursued by law enforcement officials. The publicity stunt backfired when county supervisors entirely banned automobiles from mountain roads in June 1908. The ordinance was repealed in May 1909, and by September 1909, at least two cars had assaulted the hills. On August 29, 1910, Jack Heyser made his historic and profoundly influential automobile run around the Rim and made it abundantly obvious to all that a machine had outmatched the mountains. By 1911, automobiles and auto stages were seen almost daily on mountain roads, and on July 18, 1915, the Rim of the World Drive was dedicated after having been cobbled together from much-older alignments. Today, much altered and rebuilt, the roadway continues to link all mountain communities, serving exactly the same purpose that it did in 1915 when it magically transformed the mountains into a cohesive whole. This chapter tells the exciting story of the automobile and the Rim of the World Drive.

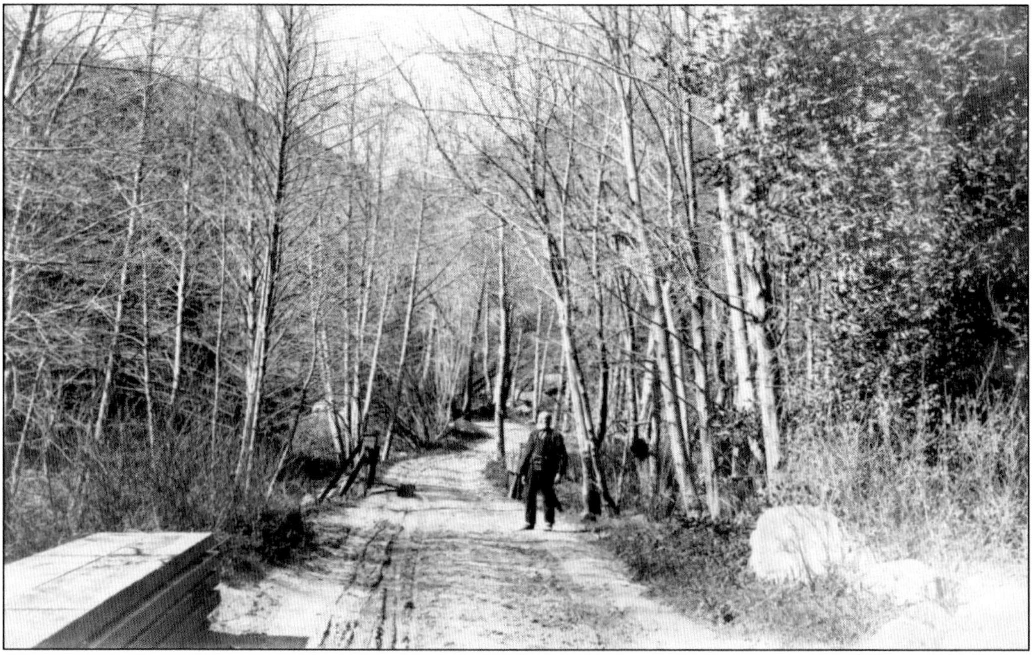

CALM BEFORE THE STORM. This March 1908 view looks north in Waterman Canyon during an Andreson family trip to Skyland in a heavily loaded wagon drawn by a pair of mules. The identity of the elderly gentleman in the road is unknown, but in less than two months, the peaceful serenity of Waterman Canyon surrounding him would be shattered by the roar of mountain-bound horseless carriages. (AFC.)

AUTO TAKES TO THE HILLS WITH A PEACE OFFICER IN HOT PURSUIT

Two automobile loads of fishermen, supposed to be from Los Angeles, at an early hour this morning were headed toward the mountains bound for the summit over the Arrowhead grade. The plans of the party were reported to the officers, and one started off horseback hoping to overtake the automobiles and prevent the ascent. As the auto had a lead of several miles it is believed that they have been able to beat the officer to the summit.

It is not generally known that though the Arrowhead road is a county thoroughfare, automobiles are prohibited from using it. There is a county ordinance to this affect, adopted in view of the danger of runaways should machines be permitted to use the road. All last night word was anxiously awaited here as to the result of the race between the machine and the mounted officer, and fear was entertained that any moment might bring news of a runaway disaster.

The names of the occupants of the machines were not learned here last night, and all is conjecture as to where they really came from.

OFFICER IN HOT PURSUIT. On May 1, 1908, law enforcement officials set off on horseback in pursuit of fishermen ignoring restrictions (autos were only allowed to the old lower toll gate) on the free county road in Waterman Canyon. William Vaughan, a prominent Los Angeles auto booster, was ringleader of the group hoping to open new automobile travel vistas. County supervisors responded by banning automobiles on all mountain roads. (TS.)

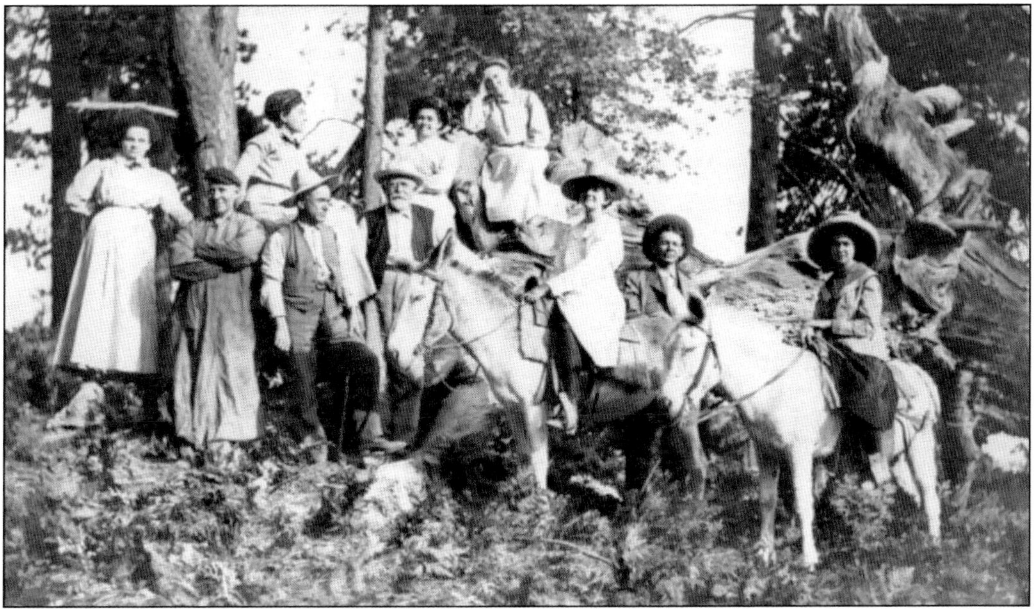

Old-Fashioned Burros in 1910. This Andreson family postcard was mailed on August 2, 1910. By this time, the county ban on automobiles on mountain roads had been lifted, but only a very few had bravely scaled the heights. Automobiles had made it to Bear Valley by way of Cushenberry Grade in 1909, but most still made their way around the mountains the old-fashioned way. This would soon change.

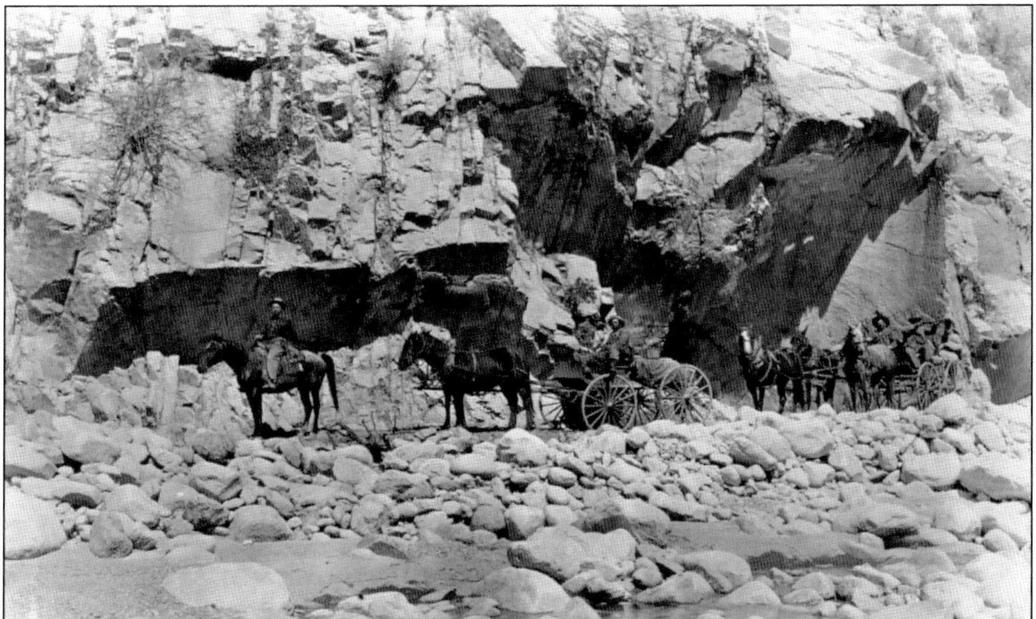

Old-Fashioned Wagons in 1910. In July 1910, the Andreson family made their last trip to the mountains in wagons. Photographs record their leisurely journey around the Rim from San Bernardino to Skyland, to Green Valley, to Bear Valley, and back down to San Bernardino. Shown here in Santa Ana Canyon, they pause for a moment on the eve of a transportation revolution only one month away. (AFC.)

SET RECORD OVER HILL ROAD

Jack Heyser Shows Ability When He Tackles the Canyon Road.

Breaking all records for successfully driving an automobile over the roughest of mountain roads, the White Steamer, driven by Jack Heyser, of Riverside, and in which George W. Wood and Opie L. Warner were passengers, accomplished what had been termed an impossible feat by many mountaineers, when it made the run Sunday from San Bernardino to Big Bear Valley, over the Santa Ana canyon road, and returned over the crest road through Little Bear Valley and Pinecrest. The actual running time was eight hours and 17 minutes and the total time consumed on the trip was 13 hours and seven minutes. Not a break down or tire puncture marred the trip, despite the fact that the course lay over what Heyser, who has driven in practically every hill climb contest in Southern California, says is the roughest he has ever seen. The course as followed by the machine is about 100 miles.

The party left San Bernardino at 8:37 a. m. and at 9.44 p. m. were back at the starting point and registered in att Hott & Winkleman's cigar store.

A Record Drive.

Before the steep Clark grade, the heaviest piece of road in the State, was reached, the men were warned to turn back by a number of mountaineers, who said they could never make it. The skillfull driving of Heyser, however, safely landed the party at the Bear Valley hotel six hours and 13 minutes after the start, three hours and 15 minutes of which was actual running time. The remainder was lost taking lunch and carrying water for over a mile to fill the tank and in taking the wrong road.

At Pinecrest, the members of the party were the guests of Dr. J. N. Baylis. Dr. Baylis is preparing to offer a handsome trophy for the winner of the proposed Pinecrest hill climb, and in which Wood and Heyser are much interested.

At various points along the route the time was certified to by reliable people, and the men are prepared to prove their claims for the trip that will probably stand for time to come as an accomplishment for steam cars.

An Impossible Feat of Mountaineering. On August 29, 1910, Jack Heyser, George W. Wood, and Opie L. Warner made a remarkable automobile run from San Bernardino to Bear Valley, to Little Bear Valley and Pinecrest, and down the hill to San Bernardino, reversing the route that the Andreson family had taken by wagon only a month before. They piloted a White Steamer, the first automobile to make the loop on what would soon become the Rim of the World Drive. Ignoring all warnings about the dangers, they made the trip in a little over 13 hours, including meals and wrong turns. At Pinecrest, Dr. Baylis welcomed them at his resort with a sumptuous meal, one of the first to recognize how closely the future of the mountains would be tied to the automobile. (TS.)

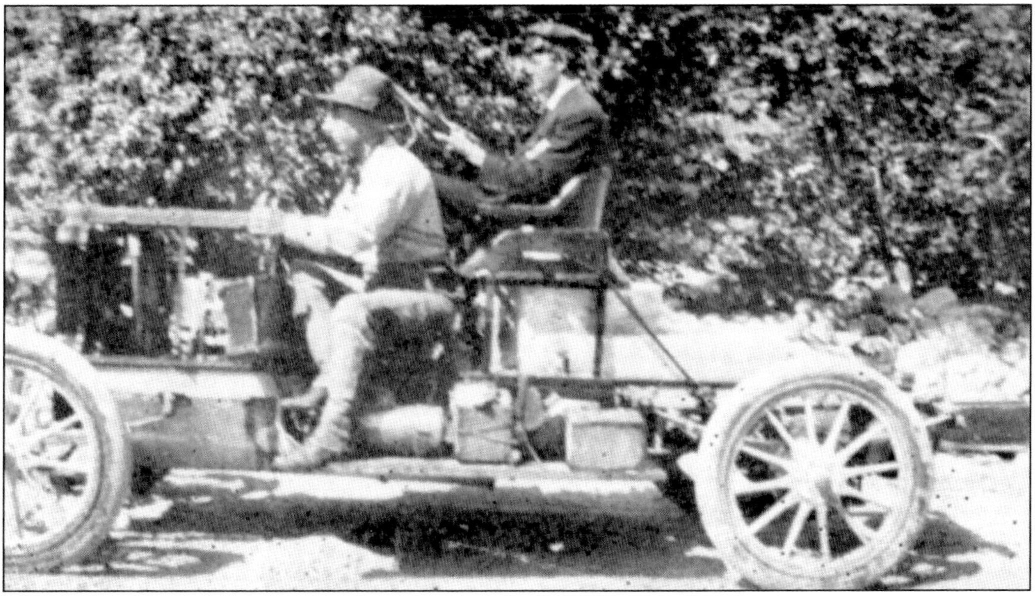

HISTORY-MAKING AUTOMOBILE. Historians always seek out single events that change history. Driven by Jack Heyser, a Los Angeles automobile mechanic, a 1910 stripped-down White Steamer (above) accomplished this historic feat. Exactly what motivated him to make the loop trip up Santa Ana Canyon (below) is unknown, but the end result was that hundreds and then thousands of automobiles would soon follow. This one event can truly be said to have changed San Bernardino Mountain history forever. Thanks to the automobile, the mountains would grow into a playground paradise for all of Southern California, eventually becoming a bedroom community for valleys below and creating what are perhaps the most heavily urbanized mountains in America. The last White steam car came off the production line in 1911, but White trucks would soon become a major part of mountain history. (ROW.)

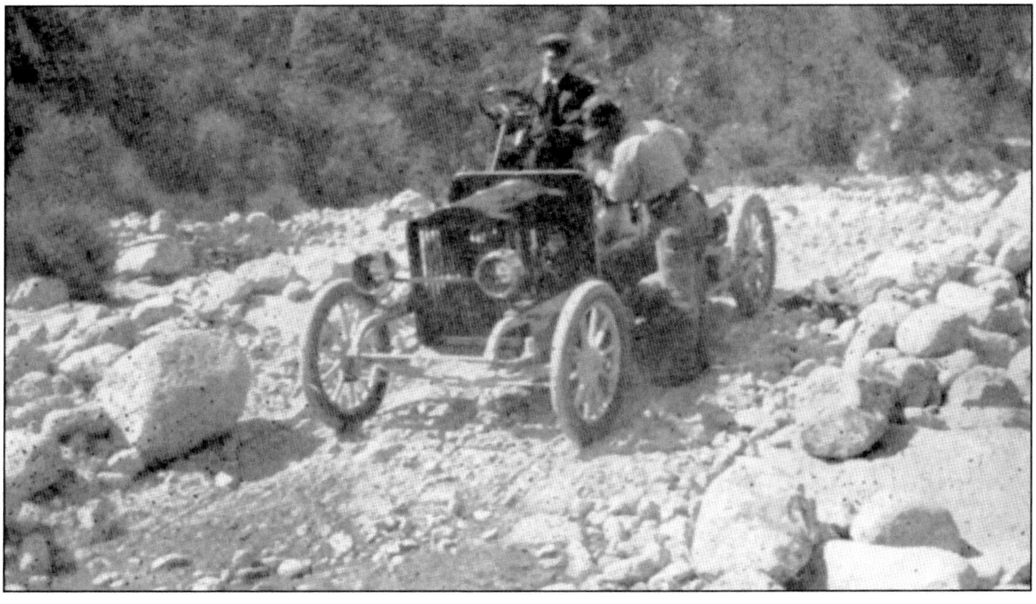

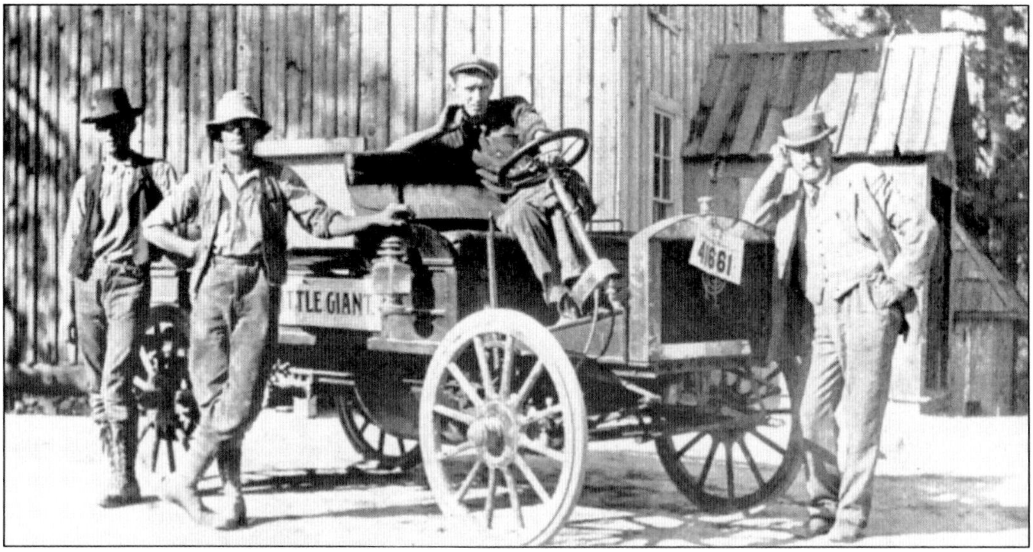

The Little Giant. In 1910, literally everyone seems to have jumped on the automobile bandwagon. This Little Giant truck is said to have hauled a record one and a half tons of cement up the Arrowhead Grade switchbacks to the Little Bear (Lake Arrowhead) dam construction site. Privately owned vehicles quickly followed, carrying mountain-bound families on vacation. (ROW.)

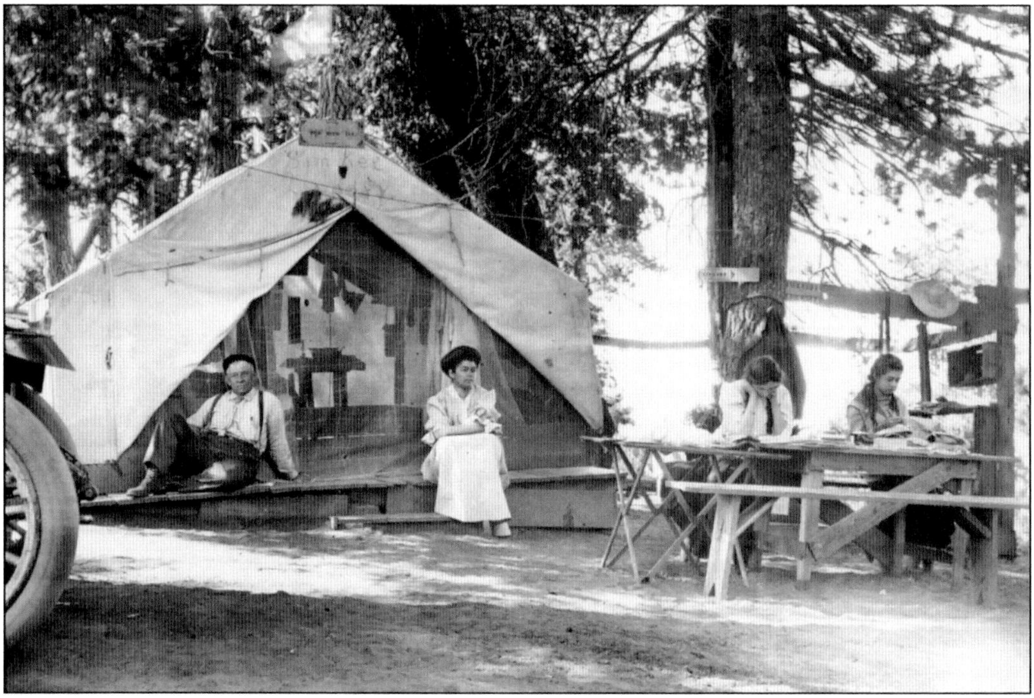

Skyland Camp 1910. Among the first to travel to the crest by automobile was the Andreson family. This view of a late-summer outing to Skyland shows the front tires of their vehicle. Only weeks before, the Andreson clan had made a tour of the Rim (see earlier Santa Ana Canyon photograph on page 29) by wagon, but from this point onward, John Anderson Jr. and family would travel by automobile. (AFC.)

PANORAMIC ROAD MAP. Mapmakers across California raced to cash in on the automobile craze. The market was almost unlimited as automobile owners were then numbered among the wealthiest of Americans, and almost no route maps existed. Published in 1913 in Los Angeles, this guide provided unusual "virtual reality" routes to various destination points as if seen from an "aeroplane," including a set of three maps leading into the San Bernardino Mountains. The text describes various resorts in the San Bernardino Mountains, including Thousand Pines, a "city of cozy cabins" with an auto stage and garage free to guests; Pine Lake (Pine Knot Lodge), "with all kinds of hunting and fishing" reached by auto stage in four hours from Redlands; Forest Home, "a real mountain camp" with daily automobile stage; Pinecrest Mountain Resort, with "excellent roads and beautiful scenery"; and Seven Oaks, in the "heart of the mountains," also connected to Redlands by stage. (TCP.)

189

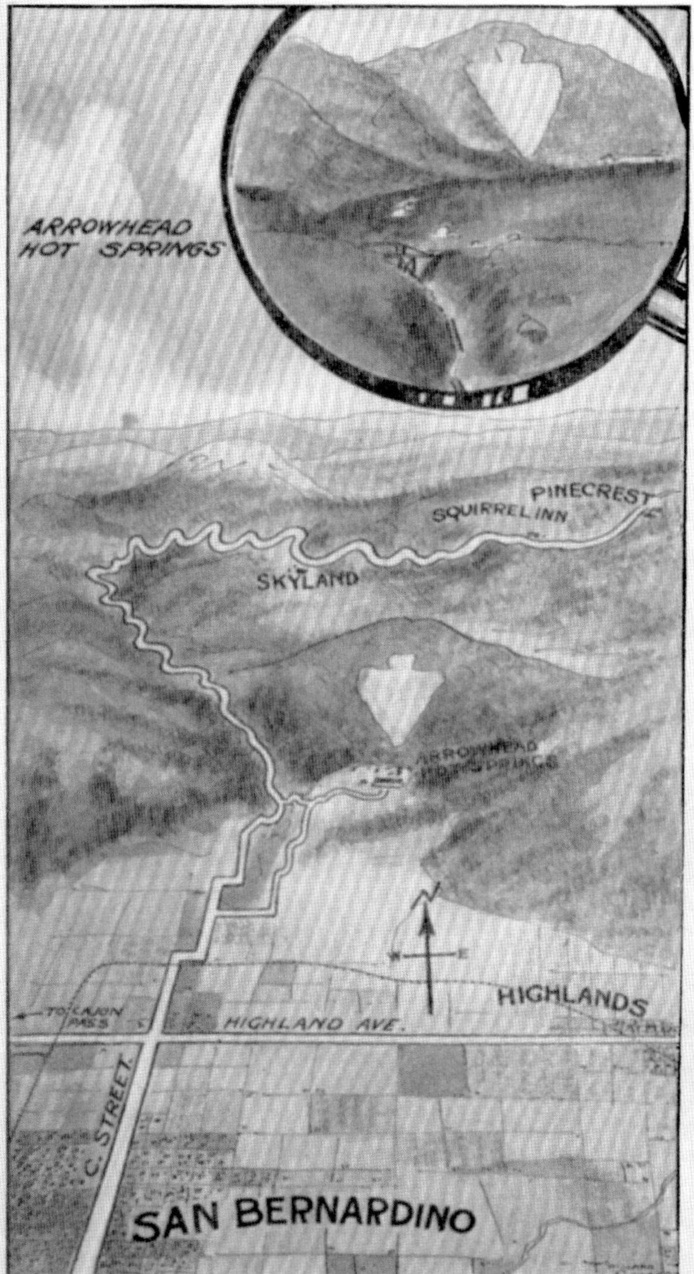

San Bernardino, Arrowhead, Skyland to Pinecrest

San Bernardino to Arrowhead, 7 miles. San Bernardino to Skyland, 13.5 miles. Skyland to Pinecrest, 4½ miles. Proceeding north on C St. at San Bernardino, follow straight out, ascending a gradual grade to Arrowhead Hot Springs. A gigantic arrowhead is erroded in the mountainside and plainly visible. A large hotel at this place, and the view is beautiful. From here a road leads to the left up Waterman Canyon to the lofty tablelands of the forests on top of San Bernardino Mountains. Here are many charming resorts and scenery is beautiful, affording many wonderful views of mountains and valleys. Roads fair, grades to 18 per cent and several dangerous curves.

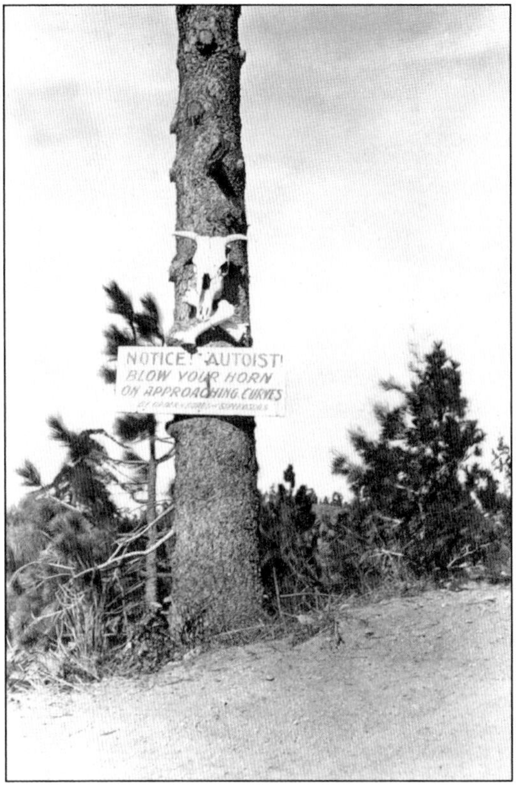

EARLY MOUNTAIN ROAD SIGN. Still leery of the dangers of allowing automobiles on mountain roads, San Bernardino County supervisors passed an order that the "autoist" must blow the horn of their car on every curve. The idea was to prevent accidents, by collision or by fright, of the horses and mules pulling hundreds of stages, freight wagons, and buggies still crowding mountain roads in this transitional period. (AFC.)

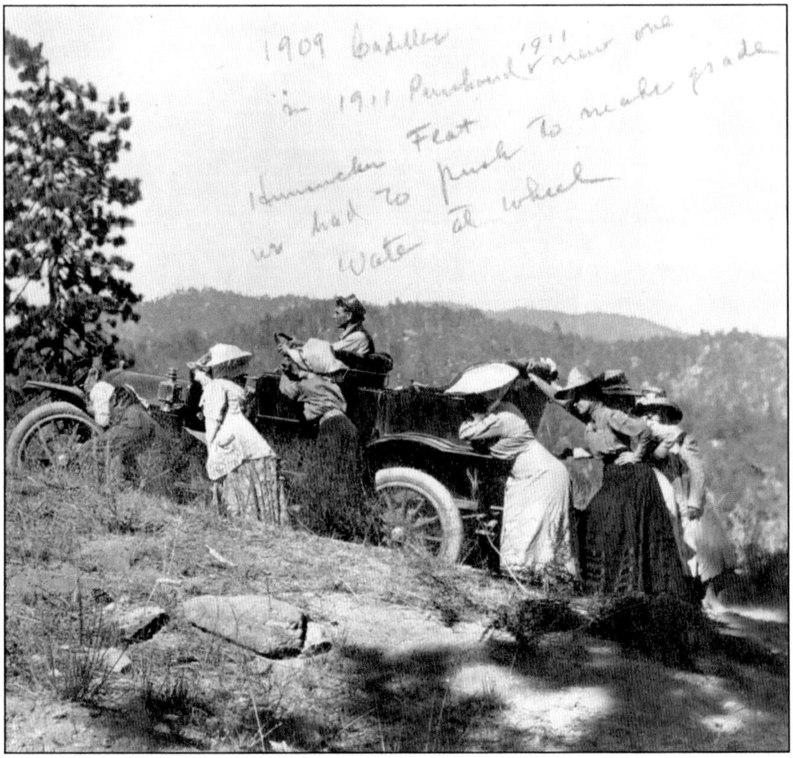

PUSHING TO MAKE THE GRADE. John Andreson Jr. owned automobiles since at least 1908, ultimately settling on the Cadillac as his car of choice, trading the old in for the new on a regular basis. However staged this view may be, it underscores the fact that many early automobiles were underpowered, and they frequently had trouble making mountain grades. Walter Kohl, an Andreson family brother-in-law, is at the wheel. (AFC.)

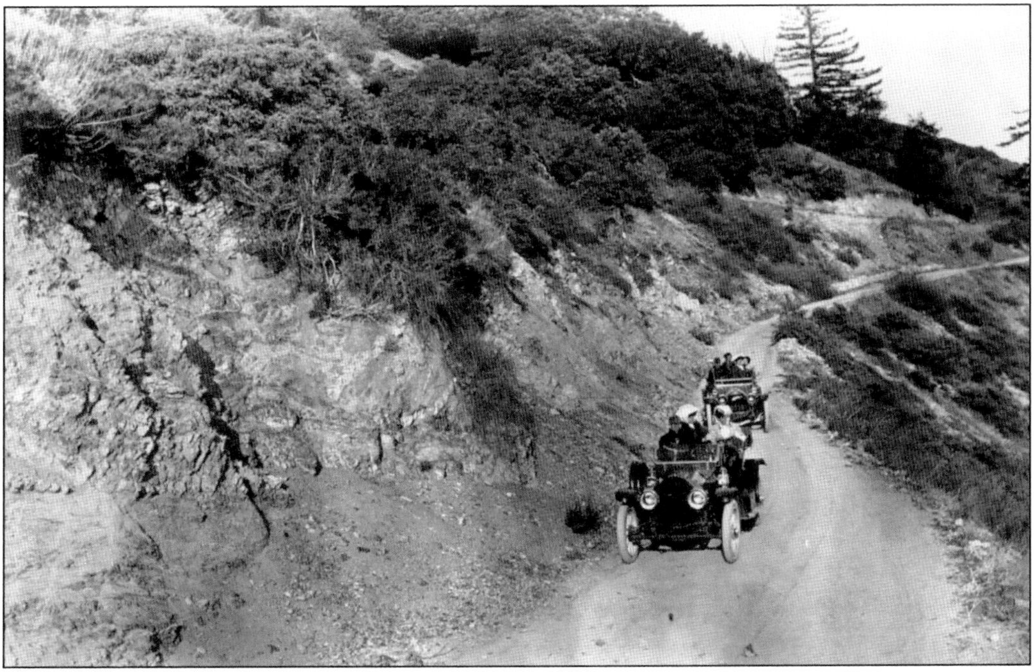

AUTOMOBILE CARAVAN IN 1911. Automobiles quickly became quite commonplace on mountain roads. Yet families still paused to take photographs on what was still regarded as a new and different adventure, much like Americans nationwide took photographs of family airplane trip departures and arrivals in the 1950s. This Andreson album memory is labeled "Arrowhead road to top of mountains 1911." (AFC.)

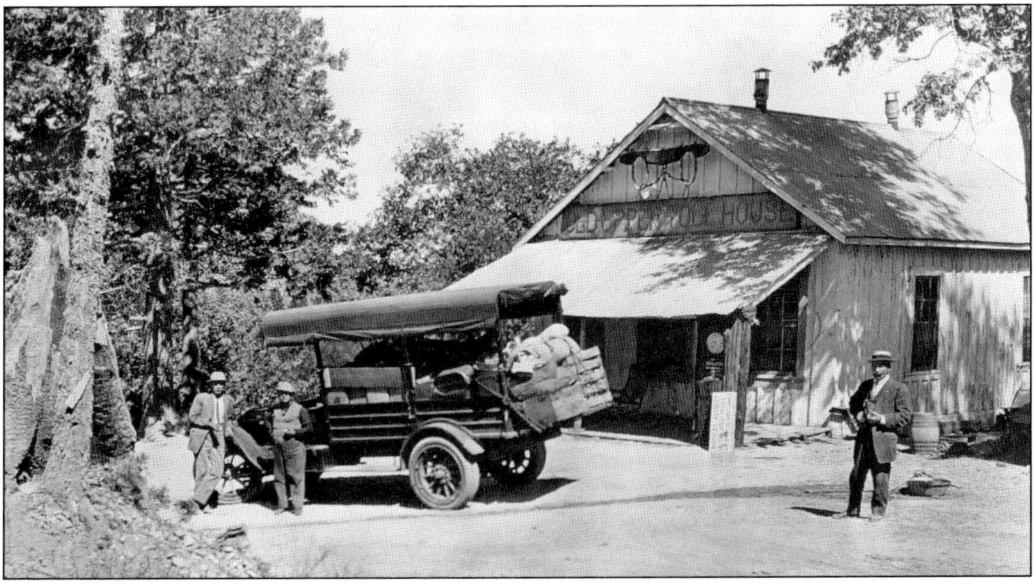

WHITE TRUCK AT OLD TOLLHOUSE. In July and August 1911, a devastating fire swept the San Bernardino Mountains. It was thought that every west-end community and resort would be lost. For 13 days, this White truck delivered men and supplies. Featured in newspaper articles as a "marvel," and credited with helping to save countless lives and properties, White trucks would quickly become the mainstay of mountain freight and auto stage lines. (AFC.)

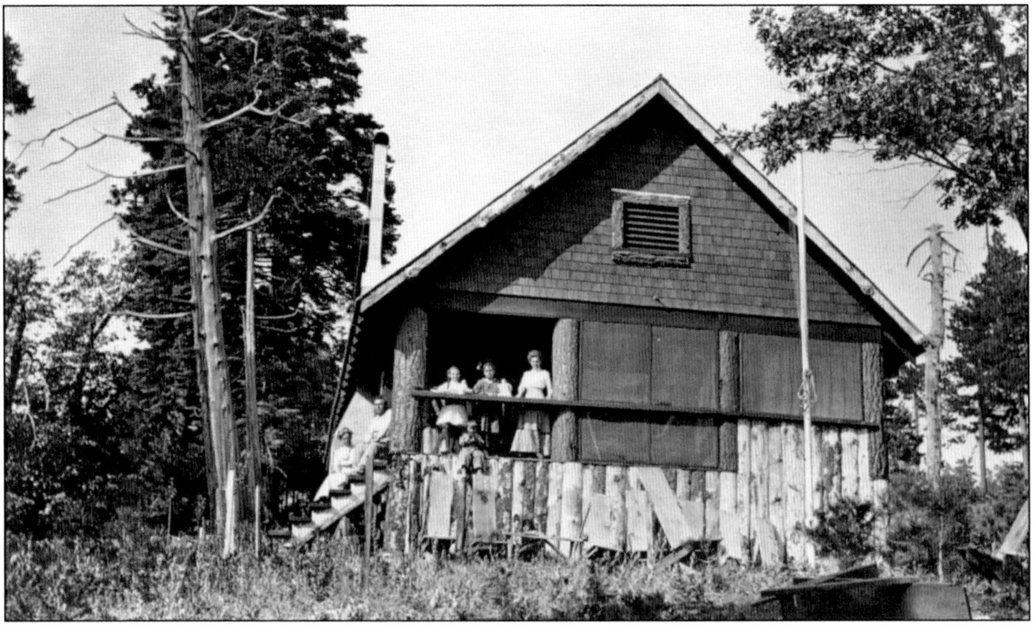

ANDRESON PINECREST CABIN 1912. John Andreson Jr. fought the horrifying 1911 fire for days without respite as a driver alongside others (rangers and mountain employees) whose duty it was to fight the fire. A wealthy man, he had no obligation yet offered use of his automobiles and helped to make supplies available. Dr. Baylis rewarded him and select others with bargain-basement leases to property at Pinecrest. (AFC.)

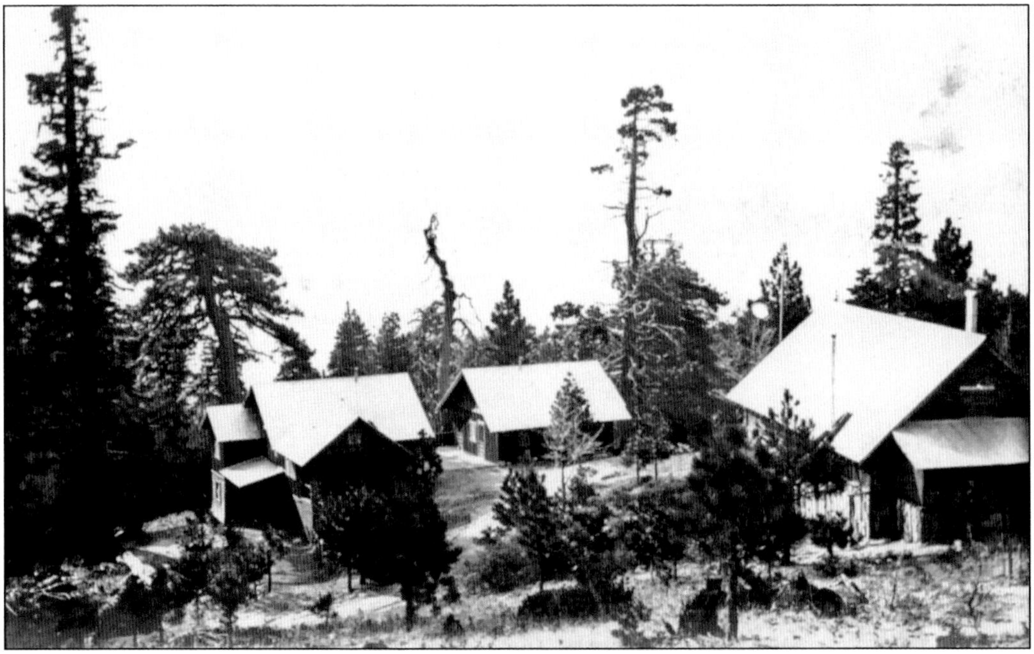

ANDRESON PINECREST COMPOUND. This 1912 family photograph is labeled the "Mountain cabins of John Andreson Jr., Walter Kohl and Roy F. Drew at Pinecrest, San Bernardino Mts." These closely related families were each rewarded in 1911 by Pinecrest owner Baylis with resort cabins. Pinecrest thus replaced Skyland as the chosen Andreson family vacation destination. (AFC.)

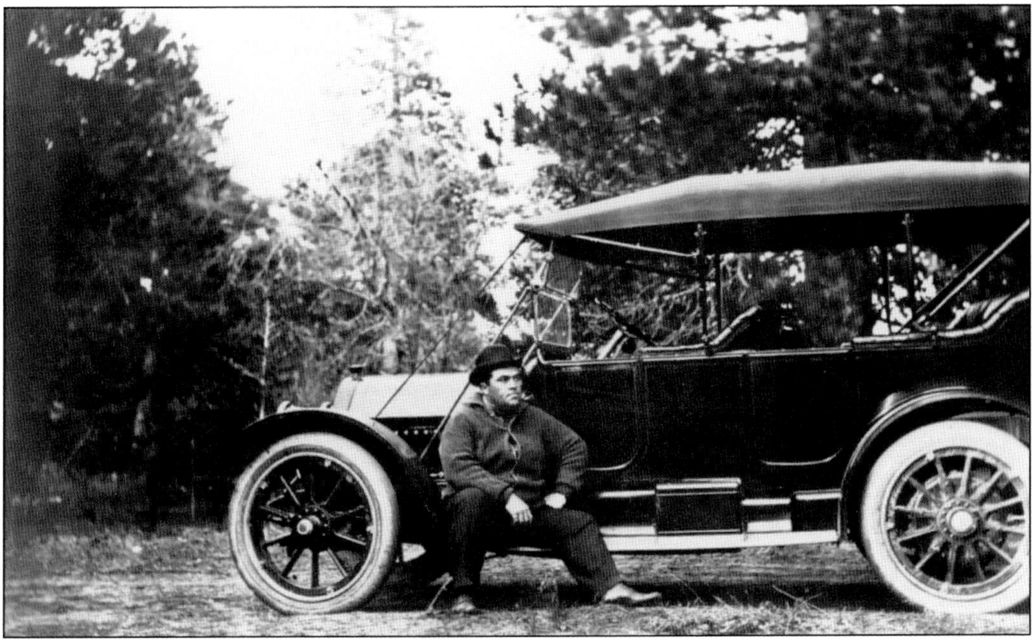

ANDRESON CADILLAC AT PINECREST. In March 1913, a proud and bold John Andreson Jr. sat on the running board of his powerful new Cadillac at Pinecrest for a carefully posed photograph. As with an Indianapolis 500 winner today, the automobile had clearly become an extension of his personality. Compare this photograph to earlier photographs of Andreson in wagons. The change is remarkable. (AFC.)

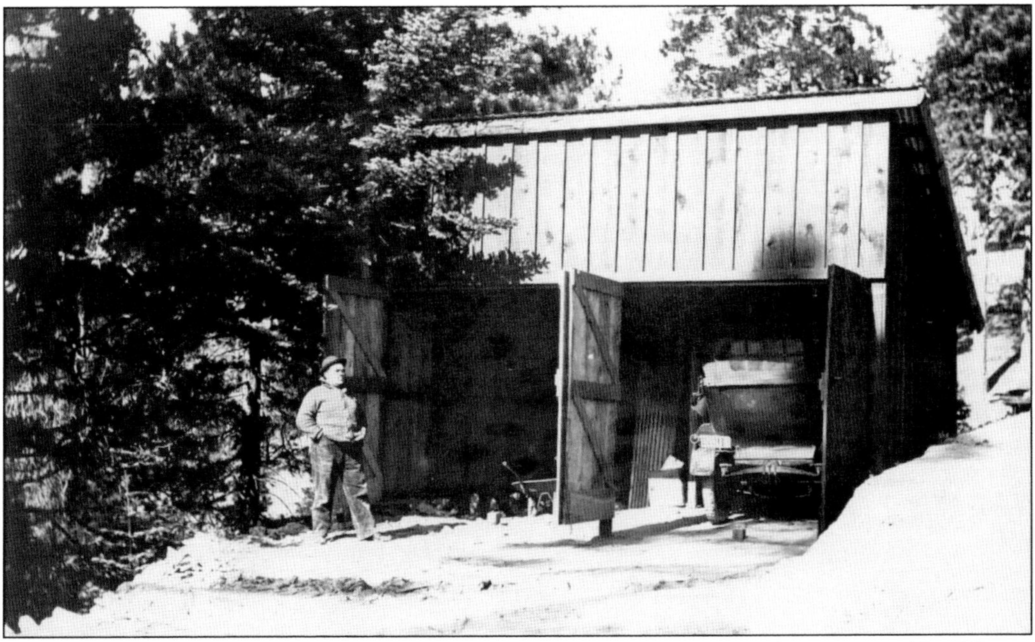

THE FIRST MOUNTAIN GARAGE? As new Pinecrest residents, John Andreson Jr. and R. F. Drew did a remarkable thing. They built a garage. Although the truth will likely never be known, this is either the very first or among the first mountain garages built by private individuals specifically for their automobiles. Even today, most mountain homes do not have a garage. (AFC.)

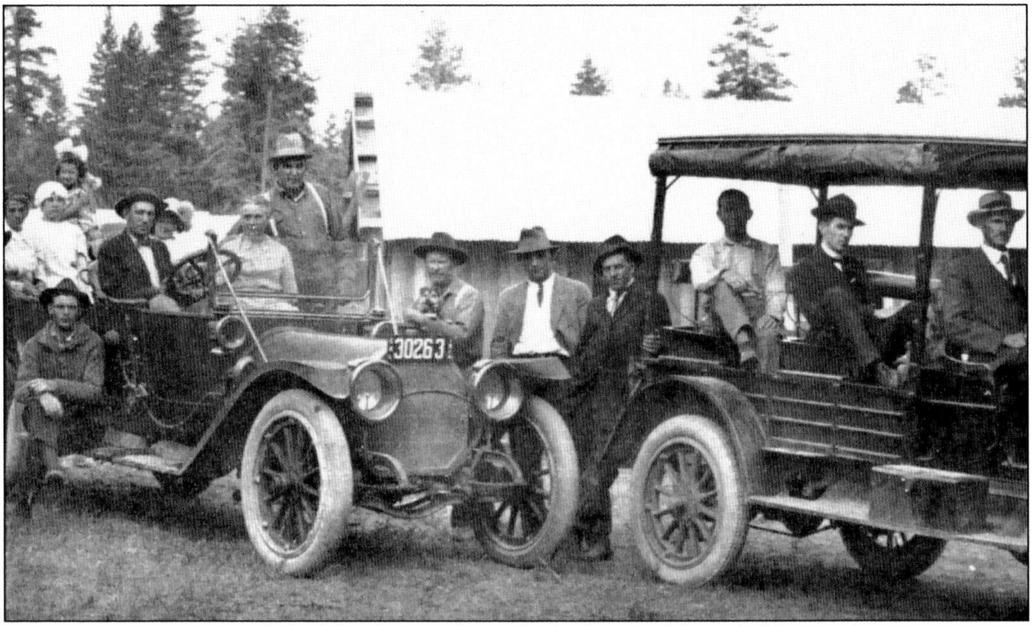

JIM JEFFRIES AND GUS KNIGHT. The world champion boxer "Gentleman" Jim Jeffries (the large man in the hat) poses here with mountain road and resort developer Gus Knight Jr. (the small man in the center holding a dog). Knight is credited, as much as anyone, with promoting the San Bernardino Mountains as a resort destination and the subsequent establishment of the Rim of the World Drive. (ROW.)

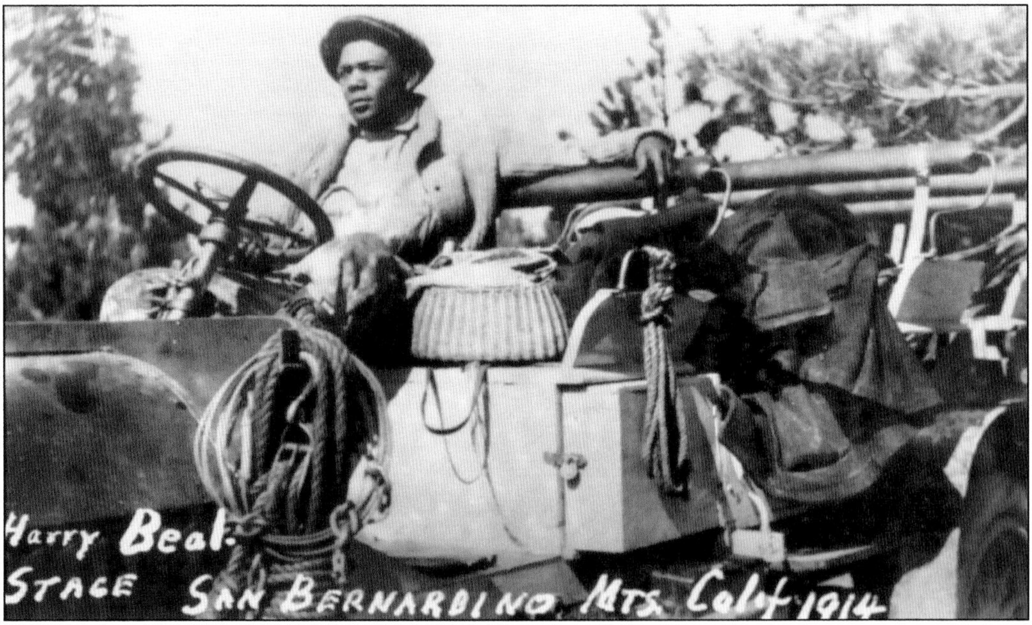

HARRY BEAL—PIONEER MOUNTAIN DRIVER. Harry Beal is shown here in a candid 1914 view. Beal, an African American, was a driver for the first mountain auto stage line. Prior to this, he had been a chauffeur for a prominent family in Redlands. All drivers carried a large block-and-tackle (like a winch) for emergencies, and it must be assumed that Beal was also a fisherman (see the creel).

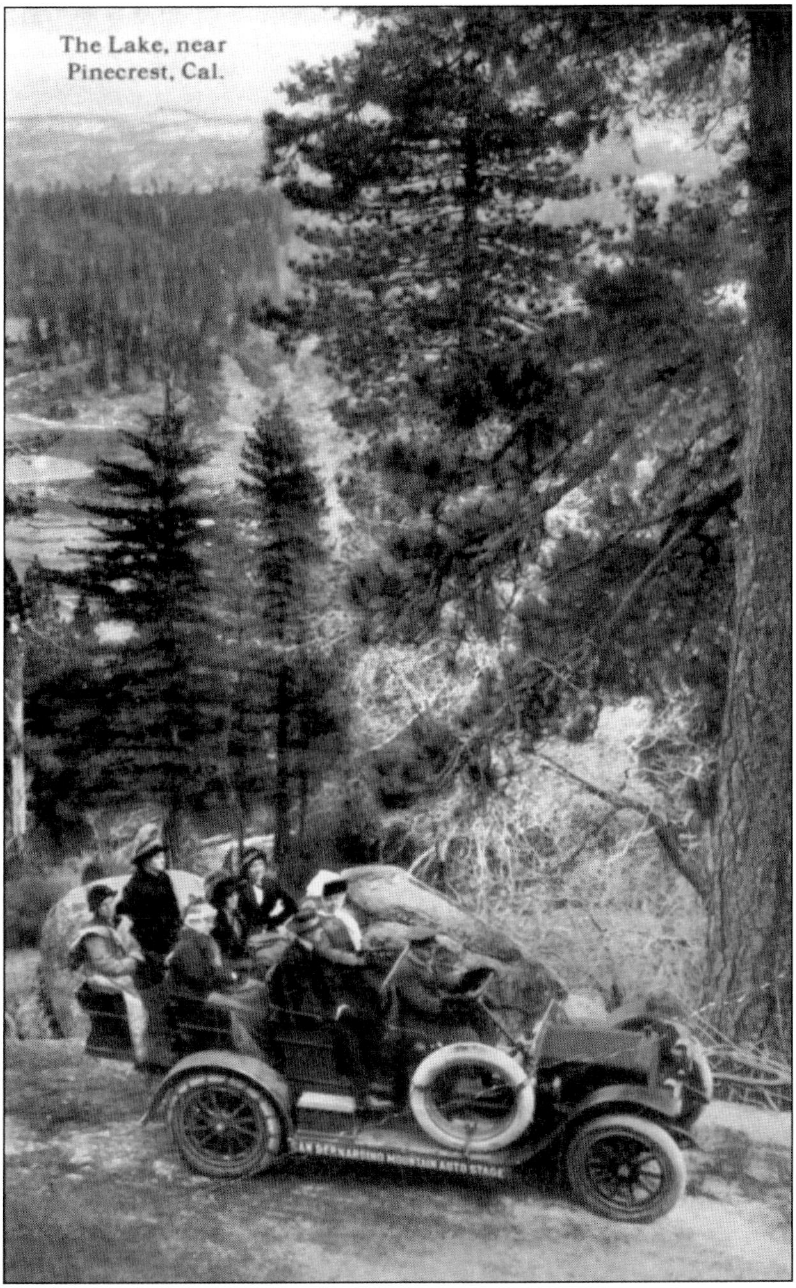

SAN BERNARDINO MOUNTAIN AUTO STAGE. An auto stage operated by Kirk R. Phillips provided service to Pinecrest, Skyland, the Squirrel Inn, and Little Bear Valley as early as 1911. By 1912, a second auto stage line, owned by Brooks and Shay, was organized to provide service to Bear Valley. Each company used powerful White trucks, with special coach bodies manufactured by the Pioneer Commercial Auto Company, to carry as many as 15 passengers and their luggage up steep mountain grades. The term *stage* was used interchangeably with *bus* until at least the mid-1940s. By 1925, the Rim of the World Drive was accessible to most Southern Californians in just a few hours. One could leave Los Angeles, for example, at 7:00 a.m., arrive in San Bernardino at 10:00 a.m., reach Pinecrest at 12:00 noon, and relax at Arrowhead Lake at 12:45 p.m. (CC.)

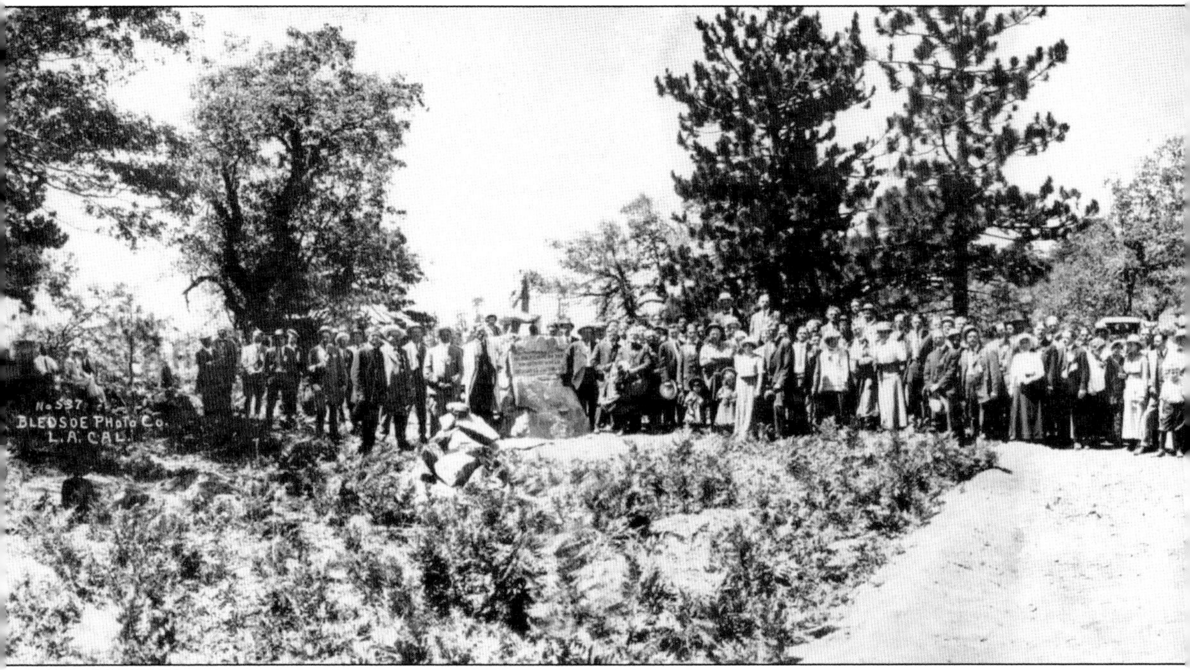

RIM DEDICATION AND SWITCHBACKS. From 1905 to 1913, the County of San Bernardino slowly purchased toll and lumber roads to assemble the Rim of the World Drive. On July 18, 1915, a group of politicians, mountain enthusiasts, landowners, newspapermen, and automobilists gathered (above) for the dedication of what county supervisors had officially named the San Bernardino Mountain Crest Highway, a landmark event seen in this previously unpublished panorama. As

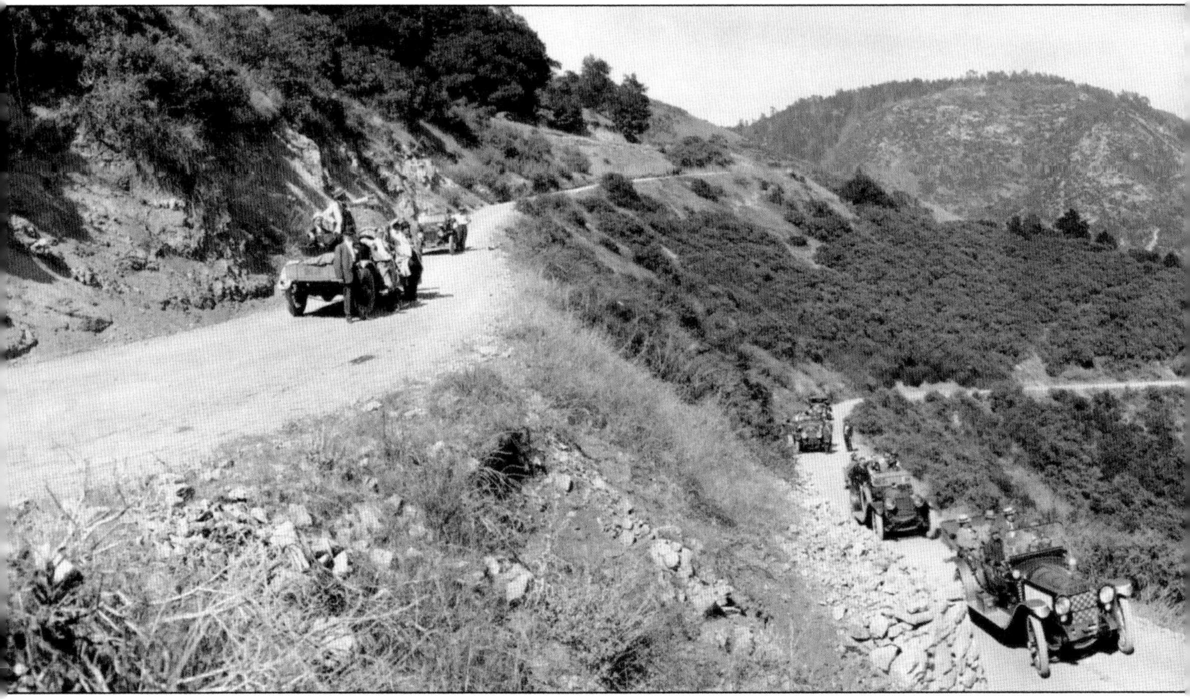

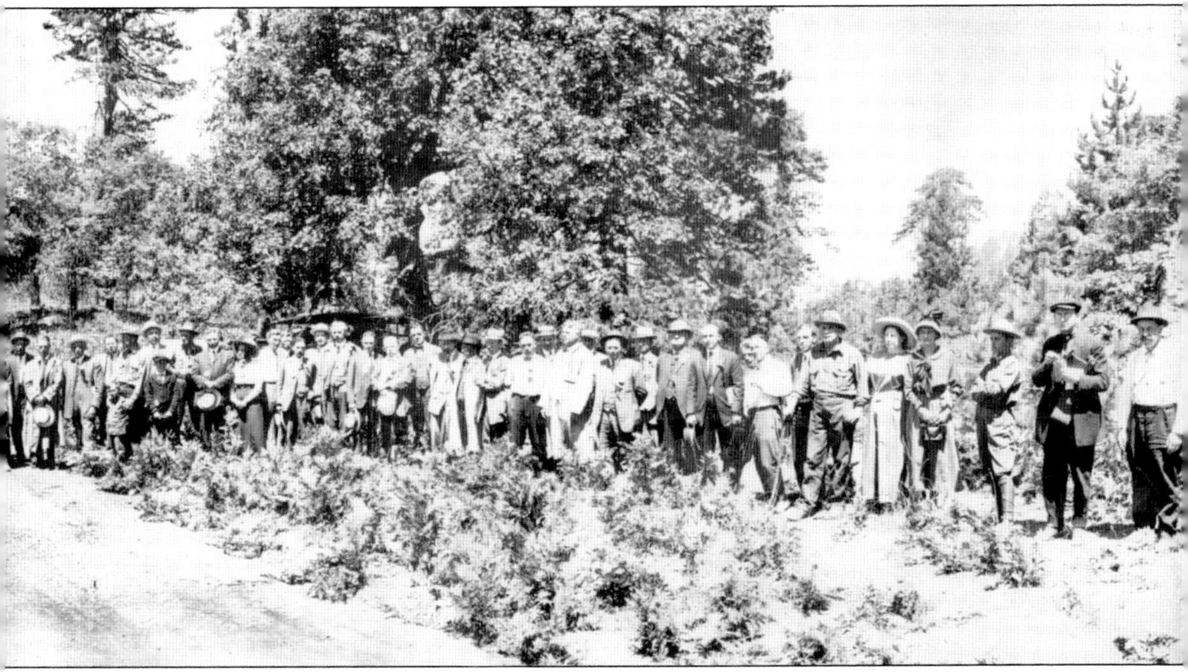

it was already nicknamed the Rim of the World Drive, in an eloquent address, John Steven McGroarty (named California poet laureate in 1933) proclaimed, "I baptize thee 'Rim of the World' tell thy story to the children of the earth as they pass this way." The panorama of the Waterman Canyon switchbacks (below) was taken in 1915 by the same photographer, recording one of the most difficult portions of the road as it first opened. (AFC and BP.)

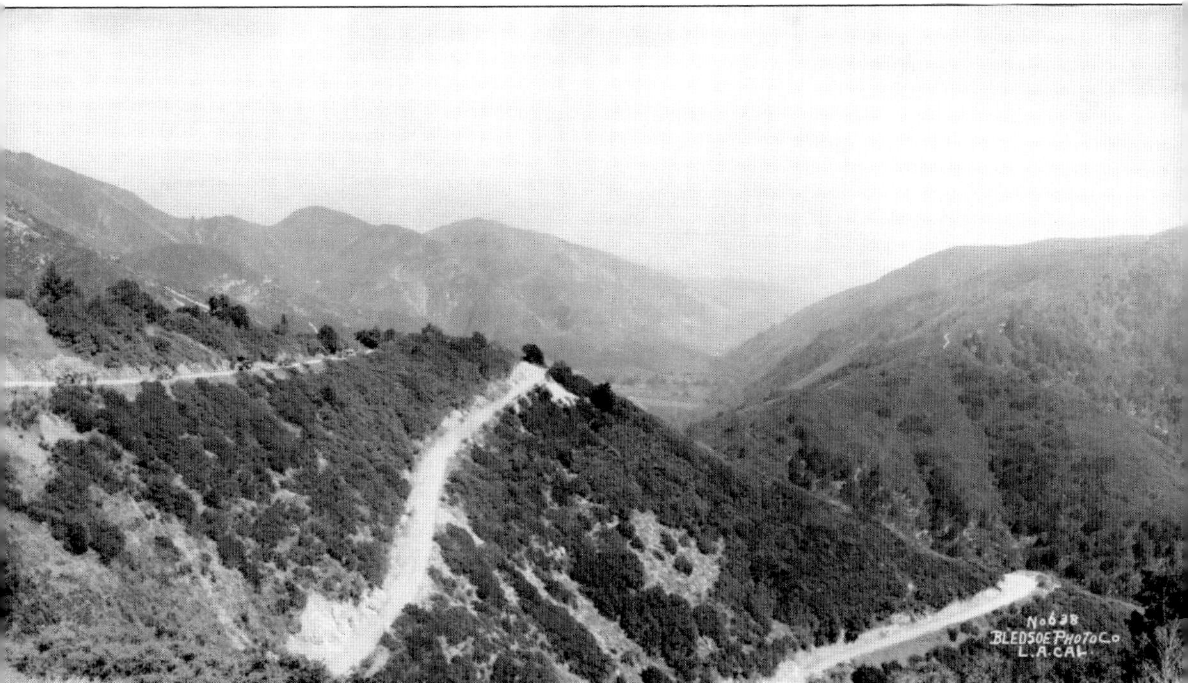

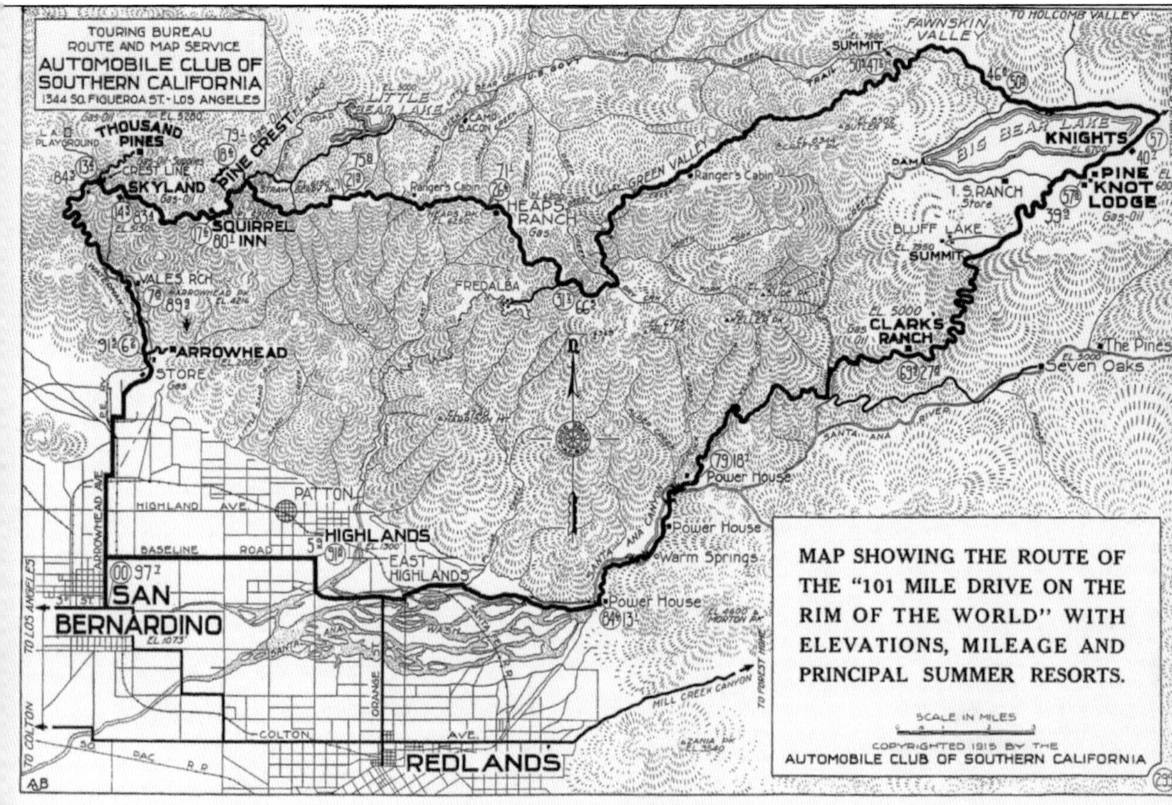

A 1915 RIM ROUTE MAP. This wonderfully detailed map depicts the original Rim of the World Drive. Beginning in the early 1890s, essentially the same route was traveled by buggies, wagons, and mules. It was not until 1913, when the last critical link was acquired as a free county road, that county construction began on the Rim of the World Drive. There were relatively few locations to stay and get gas and oil along the route when this map was published in 1915, making the drive a true adventure. Explosive growth and development soon followed, both in the mountains above and in the valleys below. The economic effects of opening the Rim of the World Drive, heralded as one of the nation's premiere mountain motor highways and as one of California's most beautiful and scenic drives, were soon felt as far away as Los Angeles when savvy real estate investors began eyeing undervalued mountain property. Accessibility would, for example, later make Lake Arrowhead an especially attractive investment. (ACSC.)

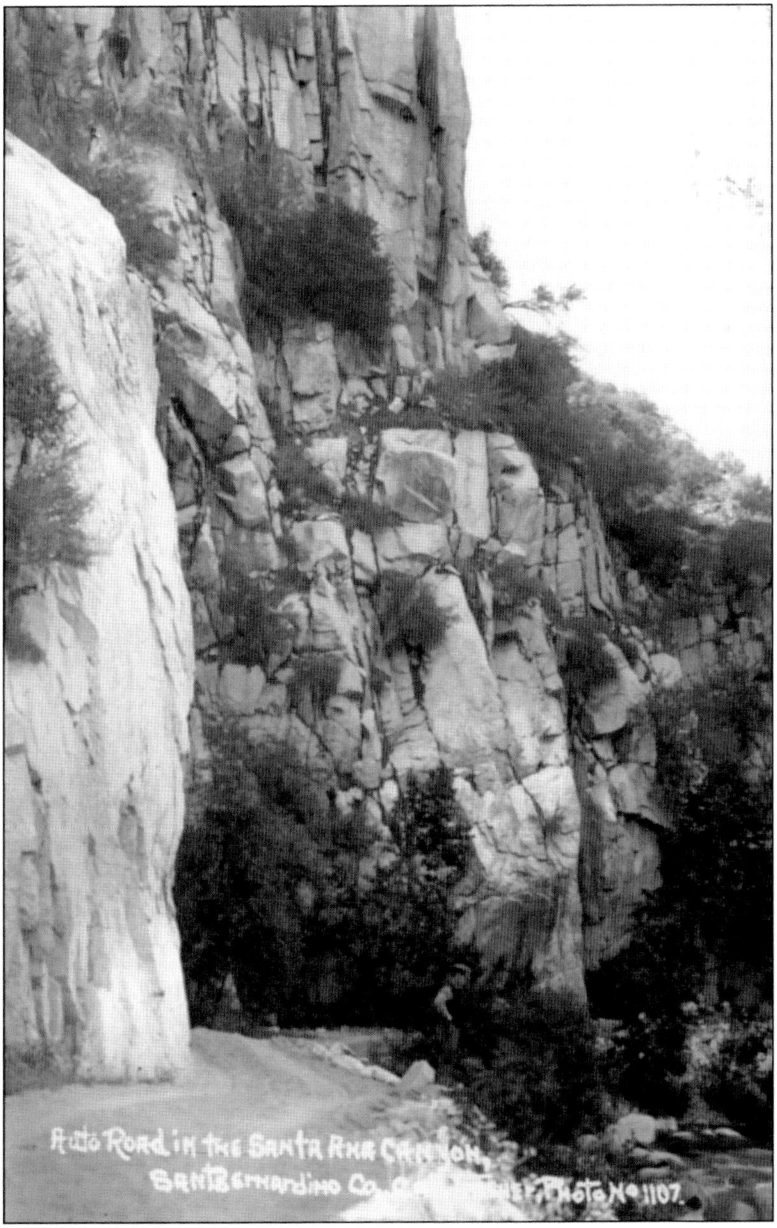

Steep Santa Ana Canyon Walls. This rare image depicts one of the steepest sections of the original "Auto Road in the Santa Ana Canyon." It is also one of the first Frashers, Inc., photographs ever taken in California, for the address of the studio listed on the back of the card is in Wapato, Washington. The Santa Ana Canyon portions of the Rim of the World Drive were entirely destroyed by massive flooding in January 1916, when record rain totals fell in the Southland. The destruction was absolute, and after giving careful consideration to cost and convenience, county highway department engineers determined those portions of the roadway passing through Santa Ana Canyon could not be repaired. A decision was made to realign the original 1915 Rim of the World Drive to a location along Mill Creek and Mountain Home Creek. The new alignment was not the most direct route and it wasn't the best grade, but at least it didn't run through a narrow canyon with walls reminiscent of the Grand Canyon. (FI.)

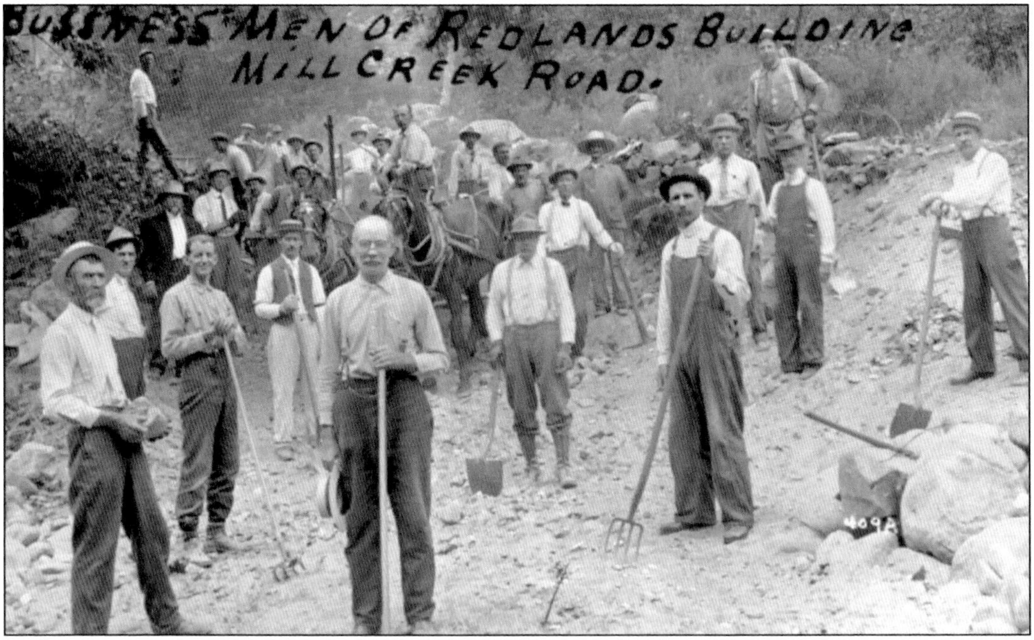

BUILDING MILL CREEK ROAD. A group of Redlands businessmen and politicians quickly proposed to county supervisors that a new Rim of the World Drive alignment be built to replace the one devastated by flooding in January 1916. Supervisors agreed, and construction began immediately with some help from the men of Redlands (above) in an obviously posed shot (note the lack of sweat stains) and a much more substantial commitment of convict labor. Rushed to completion in 1916, the incredibly narrow alignment (below) with its steep grades and switchbacks was less automobile-friendly than the original. It did have one big advantage, however, in that it was much less prone to flooding and could be driven year-round. Finally, it brought the Rim of the World Drive much closer to Redlands than the original 1915 alignment and brought revenues to the pockets of the same businessmen who proposed the realignment.

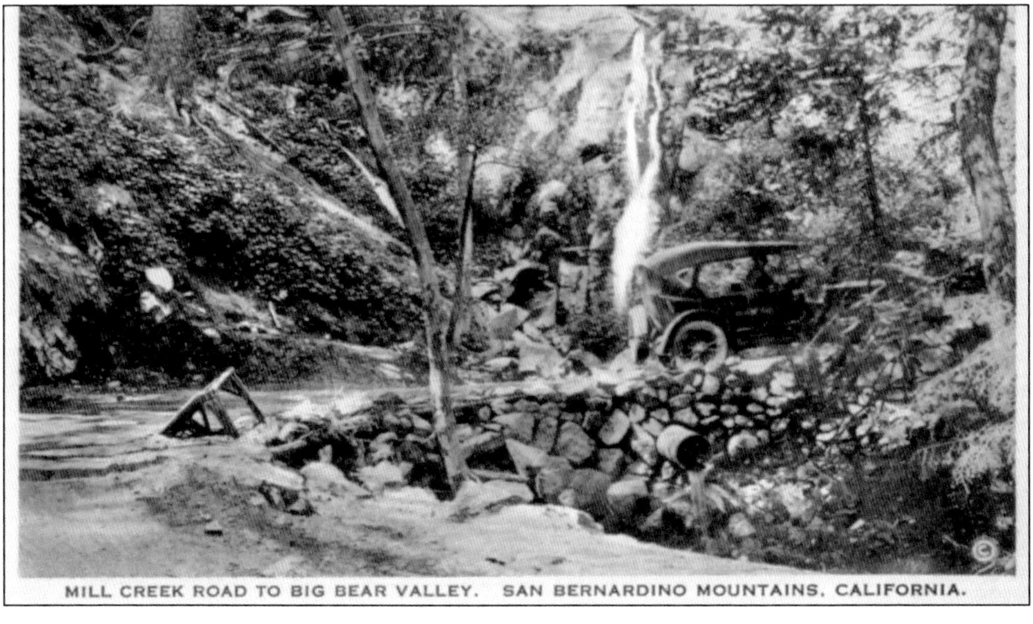

MILL CREEK ROAD TO BIG BEAR VALLEY. SAN BERNARDINO MOUNTAINS, CALIFORNIA.

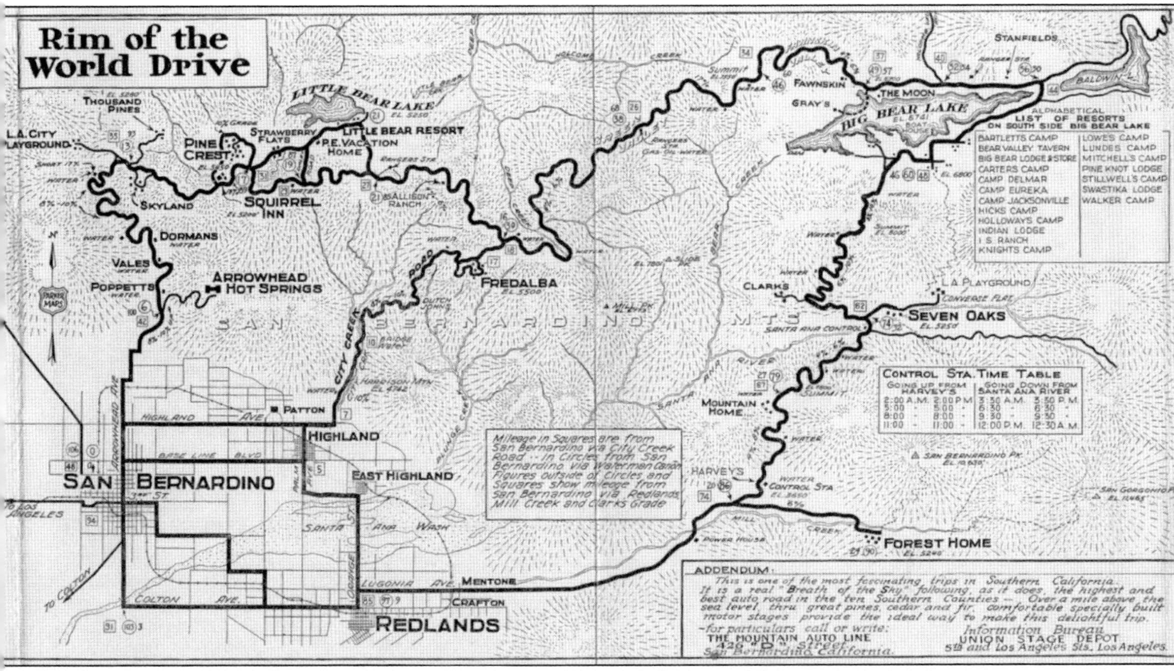

Rim Drive Realigned. Taken from a 1920 Rim of the World Drive Mountain Auto Line brochure, the above map provides an overview of San Bernardino Mountain resorts and roadways after realignment following the 1916 flood. Compared to the previous 1915 Rim alignment map, it is clear that a staggering number of changes have taken place across the mountains in just five years. First, the total number of mountain resorts catering to the tourist trade has more than doubled. Second, new feeder roads have been developed, creating an interconnected mountain roadway network with the Rim of the World Drive as the backbone. City Creek Road, also rebuilt by the county beginning in 1916, is an excellent example as it connected directly to the Rim of the World Drive, providing an alternate route to both Big Bear and Little Bear Lakes. As an interesting fact, the length of the original "101 Mile Drive on the Rim of the World" had increased to a total of 110 miles. (MAL.)

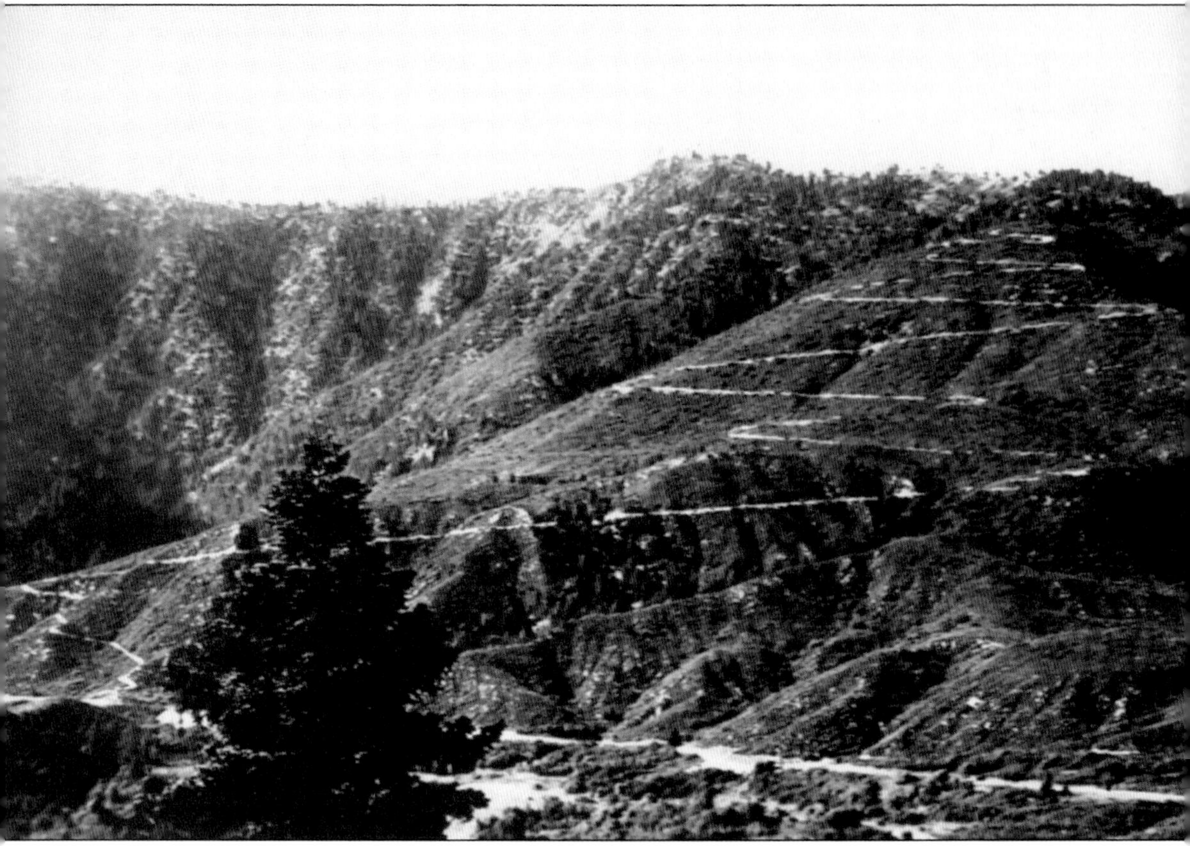

CLARK'S GRADE. The most famous grade on the Rim of the World Drive was Clark's Grade. Built by Hiram Clark, owner of a ranch at the base of the grade and an investor in the 1899 Bear Valley and Redlands Toll Road Company, it was a dizzying set of switchbacks leading from the Santa Ana River far below to the summit above at 7,900 feet. The almost unimaginable ascent was often used to test cars. In 1918, for example, David Fassett of Los Angeles tested the new Reo "light four" on the challenging grade, calling the performance "amazing." First improved in 1914 prior to the opening of the Rim of the World Drive, Clark's Grade was perpetually rebuilt and improved by county crews and prison gangs. Not until 1930 were federal moneys made available to eliminate this motorist's nightmare. It is the subject of literally hundreds of postcard views. (AFC.)

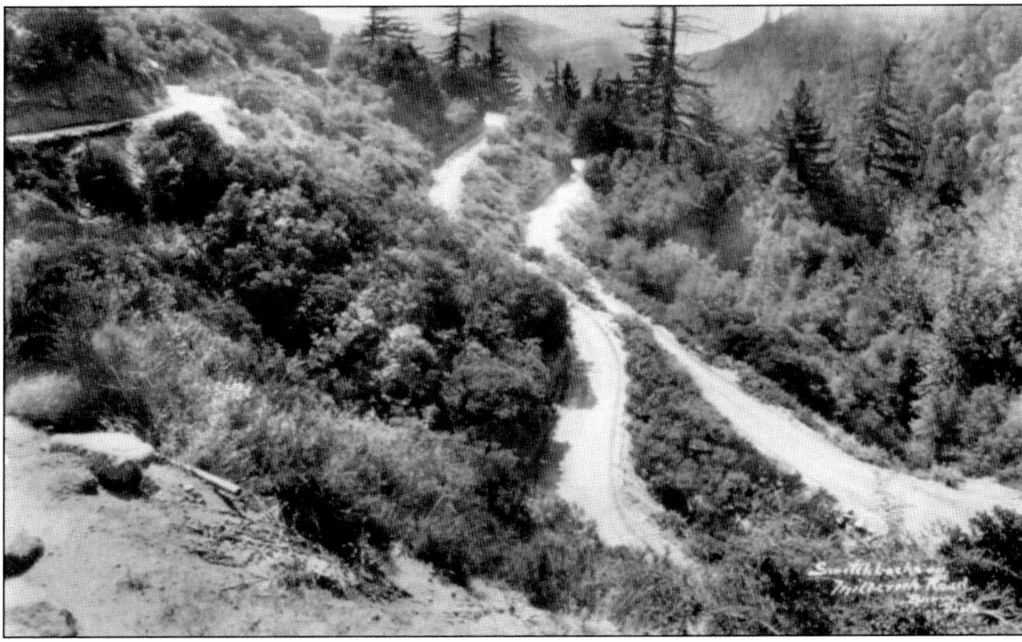

MORE MOUNTAIN SWITCHBACKS. Switchbacks and mountain roads simply go hand in hand, and the San Bernardino Mountains are no exception. Prior to the widespread use of dynamite and heavy machinery (affordable only to federal agencies, railroads, and mining companies), virtually every mountain road was built as simply as possible. Expensive cuts deep into hillsides or building cantilever roadways to achieve a better grade were not an option for most counties. Switchbacks were found, therefore, across the San Bernardino Mountains in Waterman Canyon, Mill Creek (above), City Creek (below), Mountain Home Creek, Cushenberry Grade, and, of course, Clark's Grade. A challenge to even the best of drivers in inclement weather, they were the stuff of legend, the grist of a veritable paper mill of newspaper articles, postcards, and letters home. (Above and below BS.)

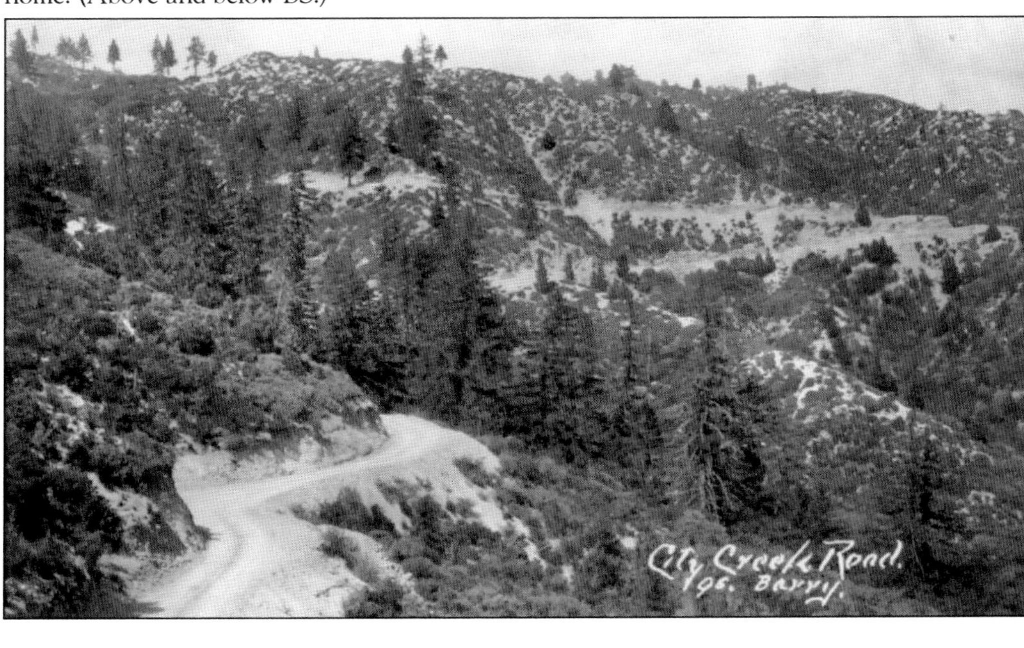

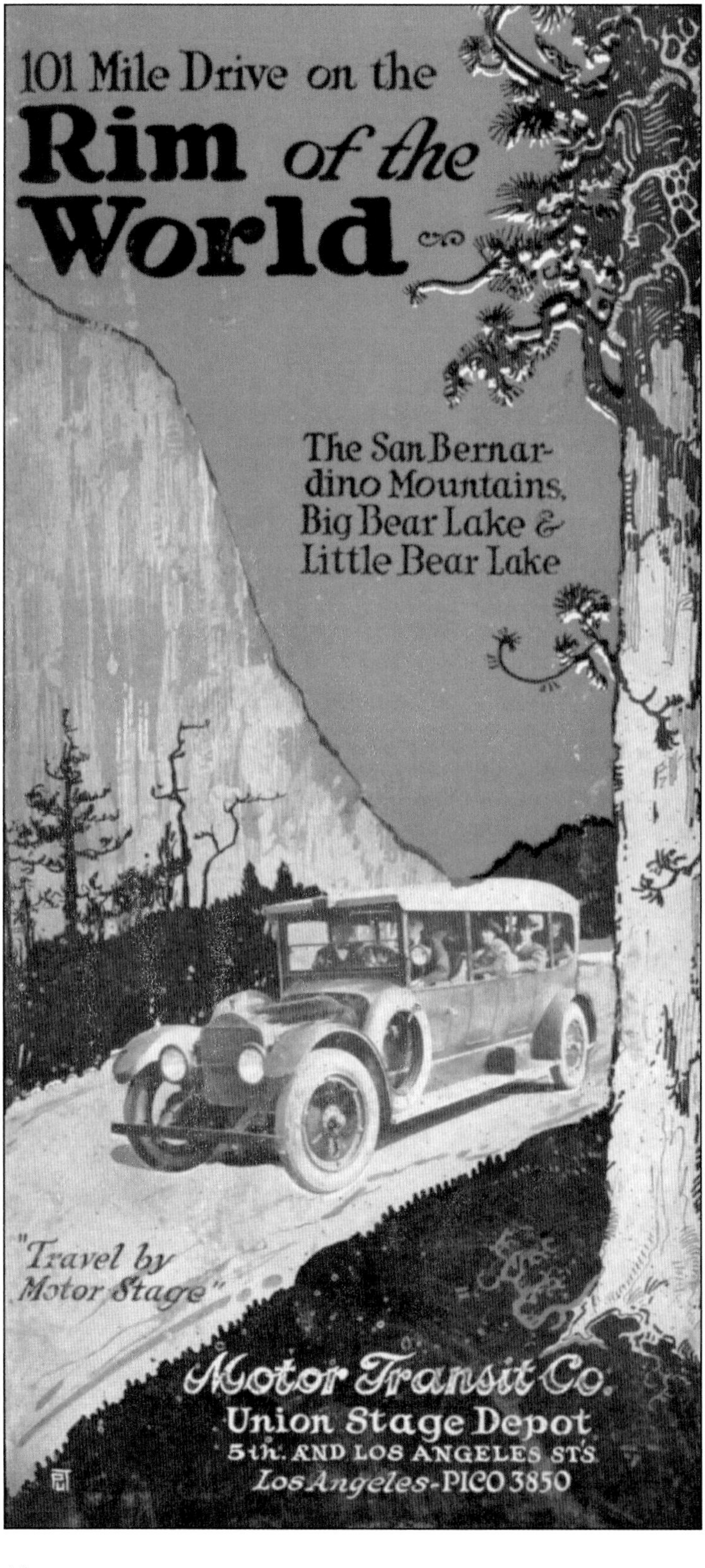

TRAVEL BY MOTOR STAGE. Artistically designed brochures were produced by various companies competing for the San Bernardino Mountain tourist dollar. From the very beginning, designers plastered the name "101 Mile Drive on the Rim of the World" on everything they could. Almost everyone in Southern California had heard of the roadway, and by the mid-1920s, it had become a premier vacation destination. This brochure advertises the Rim of the World Drive as "the longest and highest automobile mountain road in the United States. For 101 miles, stages pass through a panorama of mountain grandeur." From Los Angeles, it was a two-day round-trip to Big Bear Valley by way of Crestline, Little Bear Valley, and Fawnskin. Including connecting to the separately operated mountain system in San Bernardino, the round-trip fare from Los Angeles was $12.55. The Rim of the World Drive had already become much more affordable. In 1915, for example, a round-trip from San Bernardino to Bear Valley alone cost $12. (MTC.)

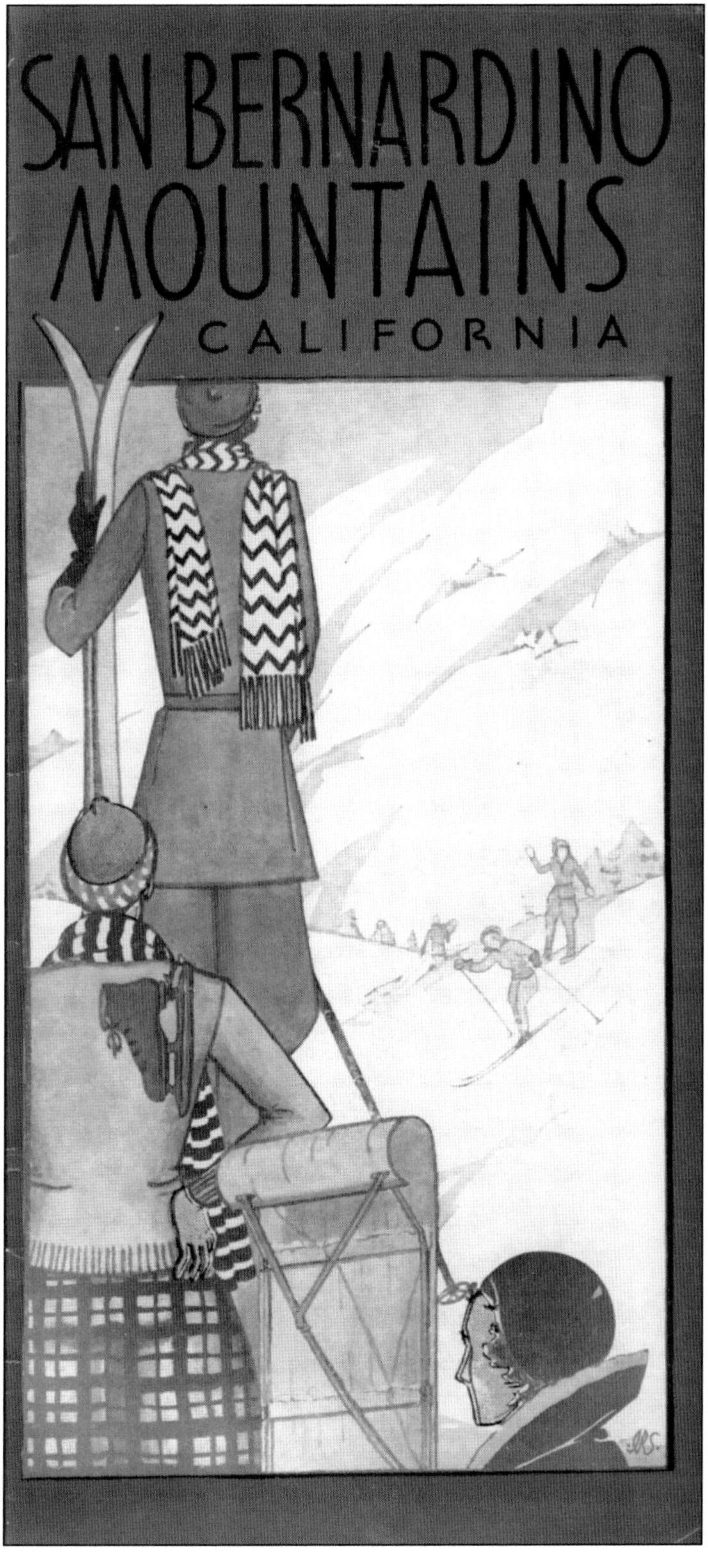

RIM LEAGUE BROCHURE. The amazing art deco–designed brochure was the brainchild of the Rim O' the World League, an organization dedicated to "secure by united effort the best and highest advantage for the entire San Bernardino Mountain District, to herald to all the earth the charms of its matchless resorts and playgrounds." Three league districts—Crest Forest, Lake Arrowhead, and Big Bear—acted together for perhaps the first time to trumpet the San Bernardino Mountains. Not surprisingly, the Rim of the World Drive was the key to their entire promotional scheme. They write, "From the time you enter this Mountain Wonderland, you will become impressed with the fact there is something primeval about the surroundings . . . and along the scenic RIM OF THE WORLD DRIVE is revealed the grandeur of nature." The purple prose complements the impressive cover, although the central point of interest here is that the Rim of the World Drive was seen by the brochure authors as the "glue" that kept their organizations together. (RWL.)

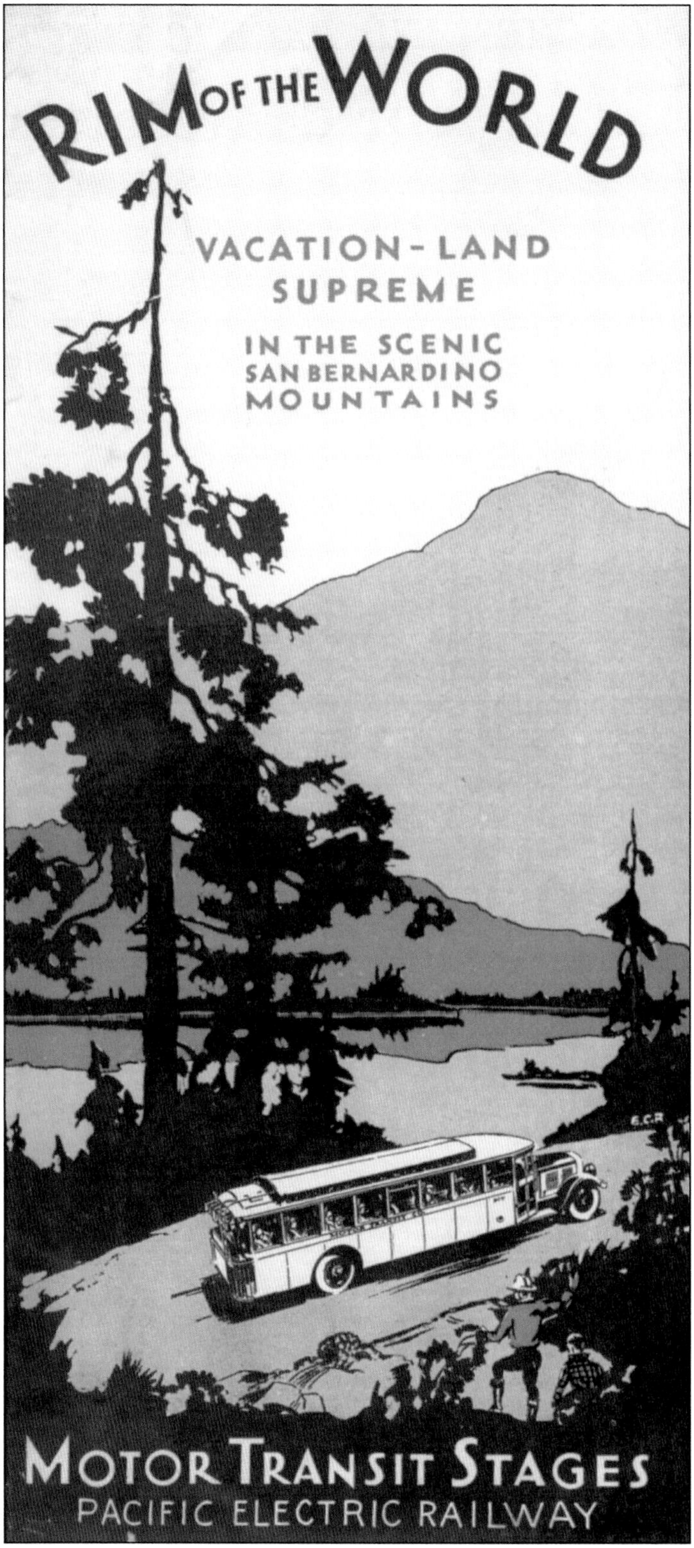

EXTRA-LOW FARES TO RIM RESORTS. By the 1930s, the San Bernardino Mountains and the Rim of the World Drive were linked together as a single identity in the public mind. The primary purpose of this 1930 brochure was to convince vacationing Angelinos to take Motor Transit Coaches and/or the Pacific Electric Railway to San Bernardino, and to continue on to mountain resorts by "Transit Stages." All routes leading to "Rim of the World Resorts" were covered, including those leading up Waterman Canyon, City Creek, and Mill Creek. "Unusually low rates" were offered in an effort to entice those planning to drive their own automobile away from the idea. Owning an automobile was becoming affordable for most Americans, and transit companies were fighting an increasingly uphill battle. After completion of the high-gear road in 1933, it was a losing battle. The private automobile was quickly becoming the preferred mode of transportation across America. (MTC.)

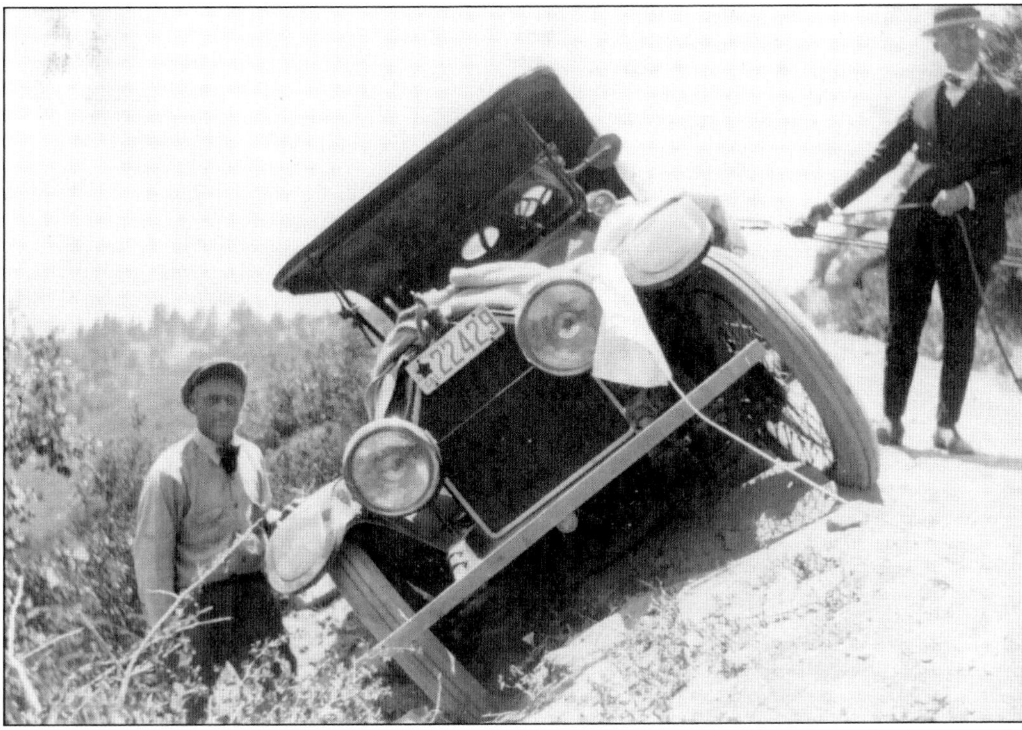

Accidents Happen. Automobile accidents and breakdowns occurred on a regular basis on the Rim of the World Drive. Included in this potpourri were flat tires, boiling radiators, slipping over the edge, and running into everything from trees to boulders to other cars. This unfortunate driver appears to have simply cut too close to the edge, a common problem when guardrails didn't exist and roads were exceedingly narrow.

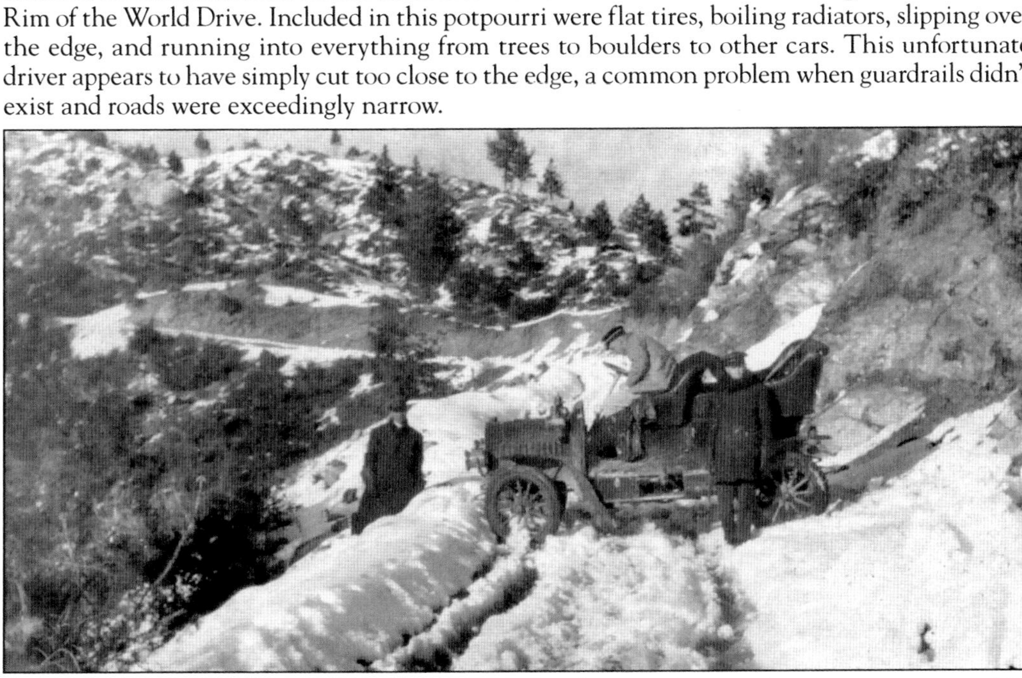

More Accidents Happen. This is one of the earliest known photographs of a winter automobile "accident" on the roadway that would become the Rim of the World Drive. Winter has always posed something of a problem for mountain residents. These adventurers got this far without chains and had to turn around.

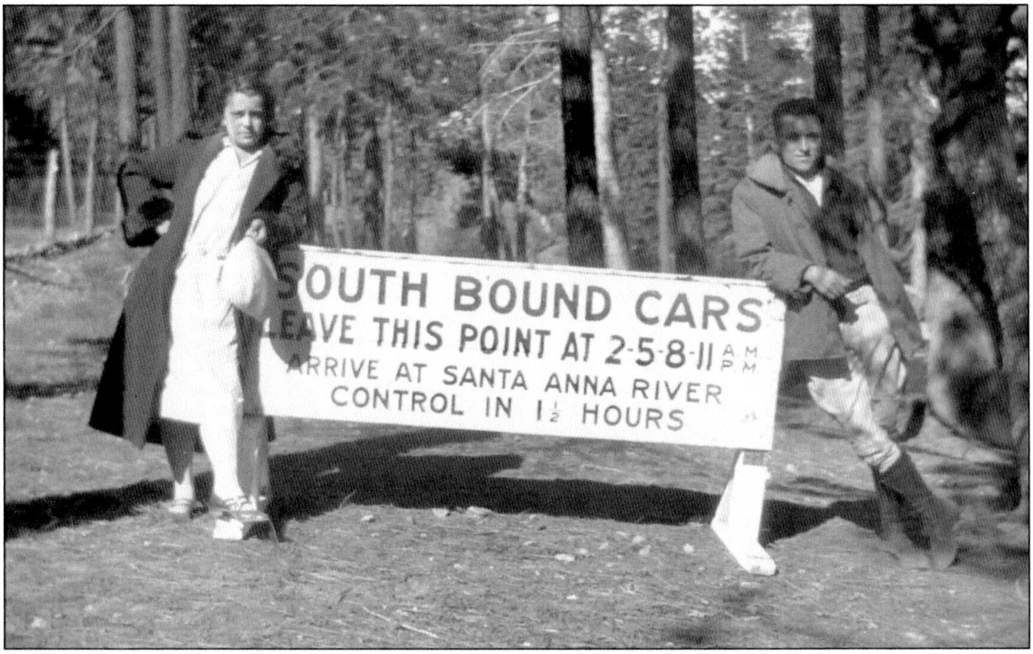

CONTROL SIGN AND LINES. The Rim of the World Drive was realigned up Mill Creek and Mountain Home Creek in 1916. The new road was both narrow and steep, and control stations (above) were established by the board of supervisors when snarled traffic and numerous accidents prevented orderly travel on the highway. Traffic was strictly regulated heading both up and down the hill (northbound and southbound) at specific intervals both day and night. Cars entered the control area in order of their arrival; speed limits were initially fixed at 15 miles per hour; slow vehicles had to give way allowing faster cars to pass; and if a vehicle couldn't make the control grades in one and a half hours, they had to pull over until the next cycle. Long lines (below) were the norm on the Rim of the World Drive.

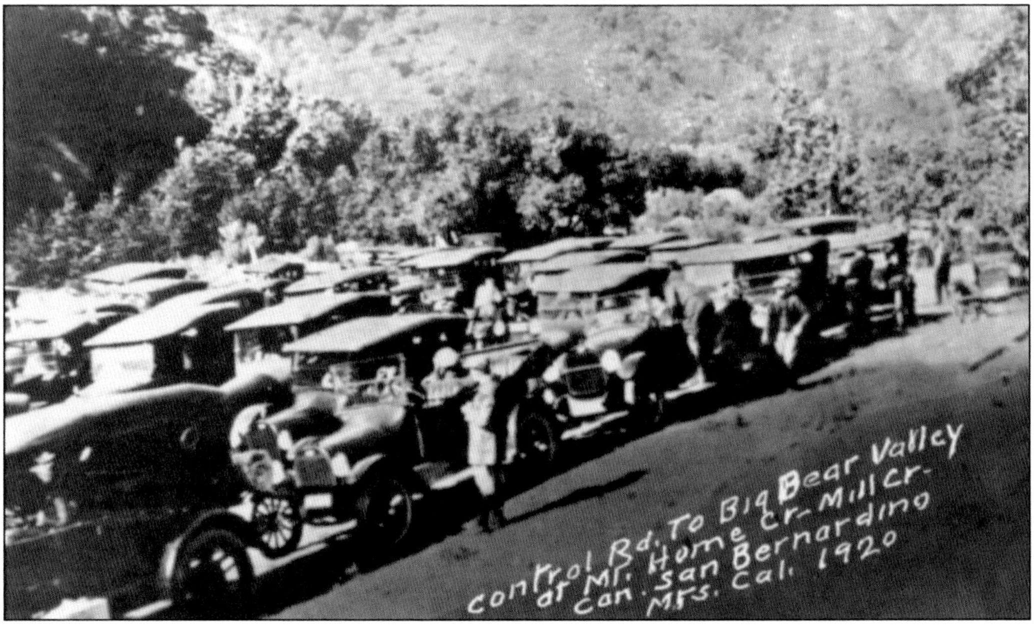

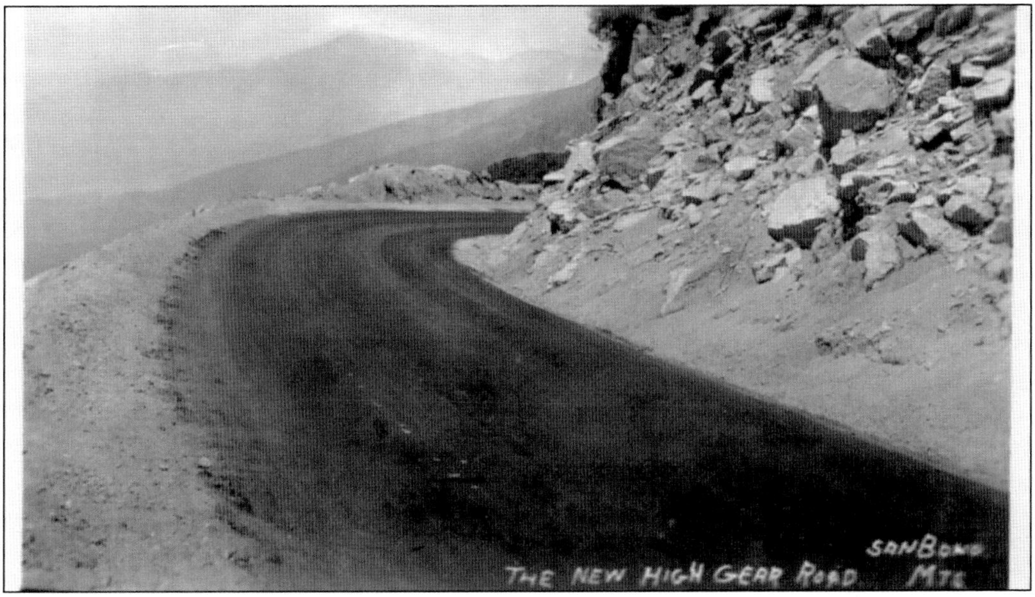

THE HIGH-GEAR ROAD. Construction of the high-gear road on the Rim of the World Drive was a genuine breakthrough. First planned in the mid-1920s, construction was underway by 1928, the switchbacks were eliminated by 1931, and the completed highway was officially opened on October 21, 1933. The view above, taken immediately after opening, clearly shows just how difficult construction was (the road was literally carved into the mountainside) and how precipitous the drive was. Highway safety improvements continued throughout the mid-1930s, including construction of rock post and chain-link guardrails. The back of the linen postcard below reads, "The Road to San Bernardino Mountain Resorts: This glorious scenic drive over the high-gear state highway leads to the beautiful land of sky-blue waters in the San Bernardino Mountains, the famed vacation spot above the clouds." (Below CC.)

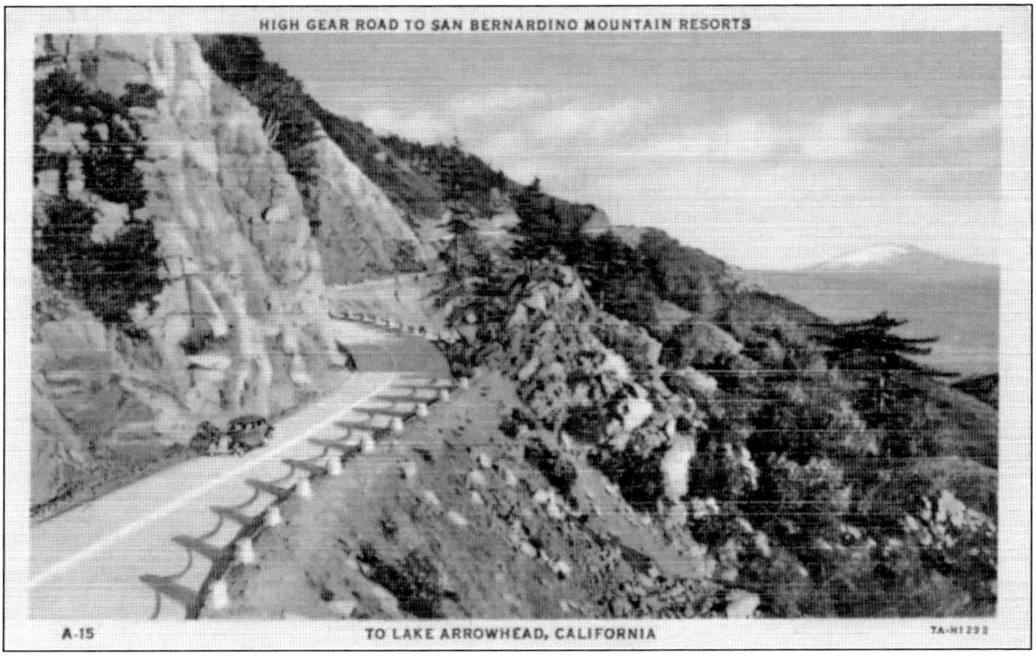

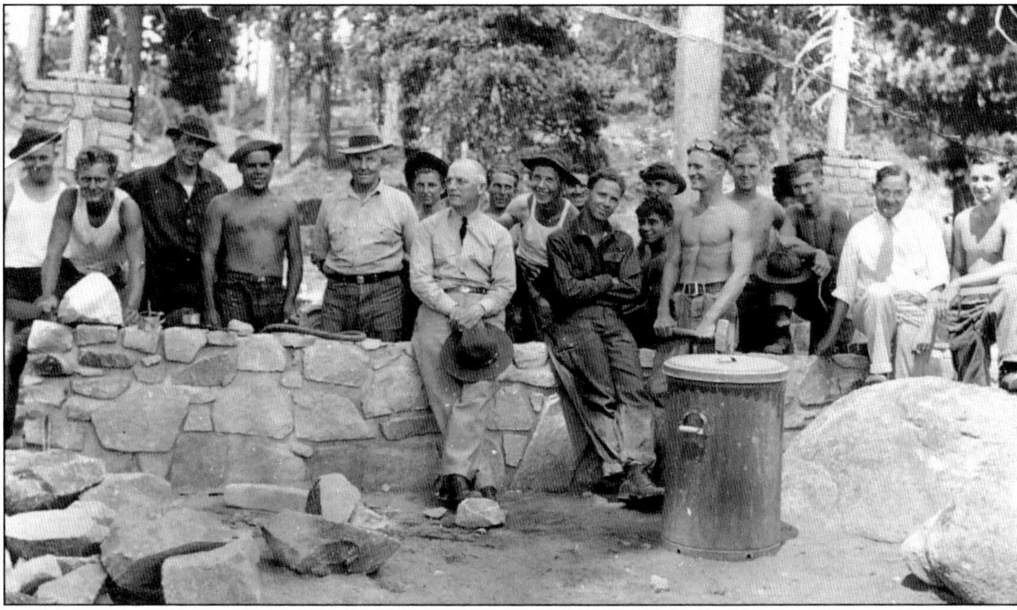

BUILDING BAYLIS PARK. Some of the most scenic components of the Rim of the World Drive are red-rock turnouts, retaining walls, pillars, culverts, and even a bridge. These rustic features are found from the "Narrows" on the west to Fawnskin on the east. The rock itself is from the slopes above the south shore of Big Bear Lake. Here WPA-funded workers take a break while building Baylis Park.

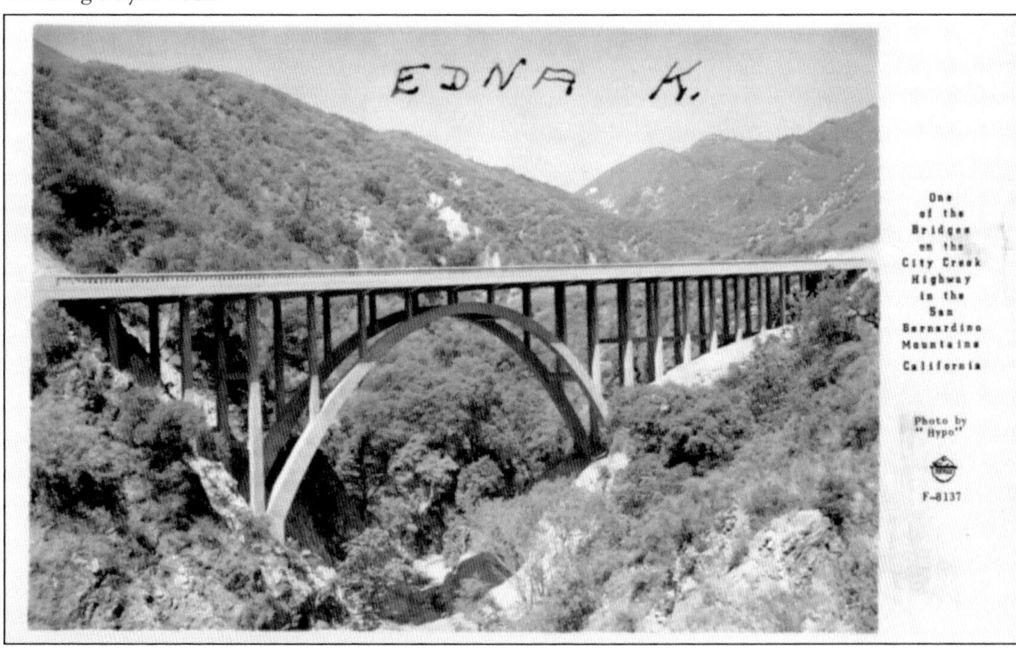

IMPROVED CITY CREEK HIGHWAY. System-wide mountain transportation improvements were implemented by state highway officials across the breadth of the San Bernardino Mountains with the idea of providing high-gear highway connections throughout. This 1940s view shows City Creek Highway, begun on November 2, 1938, as a $1.5 million project linking the valley to the Rim of the World Drive. (FI.)

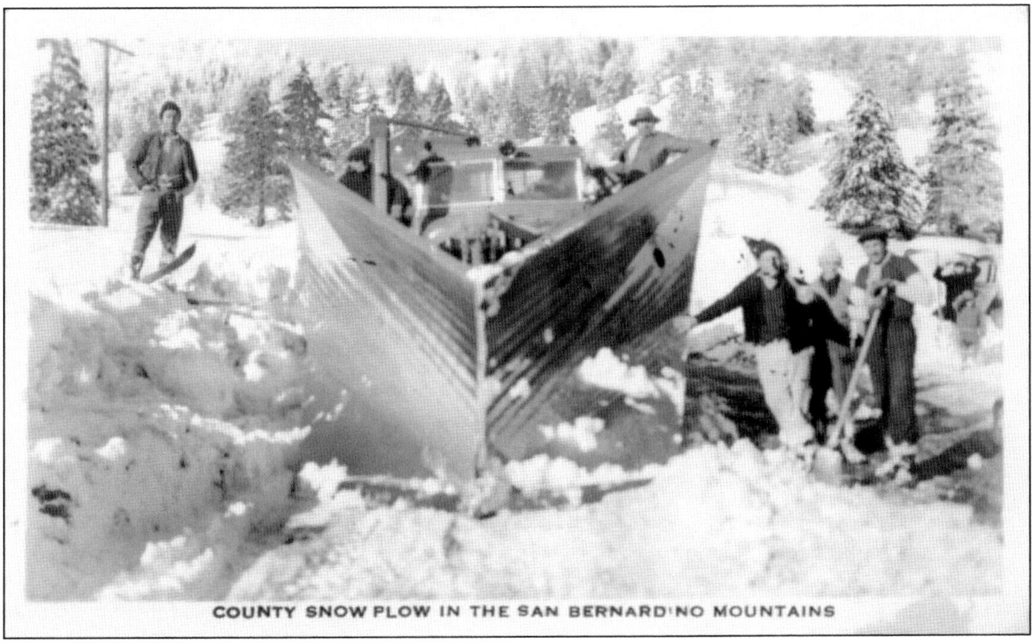

MOUNTAIN MAINTENANCE HEADACHES. The Rim of the World Drive was advertised as the highest and longest mountain highway in America. The most flamboyant brochures exaggerated (incorrectly) by expanding this claim to include the world. The word "highest" is the key here. Beginning in the early 1920s, mountain resort communities like Lake Arrowhead began to operate on a year-round basis, and pressure was put on county and state officials to keep roads open during the most inclement weather conditions. County crews (above) used large trucks with V-shaped plows, while state crews (below) had more options, including powerful rotary plows and larger work crews. Yesterday and today are much the same. It is a fact of life that the Rim of the World Drive continues to be at the mercy of the elements. (Above R; below FI.)

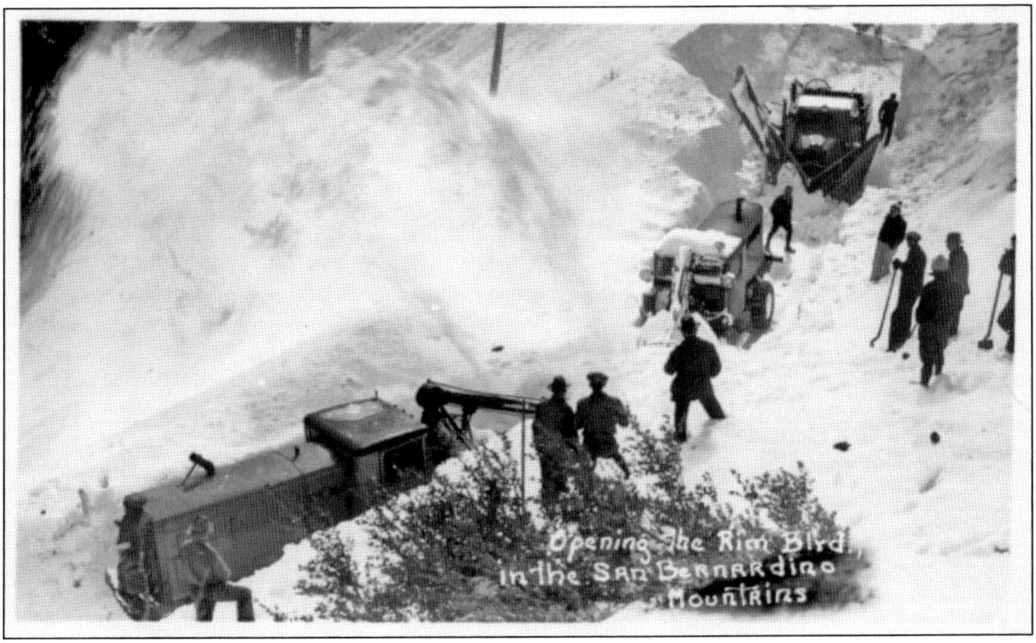

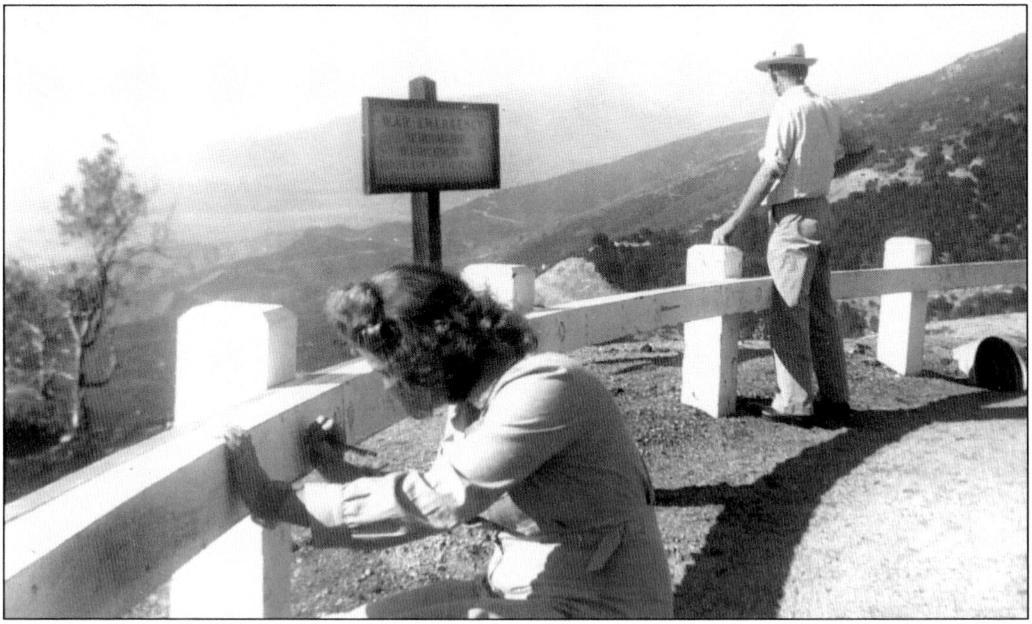

WARTIME EMERGENCY MEASURES. Taken at a turnout near the intersection of Highway 18 and Highway 138, the sign reads, "War Emergency—This Forest Area Closed—For National Defense Purpose—Trespassers Beyond This Point Will Be Prosecuted." World War II had a profound effect on mountain travel, and this photograph is a poignant reminder of this fact. Wouldn't it be great if we knew what the young woman wrote?

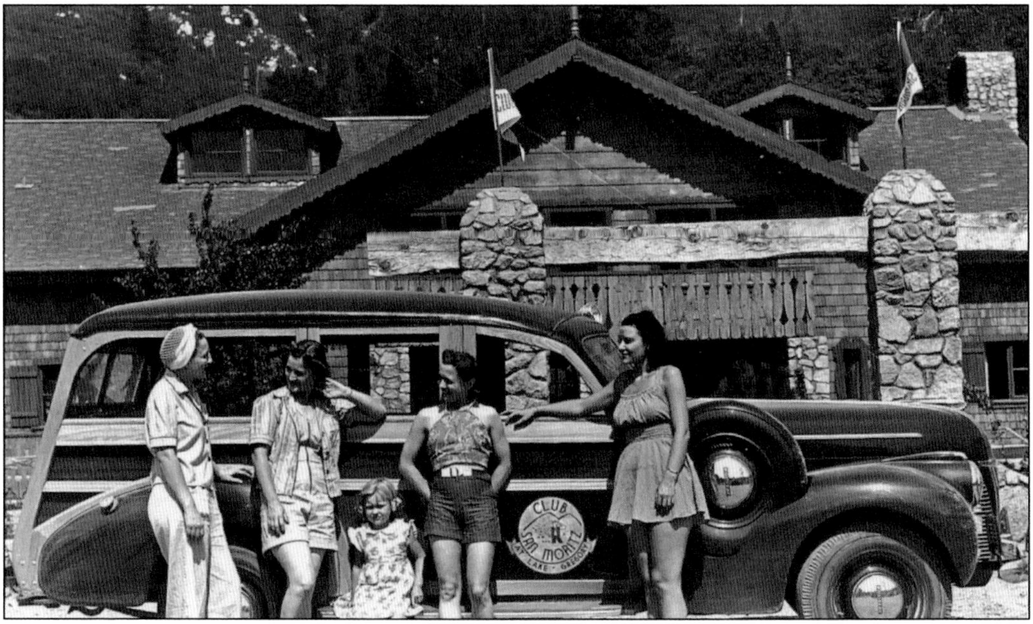

POSTWAR MOUNTAIN GOLDEN YEARS. Postwar America marks the beginning of the golden age of mountain tourism. Americans hopped into their automobiles in record numbers, heading for vacation retreats across America. Here a group of stylishly dressed ladies (outfitted as 1940s fashion plates) gather in front of the Club San Moritz in Crestline. Leaning against a classic "Woody," this image is truly worth 1,000 words.

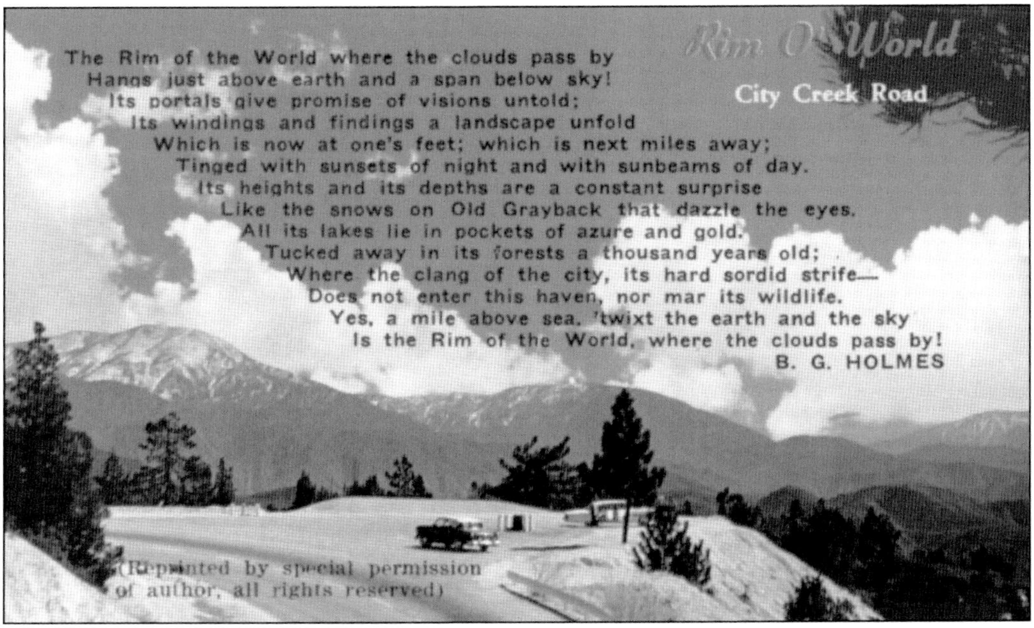

RIM OF THE WORLD SOLILOQUY. The author of this poem, Bernise Gay Holmes, was a prominent realtor and businessman originally based in Redlands. A pioneer of Bear Valley development, he subdivided Boulder Bay Park and was an early automobile enthusiast who genuinely loved driving through the San Bernardino Mountains along the Rim of the World Drive. Holmes, preferring to use the initials B. G., later moved to Beverly Hills. (WRP.)

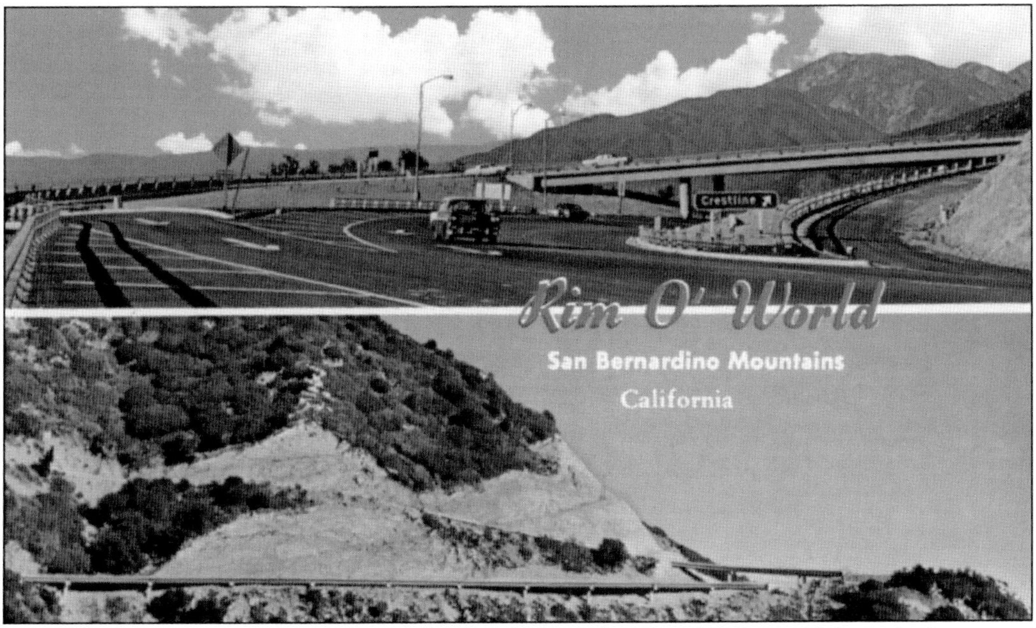

FOUR LANE MOUNTAIN SUBURBS. In the late 1960s, a four-lane Highway 18 from the bottom of the hill to the Crestline Interchange was completed. Continual improvements were, in fact, made along the length of the Rim of the World Drive. Clark's Grade was, for example, eliminated in 1930, and in 1961, Highway 38 was opened through Barton Flats to Big Bear, ending decades of planning and construction. (WRP.)

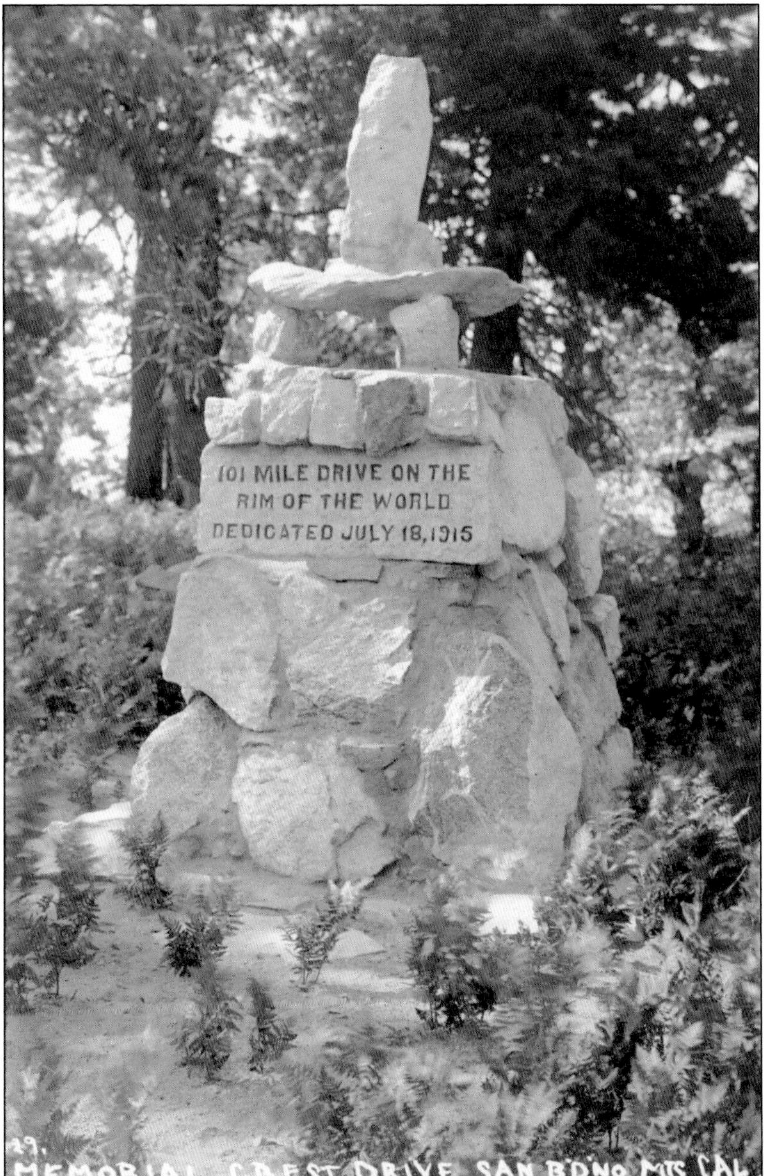

ORIGINAL RIM MONUMENT. Remarkably, although moved and entirely rebuilt, this monument is still standing. Located on the south side of Highway 18 between Rim Forest and Baylis Park, it is in a decidedly precarious condition today. The stone plaque reading "101 Mile Drive on the Rim of the World, Dedicated July 18, 1915" appears to be the only remaining original feature. The Rim of the World Drive itself, despite alterations and realignments, continues to survive and serve the San Bernardino Mountains in exactly the same capacity that visionary county planners envisioned over 100 years ago when, prompted by increasing pressure on the part of wealthy and influential citizens, they began to assemble the various component parts of the future public highway. Today one can still take an amazing automobile tour on the Rim of the World Drive, and the long-term preservation of the historic highway has recently been given consideration by state officials and local historical societies. Hopefully, this landmark monument will continue to survive along with the rustic qualities of the roadway itself.

Three

Historical Tour around the Rim

This chapter tells the story of select Rim of the World Drive landmarks, resorts, geographic features, and communities. Here we take a historic tour through time on the most popular San Bernardino Mountain highway, as illustrated by maps, photographs, postcards, and brochures. The tour begins in San Bernardino, heads uphill to Crestline, then easterly along the crest with a detour to Lake Arrowhead communities and resorts, back on the crest to Running Springs, Green Valley Lake, and Snow Valley, then around Big Bear Lake communities and resorts, and finally downhill by way of Barton Flats and Mill Creek on the way to Redlands. Images included in this chapter range from *c.* 1915 to the very early 1960s, or from the year that the historic roadway was dedicated to the end of the postwar golden years.

Unfortunately, with literally hundreds of possible locations to choose from, more locations have been left out than have been included. Every effort has been made to feature those communities that are actually on the Rim of the World Drive. It is not by accident that cars, trucks, or various roadway-associated features appear in almost every image, as the modern history and development of the San Bernardino Mountains is tied to that of the automobile in every imaginable way.

Each image in this chapter is linked to the history and/or evolution of the Rim of the World Drive, and each tells a story. Some reveal amusing surprises (see Santa's Village and the burro rides), while others simply illustrate just how pervasive the long-term impacts of a road can be. Enjoy this armchair tour of the most interesting and historic San Bernardino Mountain highway.

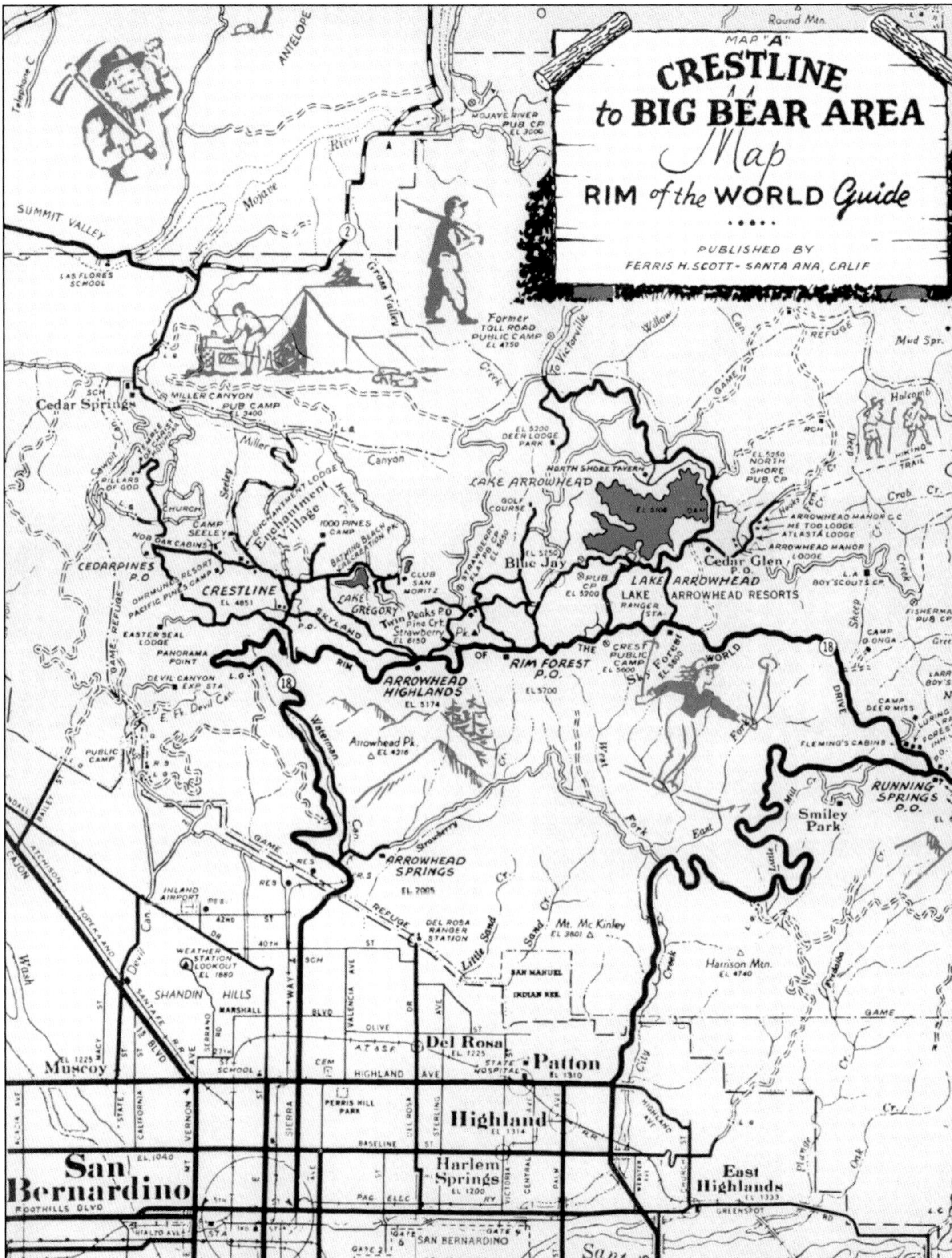

RIM OF THE WORLD GUIDE MAP. Ferris H. Scott of Santa Ana, California, began publishing a series of comprehensive Rim of the World guides to the San Bernardino Mountains in the early 1950s. A key feature was a set of maps depicting hundreds of mountain locations and, most important of all, featuring the Rim of the World Drive. Scott included dozens of historic

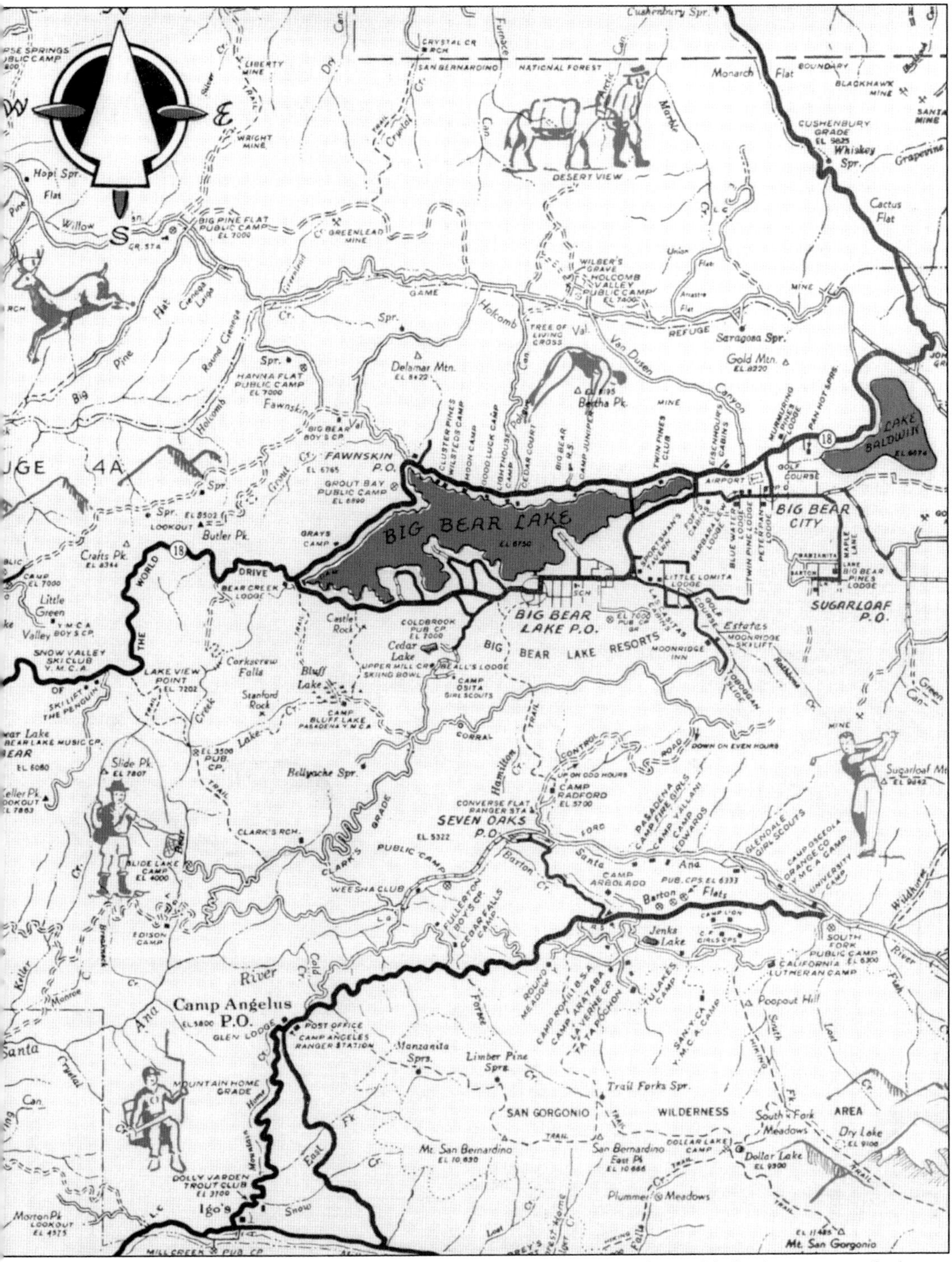

and contemporary images in his guides, many of which were also published as postcards (some appear in this chapter). This overview map is included as a historic reference point, for, when all is said and done, the best way to take a historic tour through time is to take along a historic map. (ROW.)

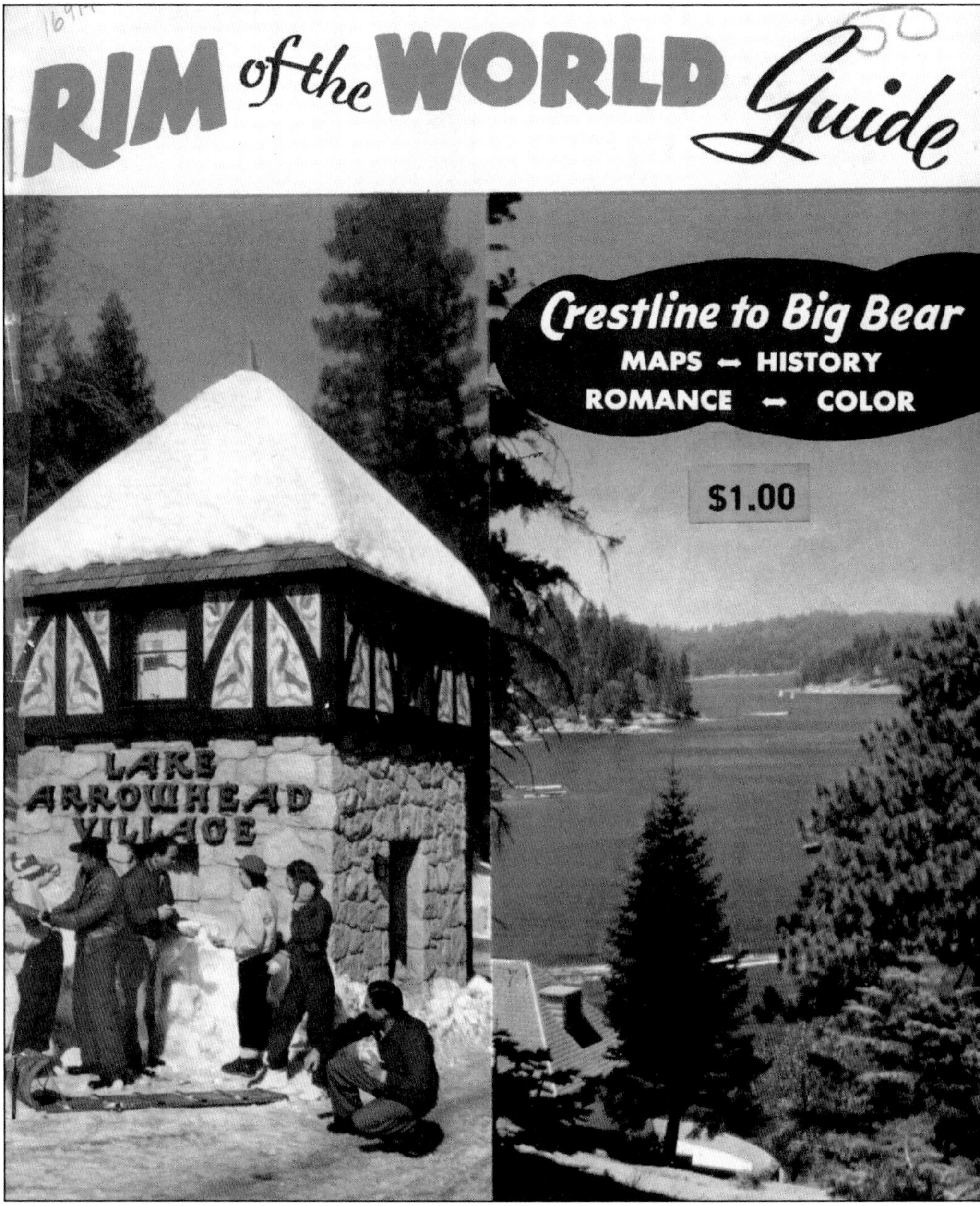

RIM OF THE WORLD GUIDE COVER. In the foreword to his 1953 edition, publisher Ferris H. Scott writes, "This book is presented with one purpose in mind: to help you obtain the greatest possible enjoyment during your visit to one of the nation's most scenic and historic mountain areas. If you are one of the three million people who will visit the Rim of the World this year, it is our desire to provide a medium whereby you may easily locate the many places of beauty and historic lore." In Scott's opinion, the Rim of the World Drive *was* the San Bernardino Mountains. Written primarily for families on automobile vacations, it is filled with language like "you will see the highways leading to the Rim O' World crowded with cars bearing skis and toboggans." Incredibly, Scott also included a brief history entitled "Rim of the World Story," detailing the growth and development of the Rim of the World Drive itself. (ROW.)

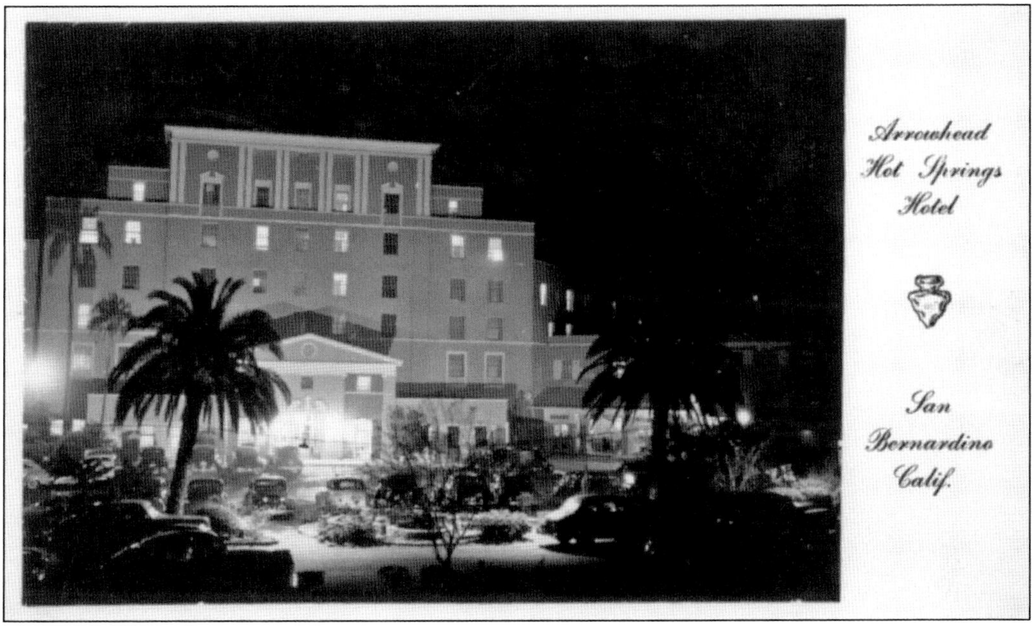

HOT SPRINGS HOTEL AT NIGHT. This is the fourth and final hotel built at this location. This photograph was almost certainly taken shortly after the opening in December 1939. As early as 1915, Arrowhead Hot Springs owners invited Los Angeles "autoists" to spend a weekend at the mountain hotel.

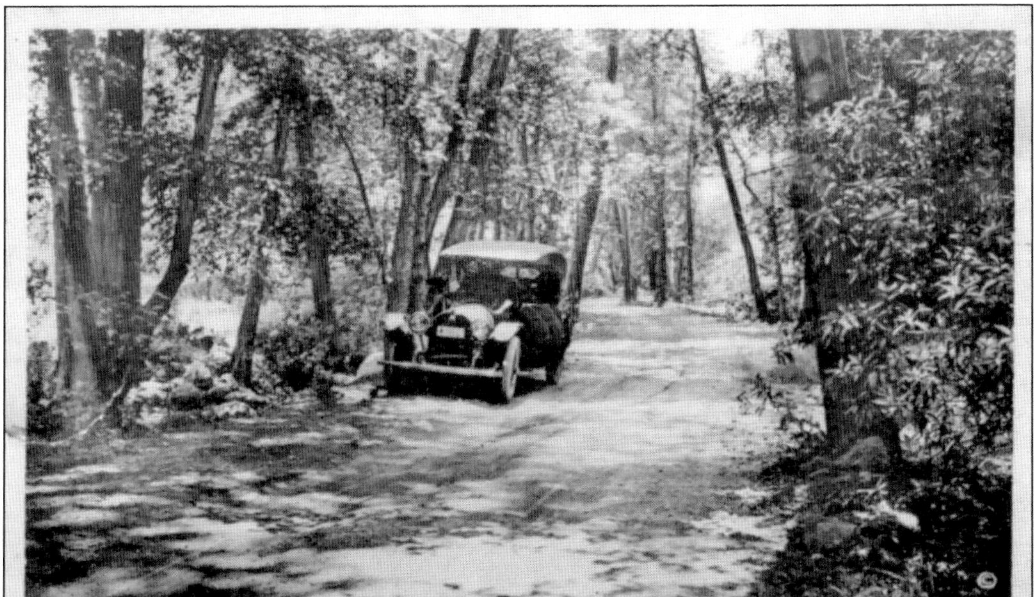

DEEP IN WATERMAN CANYON. Until the high-gear road was complete, the only route to the west-end mountains led up Waterman Canyon, where one slowly transitions from the flatlands to the highlands. Initially horses could be rested and watered amid shady groves of trees alongside the creek. Later cars would have their radiators filled and tires fixed at the same locations. (WPN.)

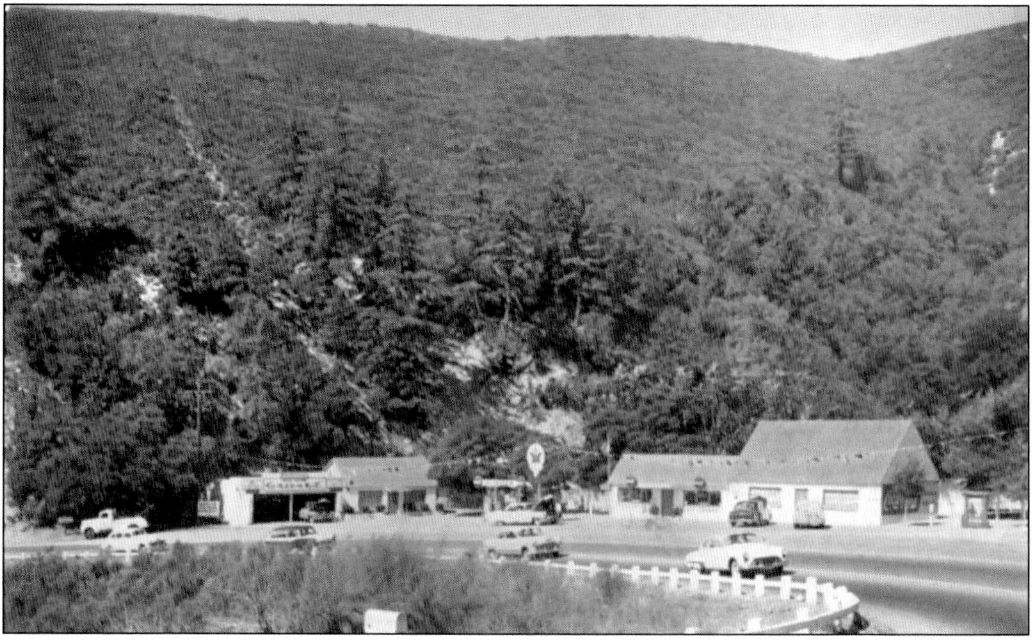

HIGH GEAR GARAGE. The back of this 1950s postcard reads: "HIGH GEAR GARAGE, SERVICE STATION—CAFÉ Day and Night Tow Service. First Stop on Rim o' the World Drive." Now a barren turnout on the four-lane highway, this landmark served mountain travelers from the mid-1930s to the mid-1960s. (R.)

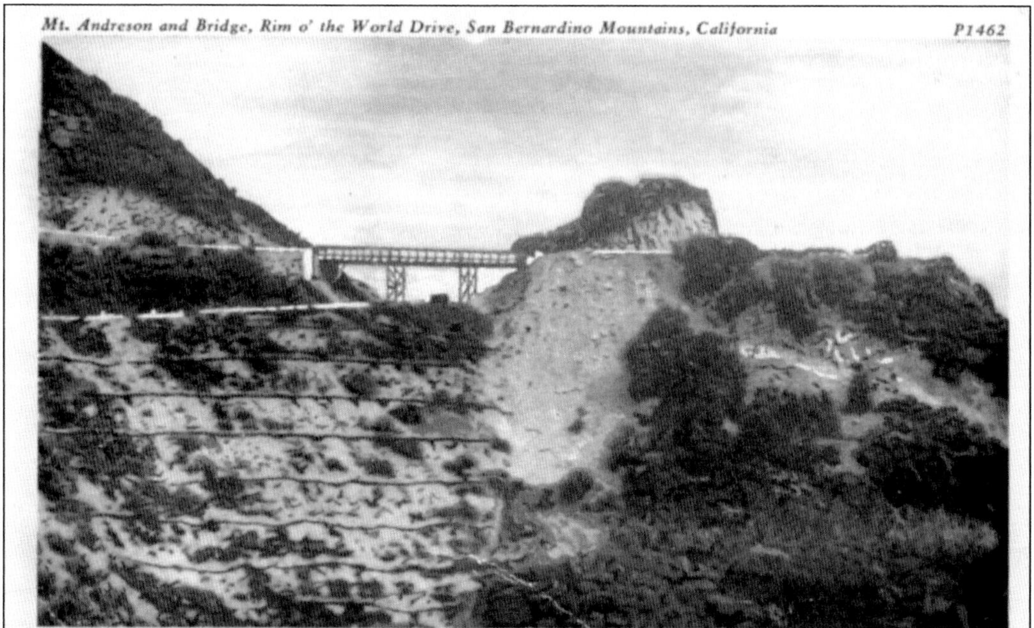

OLD MOUNT ANDRESON BRIDGE. This is the original high-gear intersection of Highways 18 and 138 on the Rim of the World Drive. An open framework steel bridge, the Crestline Bridge at Mount Andreson was named after John Andresen Jr., the source of many historic images used in this volume. (R.)

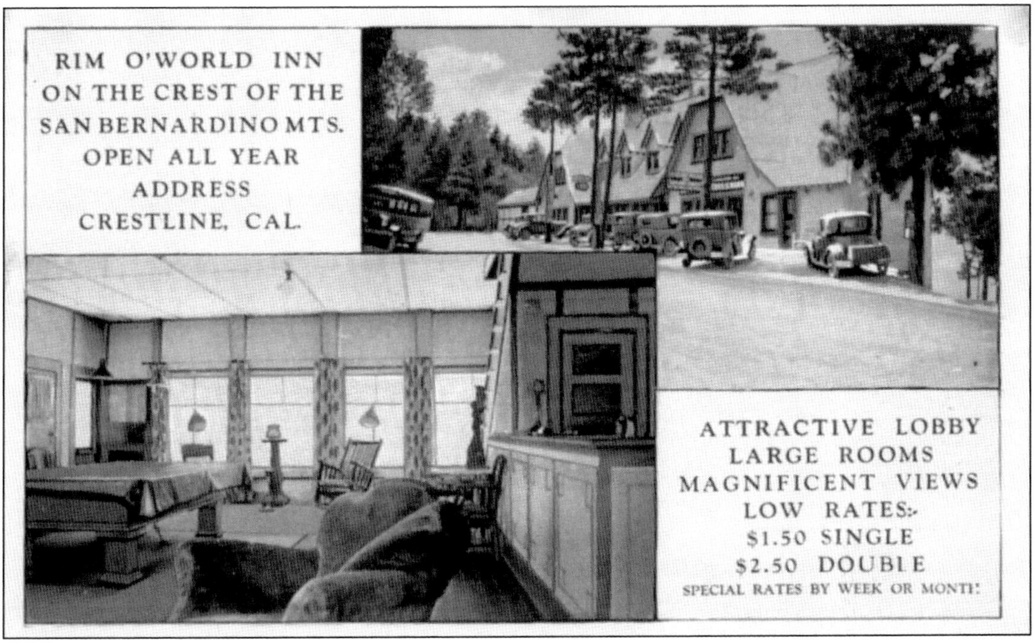

CRESTLINE RIM O'WORLD INN. Located on the Rim of the World Drive, a well-appointed inn was built by Charles Mann to attract visitors and investors. A landmark for travelers prior to construction of the high-gear road, it offered the first available refreshment on the way up the hill and the last on the way down. (BRM.)

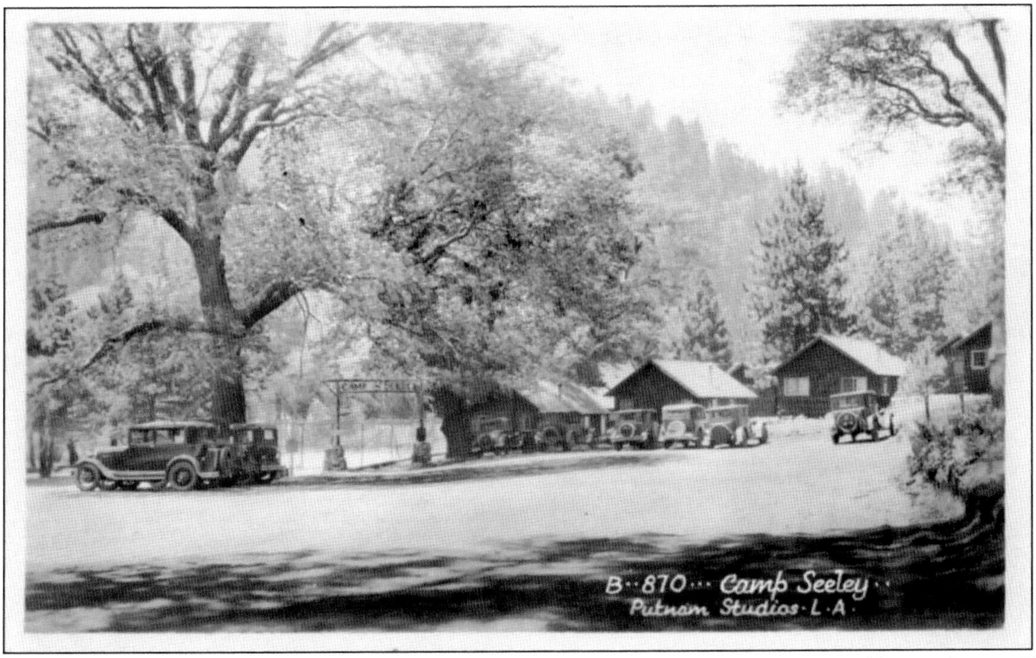

CAMP SEELEY CABINS. Built by the Los Angeles City Recreation Department and located just off the Rim of the World Drive, Camp Seeley has been a popular mountain destination from 1914 to the present. Scenes from the 1998 remake of the movie *The Parent Trap* were filmed here. (PS.)

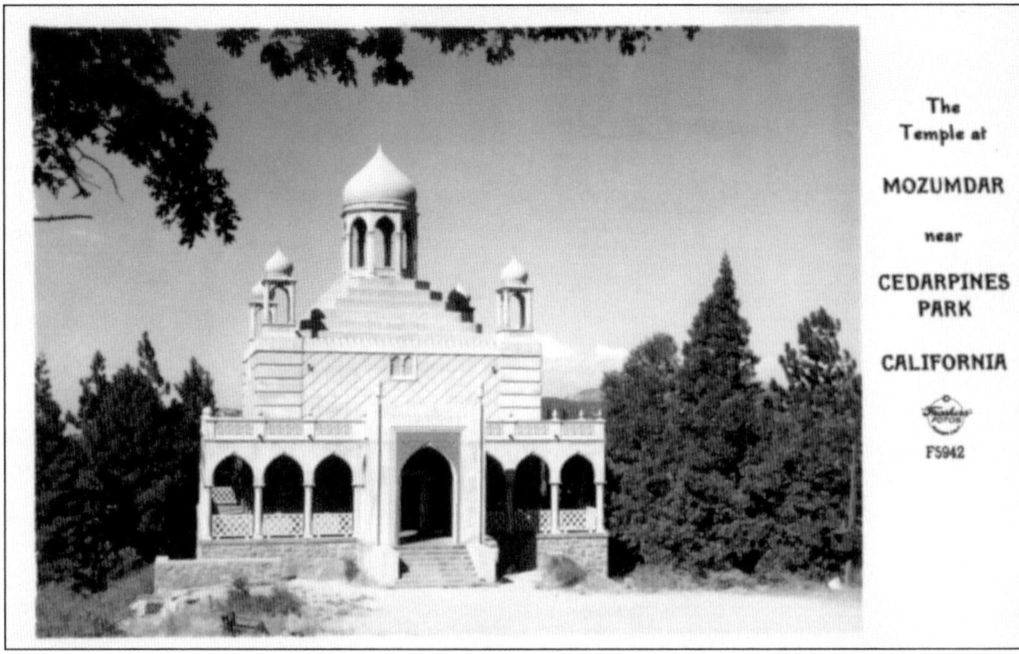

MOZUMDAR AT CEDARPINES PARK. Featured in the 1953 edition of the *Rim of the World Guide*, Mozumdar Temple was touted as being "a replica of the Taj Majal in India." Originally intended as a religious retreat, by 1950, it was operated as a YMCA camp. (R.)

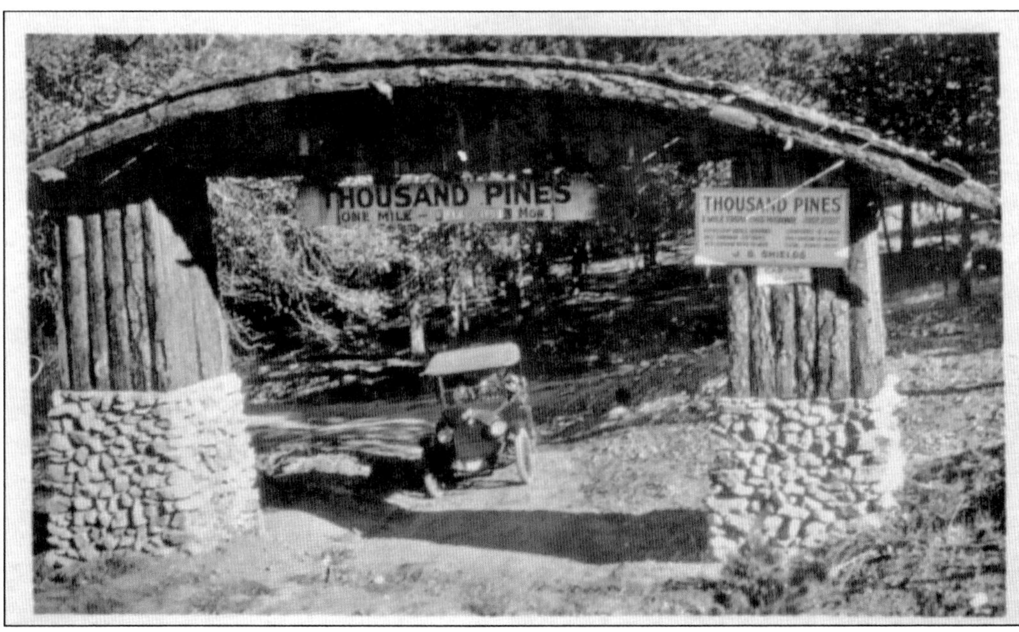

THOUSAND PINES RESORT ENTRANCE. Thousand Pines was established by Charles Brashear in 1913. A popular early Rim of the World Drive resort destination, and a scheduled stopping place on the daily circuit of the Mountain Auto Stage, it offered horseback riding, dancing, fishing, a tennis court, and cabins.

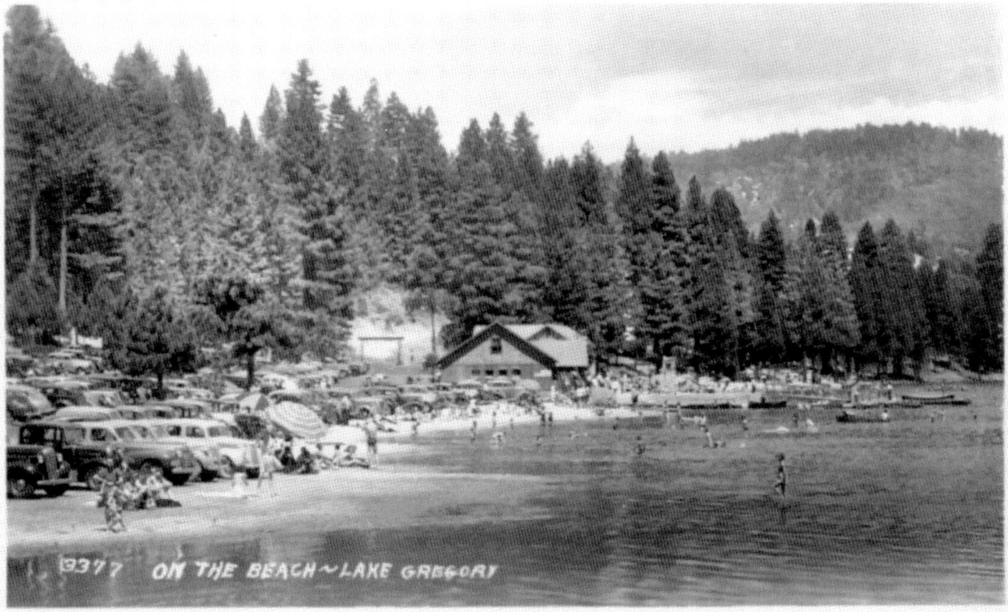

LAKE GREGORY BEACH. In the early 1940s, cars were allowed to park on the beach right up to the water's edge. This was not uncommon across the mountains (see Stillwell's in Big Bear on page 87) at this time. Completed in 1938 and entirely filled the same year in a massive flooding episode that devastated the California Southland, Lake Gregory remains a popular Rim of the World Drive destination.

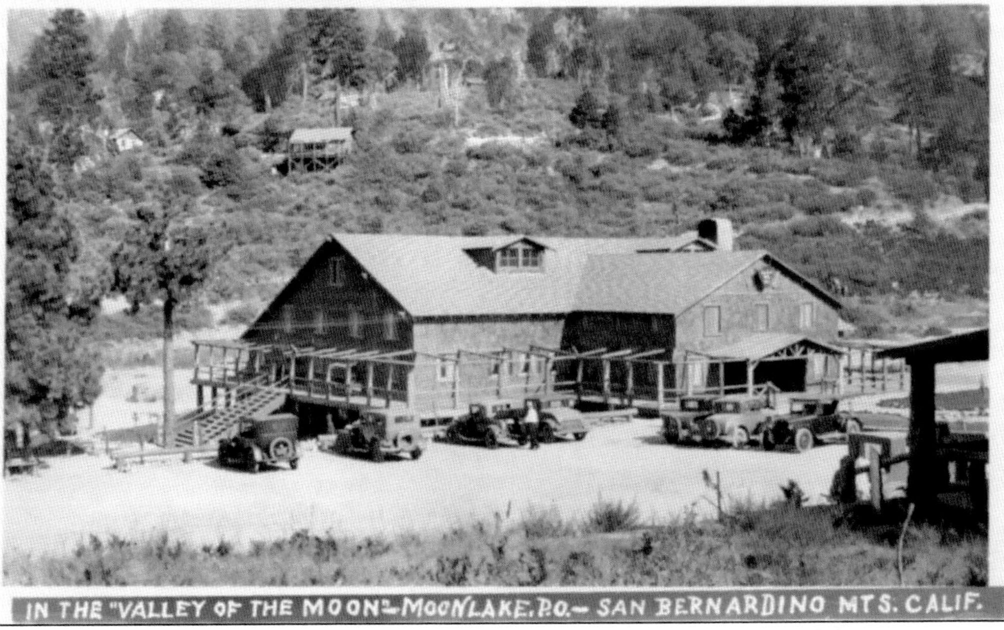

CLUB SAN MORITZ AT MOON LAKE. From 1939 until the mid-1970s, the Club San Moritz was the heart and soul of Crestline. This is the first clubhouse, originally named the Arrowhead Valley Club, at Moon Lake. Early brochures underscored just how easy it was to get to Crestline on the Rim of the World Drive.

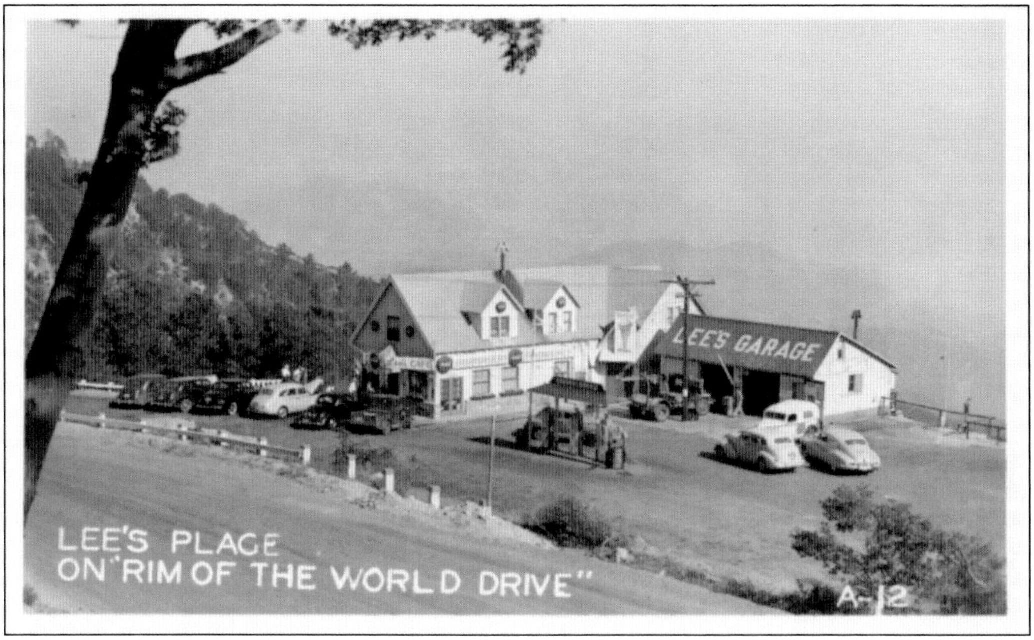

LEE'S GARAGE, 1940S. Built in 1927 as the Arrowhead Highlands Garage and originally located at the end of a cul-de-sac, Lee's Garage or Lee's Place became the first mountaintop stopping place on the Rim of the World Drive thanks to 1930s construction of the high-gear road (bypassing Crestline).

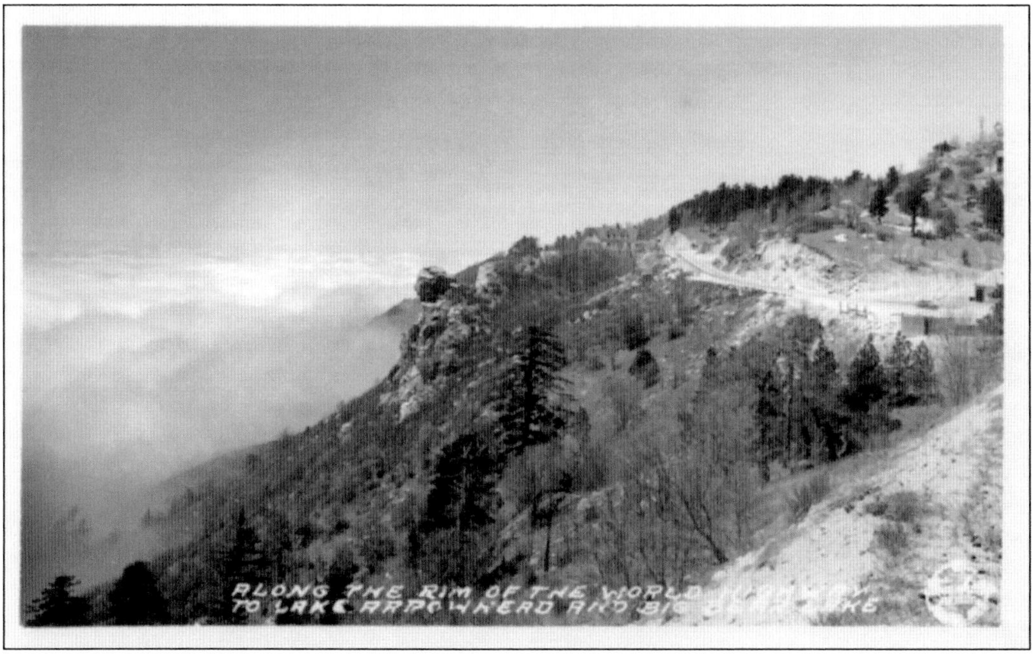

SPHINX ROCK. One of the most interesting geologic formations in the San Bernardino Mountains is Sphinx Rock, located near the intersection of present-day Highway 189 and Highway 18. Appearing in the classic 1917 movie *Eyes of the World*, Sphinx Rock has always sparked the interest of Rim of the World Drive tourists. (FI.)

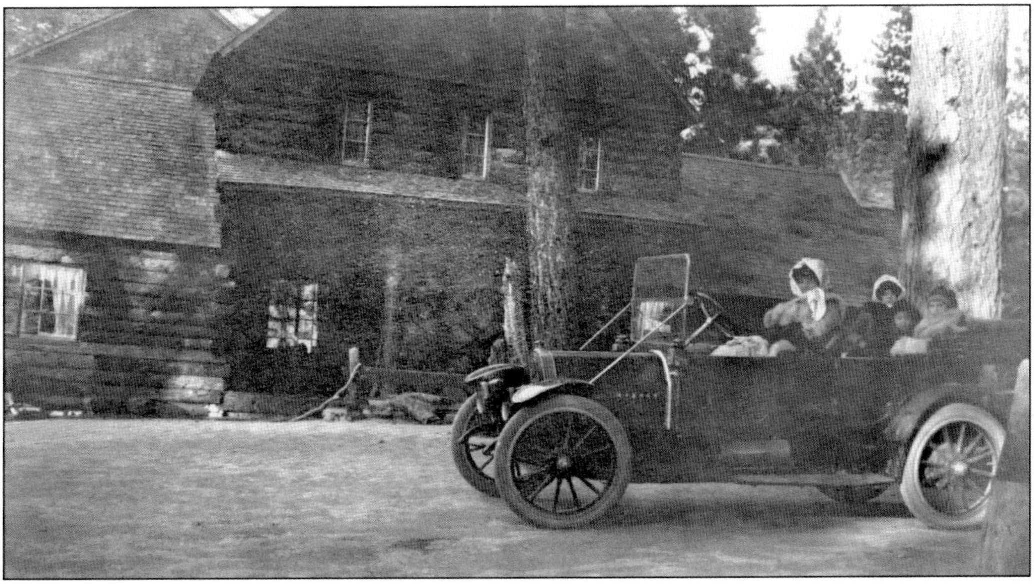

Automobile at Squirrel Inn. A private 1890s retreat built by the Arrowhead Mountain Club, the name Squirrel Inn came from a fictional hotel in author Frank Stockton's popular novel, *The Squirrel Inn*. The exclusive membership listed various high rollers from the San Bernardino area, most of whom owned automobiles like the one pictured here.

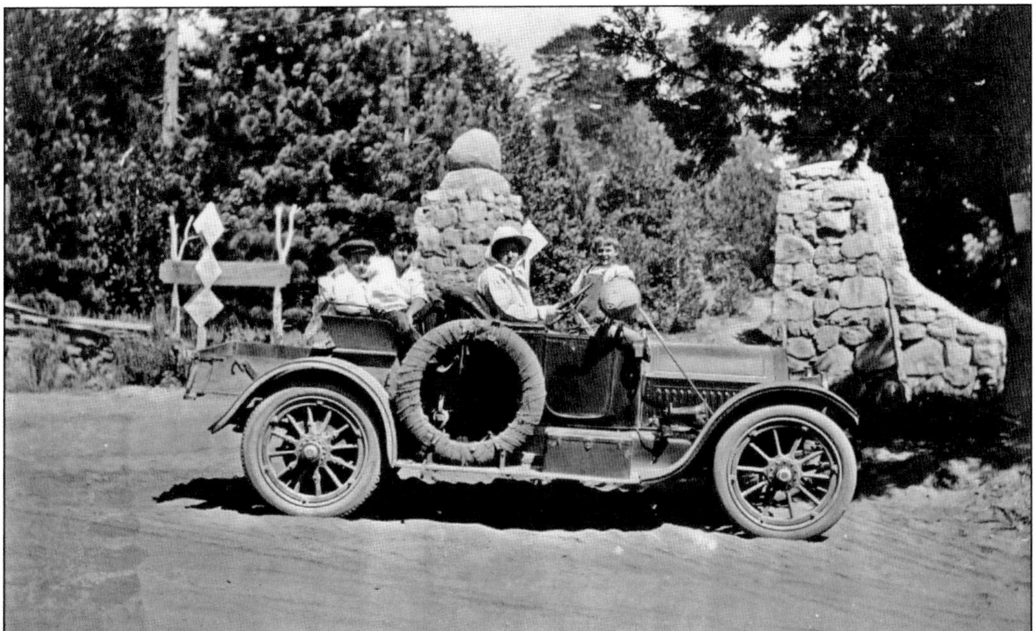

Andreson Clan at Pinecrest Gates. The Rim of the World Drive once passed through these stone pillars located off Highway 189 at Pinecrest (they still stand). In 1906, Dr. John Baylis, a visionary mountain booster often regarded as the father of the Rim of the World Drive, began construction of his resort. (AFC.)

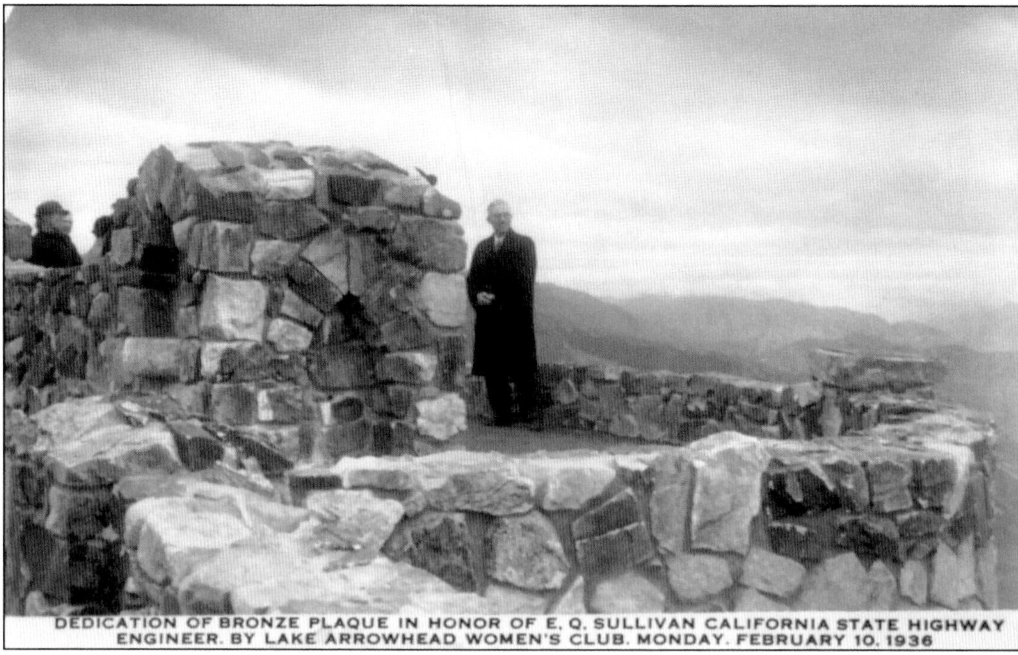

DEDICATION AT RED ROCK WALL. By 1933, the high-gear road on the Rim of the World Drive was complete. Scenic rock work and chains were later added as part of a WPA-funded program to increase the safety and beauty of the drive. On February 10, 1936, the Lake Arrowhead Women's Club honored highway engineer E. Q. Sullivan.

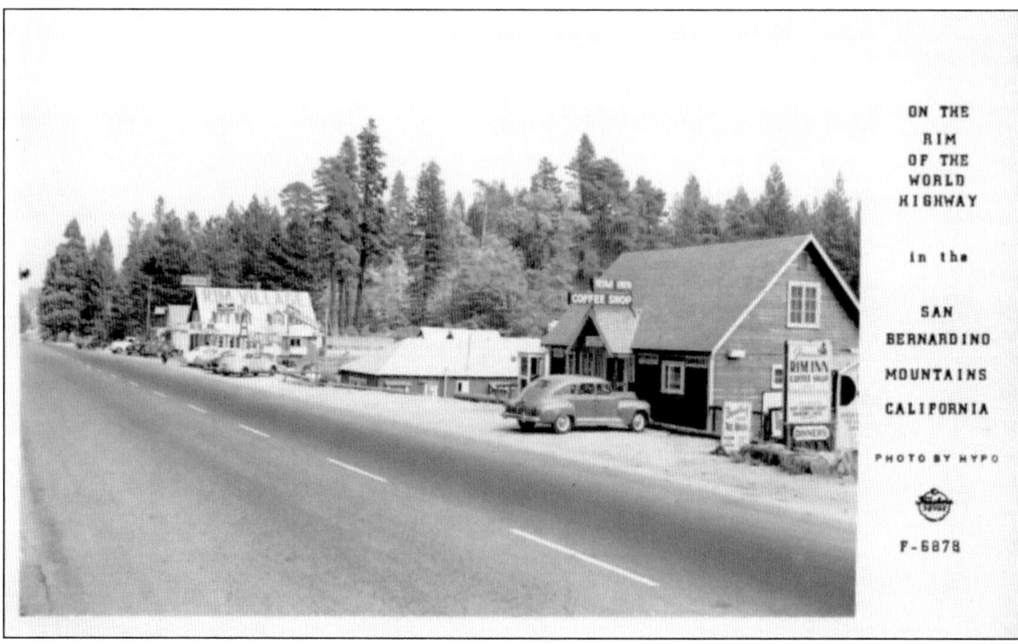

RIM FOREST, 1940S. Either the first stop or last stop on the Rim of the World Drive, depending on which way one was going, before the cutoff to Blue Jay and Lake Arrowhead, the Rim Inn Coffee Shop advertised their signature specialty item as "Hot Corned Beef Sandwiches on Rye." Ham and eggs cost 75¢. (FI.)

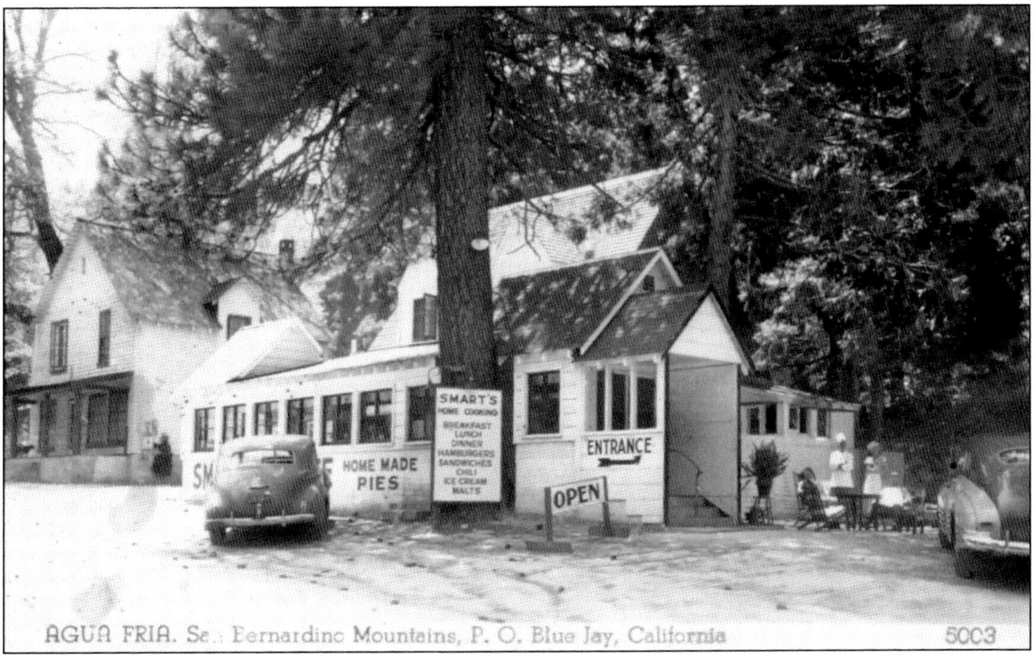

SMART'S IN AGUA FRIA. Smart's Café advertised "Home Cooking: Breakfast, Lunch, Dinner, Hamburgers, Sandwiches, Chili, Ice Cream, Malts, and Home Made Pies." A popular stop just off the Rim of the World Drive on the way to Lake Arrowhead in the 1950s, Smart's is now the hardware store in Agua Fria. (R.)

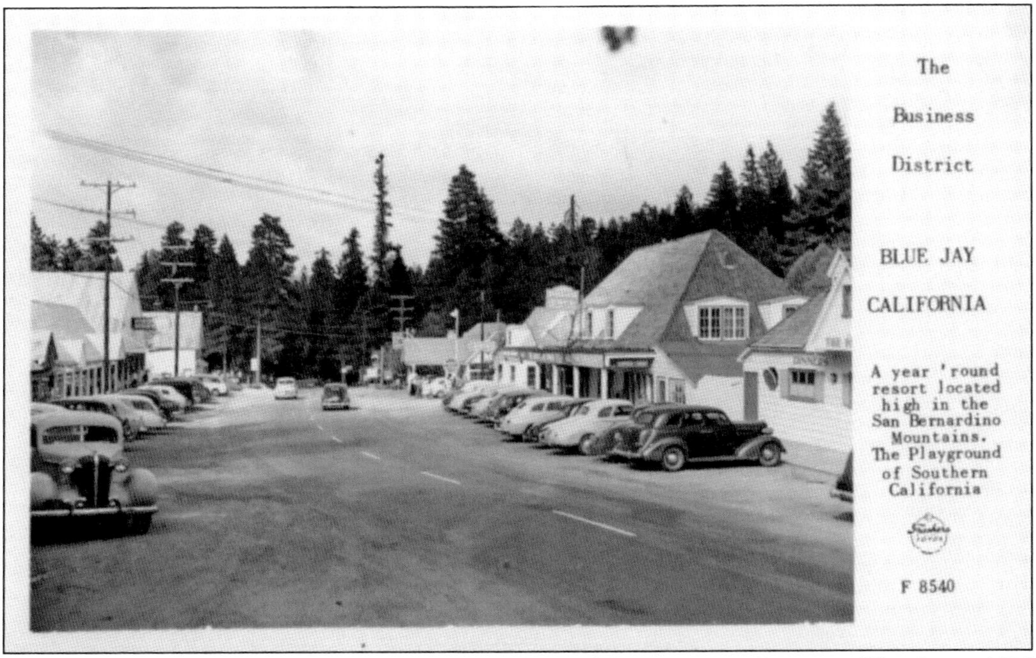

BLUE JAY BUSINESS DISTRICT. The name was changed from Wixom Corner to Blue Jay in 1924 when the post office was opened, and in 1934, Stoney Dement began to develop the business center so popular today. This mid-1940s view depicts the newly built Blue Jay shopping district. (FI.)

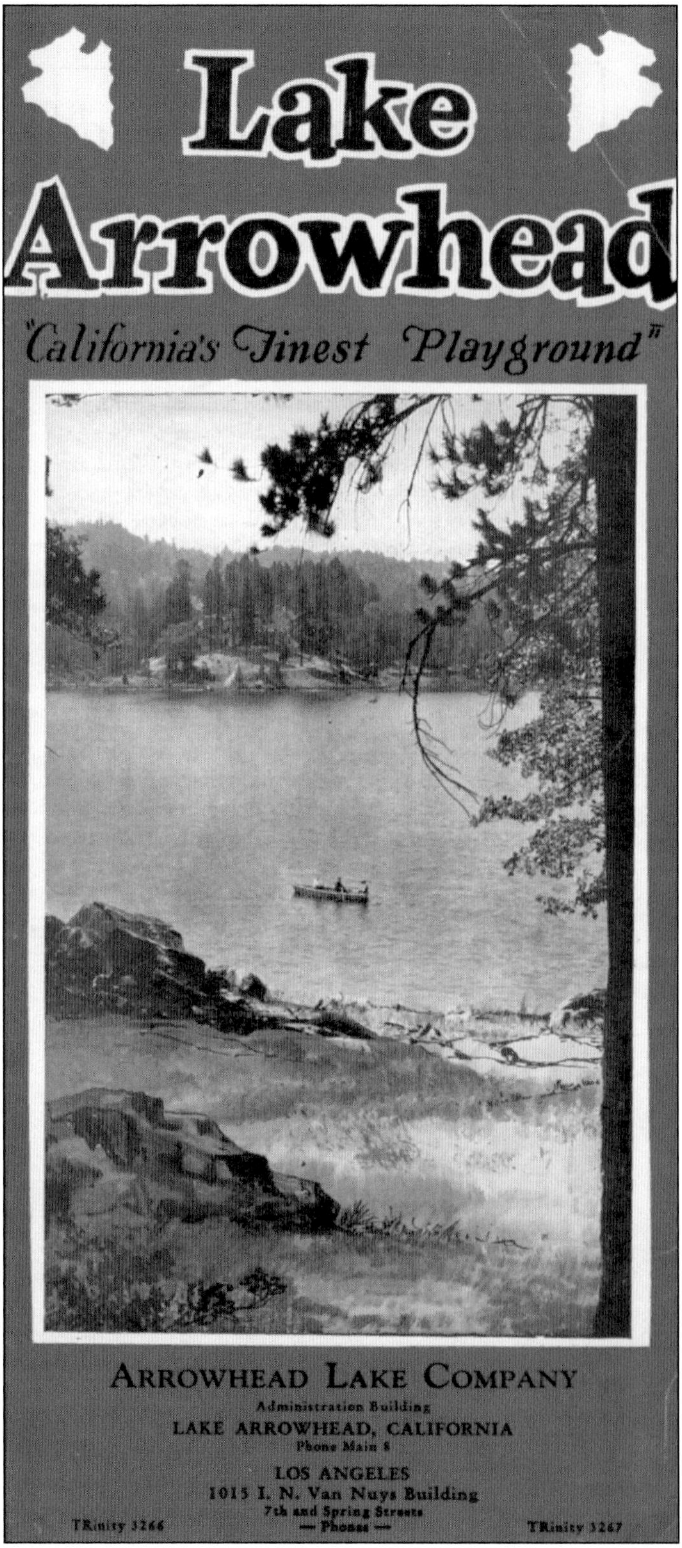

FINEST PLAYGROUND IN CALIFORNIA. Filled with inspired language, this late-1920s brochure refers to Lake Arrowhead as "Nature's greatest pleasure spot," a "pleasure land" among the "sweet scented pines" and "forest-clad mountains," where one could enjoy almost any activity imaginable at "reasonable prices" as the "owners of Lake Arrowhead have provided sites with all public utilities for purchase at prices as low as $300.00 with three years to pay." Almost lost in the fluff is an important paragraph reading, "Three broad safe roads give easy access through different sections of the mountains, and the route through Hesperia is open every day of the year. New High Gear Road will soon be a reality." The three roads were the Rim of the World Drive (Highway 18), City Creek Road (Highway 330), and the Arrowhead Road (Highway 173) from the desert. Roadway access was apparently regarded as critical to a successful sales campaign.

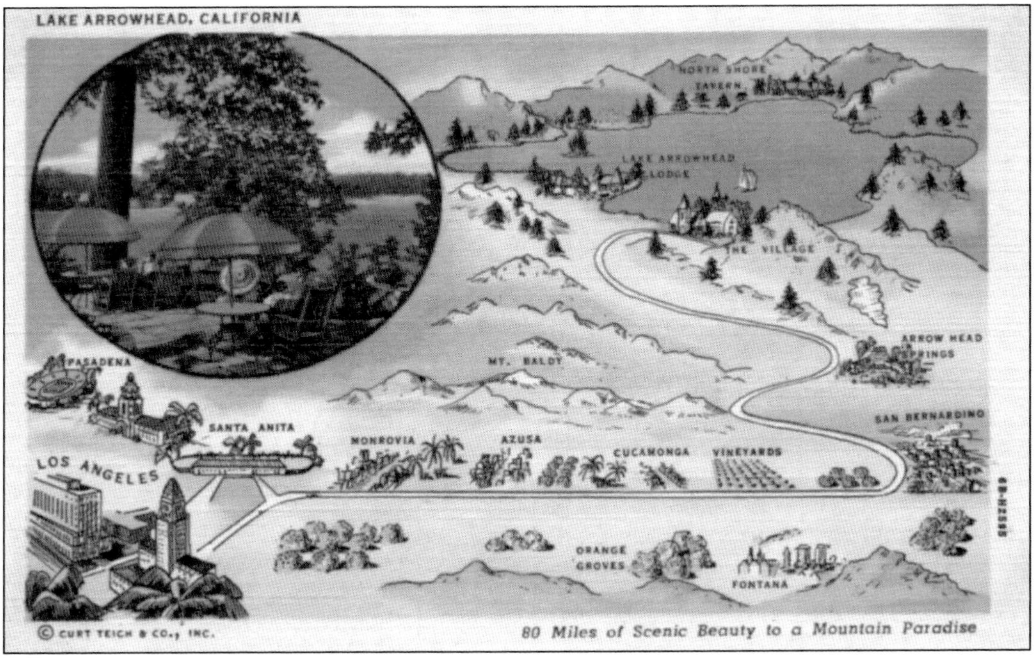

LAKE ARROWHEAD MAP POSTCARD. The back of this late-1930s postcard reads, "This glorious scenic drive to San Bernardino Mountain Resorts extends 80 miles eastward from Los Angeles . . . this high gear road." This shows exactly how the Rim of the World Drive literally tied the mountains to the rest of Southern California. (CC.)

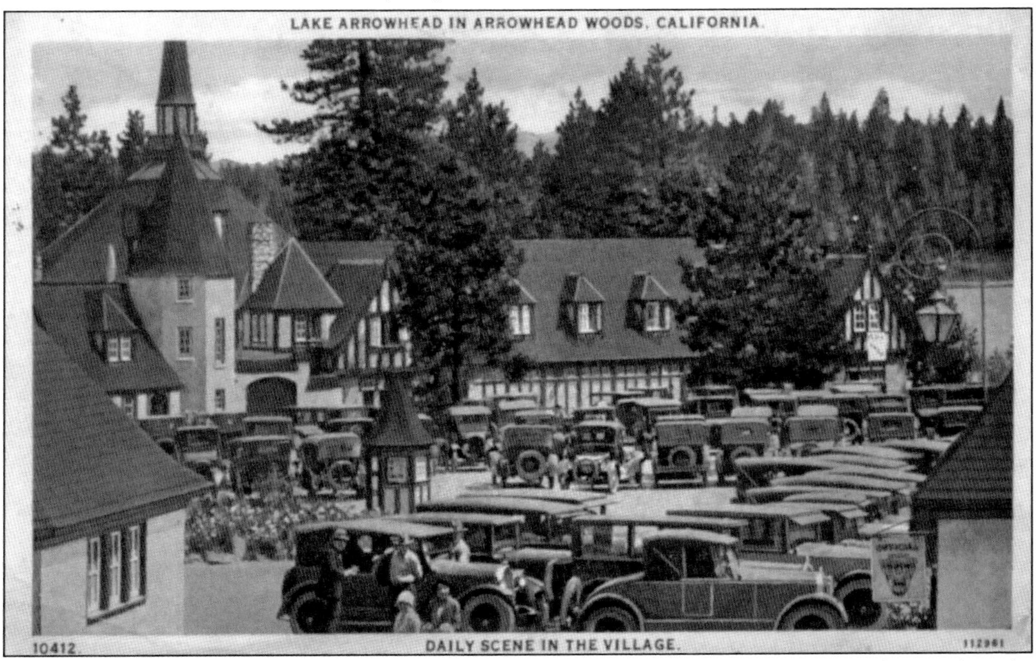

"DAILY" VILLAGE SCENE, 1920S. Printed for advertising purposes, the back of this card reads, "Here swimming, dancing, golfing, boating, fishing, tennis, horse-back riding and scenic motor drives enchant the lover of the open places." A look at the parking lot implies that many took the scenic Rim of the World Drive to reach Lake Arrowhead. (PS.)

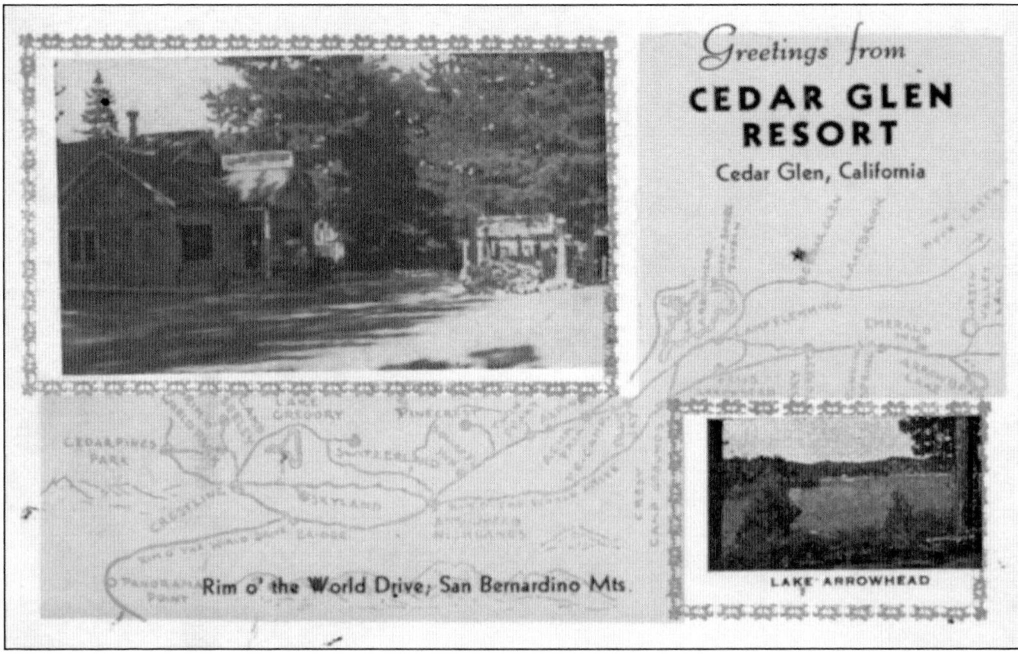

CEDAR GLEN ROUTE MAP. This is one of a series of "Rim o' the World" map cards published by Rosecraft Studios in Crestline, directing visitors to the shortest and best routes to various Rim of the World Drive communities. Cedar Glen was originally known as Camp Comfort. (R.)

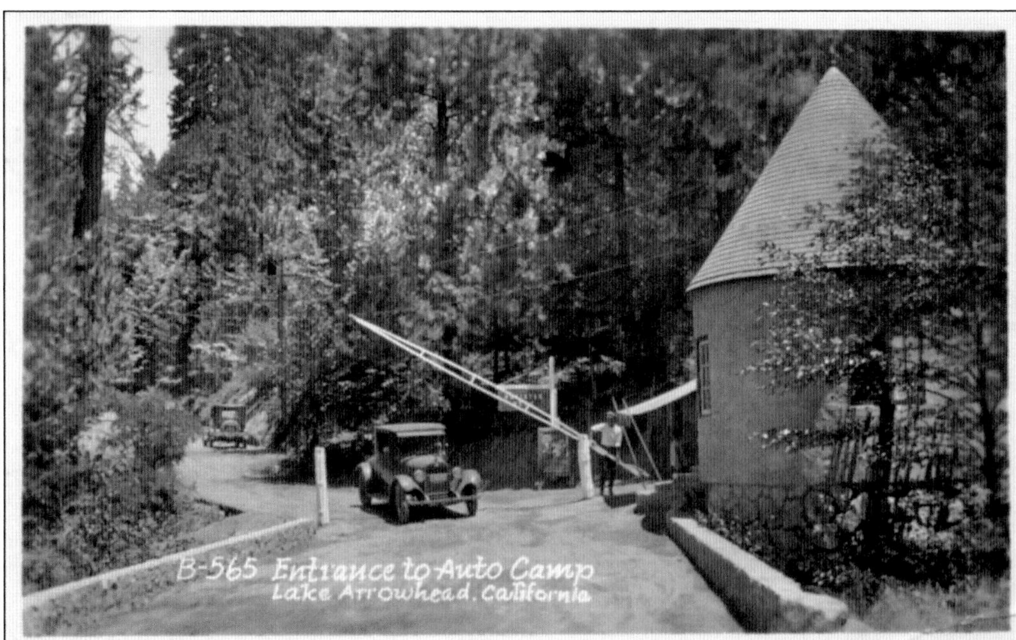

LAKE ARROWHEAD AUTO CAMP. To go "auto-camping" at Lake Arrowhead, one pretty much had to take the Rim of the World Drive. This July 1928 postcard relates, "We are up here camping for a few days, and are having a wonderful time."

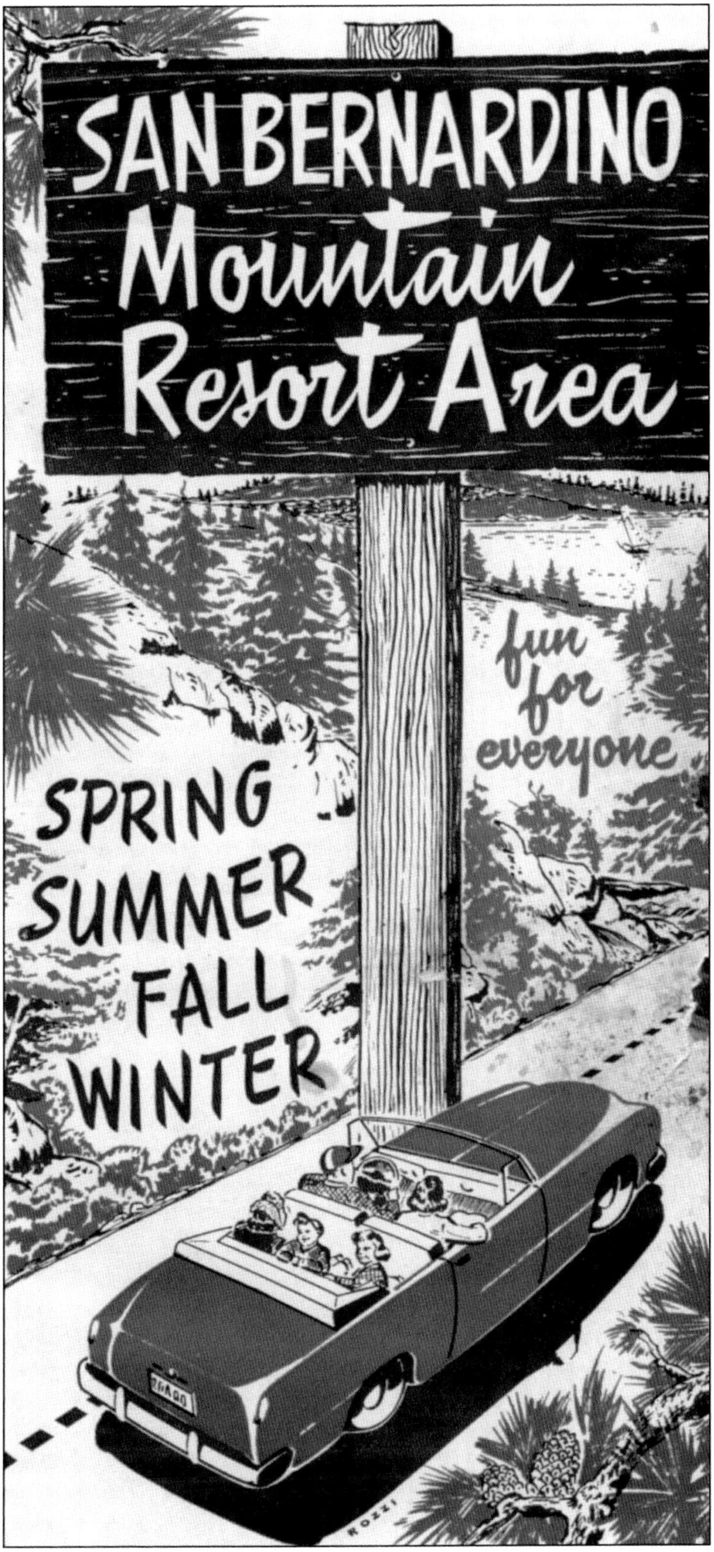

MOUNTAIN RESORTS AREA BROCHURE. Published by the Mountain and Desert Committee of the San Bernardino Chamber of Commerce, this stylish brochure simply screams 1950s family fun. The designers artistically selected a convertible to show the parents and children inside, and the carefully written text assures the reader that "smooth highways and forest roads stretch from communities in all directions, and every turn brings new delight to the motorist." By the mid-1950s, the car and the family vacation were like meat and potatoes to most Americans—people couldn't have one without the other. Interestingly, directions were given to various west-end mountain resorts on Highway 18 only. This is one of the very first brochures to drop the use of the name Rim of the World Drive and to use only the much more modern Highway 18 designator. The widespread popularity and recognition of the Rim of the World Drive as a place-name and a regional identity would, however, ensure its continued use. (SBC.)

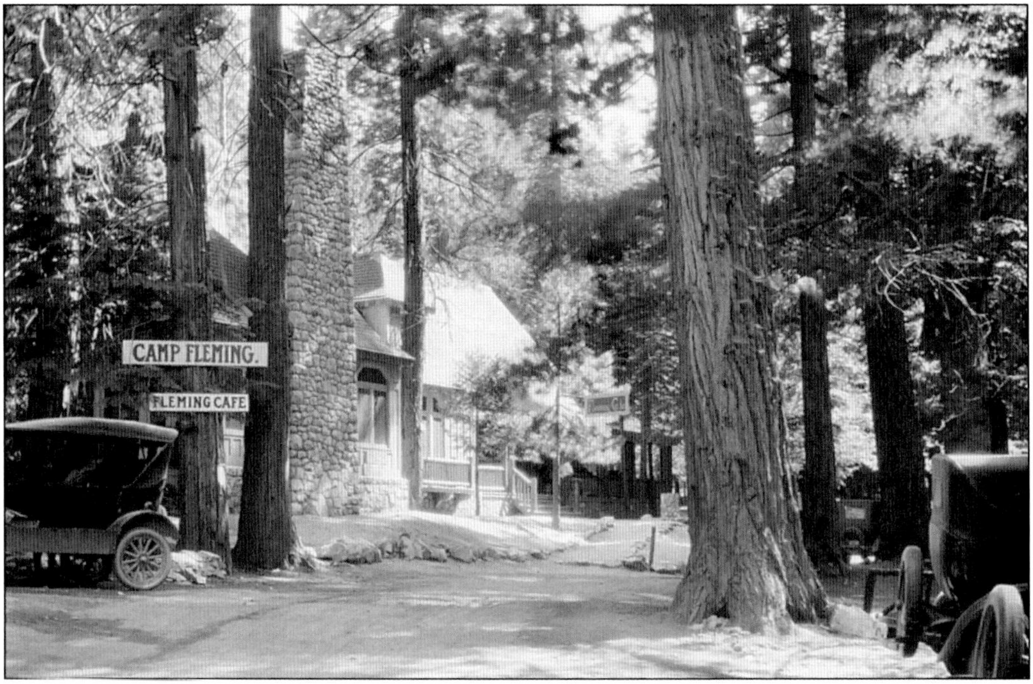

CAMP FLEMING. For decades, Camp Fleming was the premier Lake Arrowhead resort for the masses, where frugal travelers could visit an expensive place on a tight budget. One simply loaded the family car with cooking gear and bedrolls, drove it up the hill on the Rim of the World Drive, and settled in for an affordable week's rest.

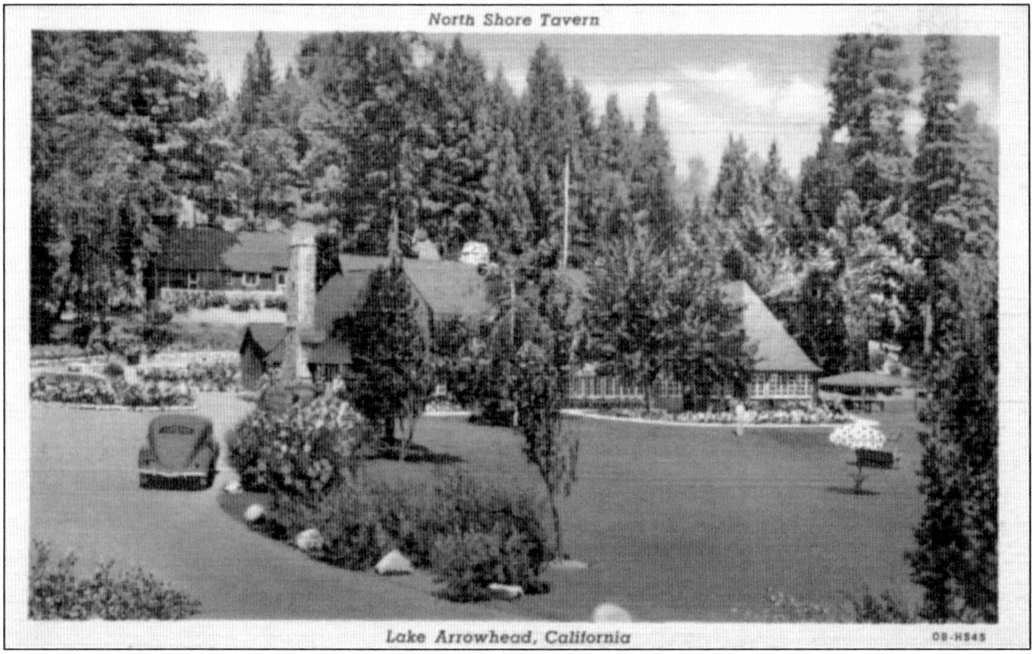

NORTH SHORE TAVERN. At the other end of the vacation spectrum was the North Shore Tavern, originally known as the Clubhouse. The back of this 1930s postcard noted the advantages of getting here "over a high gear state highway," otherwise known as the Rim of the World Drive. (CC.)

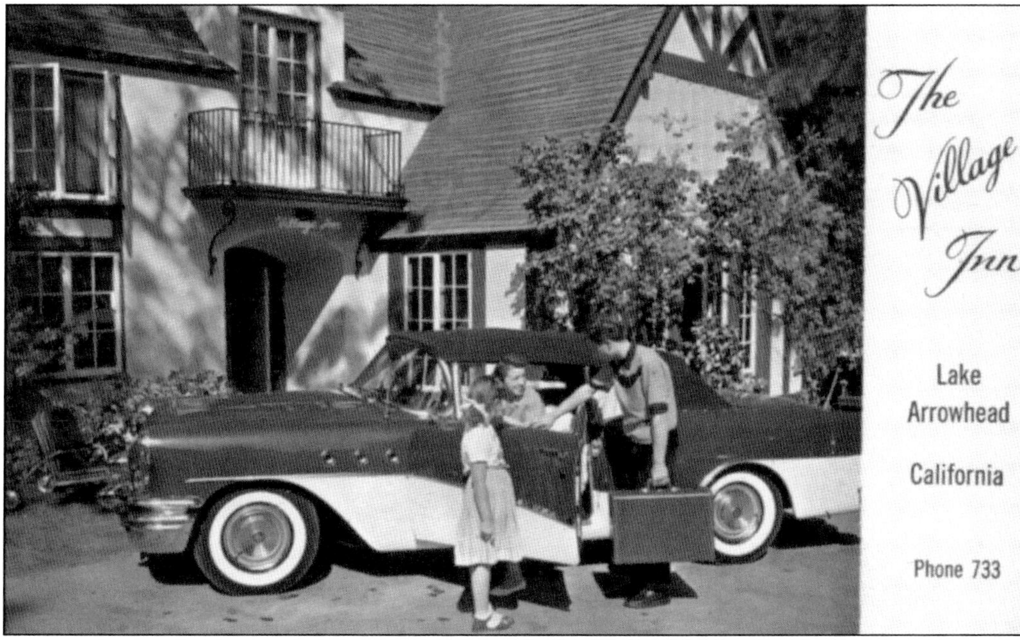

AN AUTOMOBILE CLASSIC. Originally known as the Mountain Lake Club, by the late 1920s, this once private resort was known as the Village Inn. The inn was advertised as a restful, all-year resort close to all Lake Arrowhead social activities and easily reached by the high-gear road. Here a family arrives in what is today regarded as a 1950s classic. (CB.)

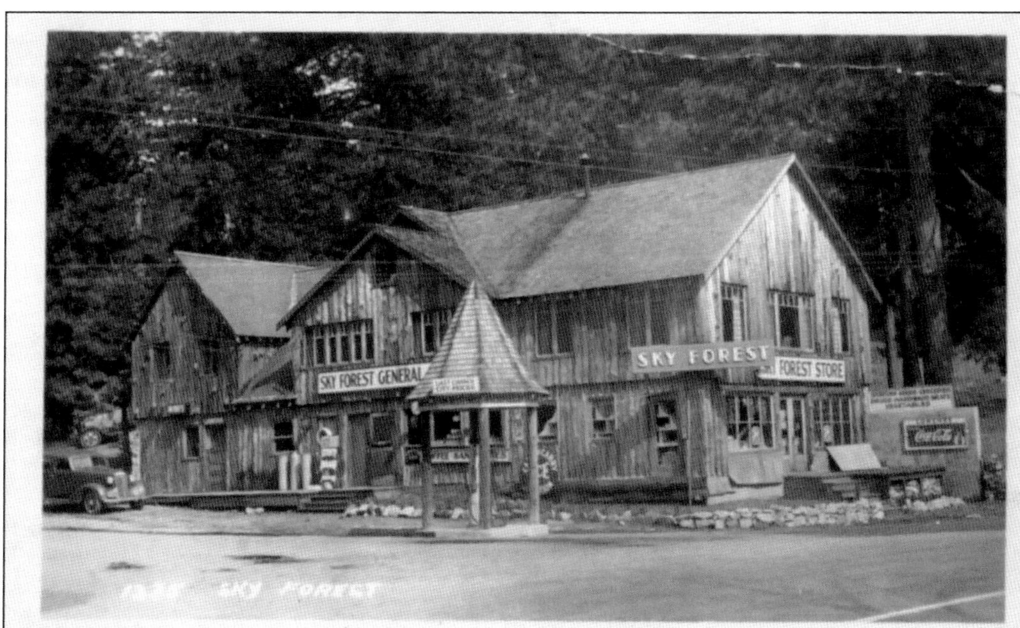

SKY FOREST STORE. Unfortunately, this Rim of the World Drive landmark is no more. Located on the Rim of the World Drive, this store sold just about everything, including groceries, drugs, hardware, meat, vegetables, wines, liquors, and gasoline (note the hand-pump under the gazebo), as well as automobile parts.

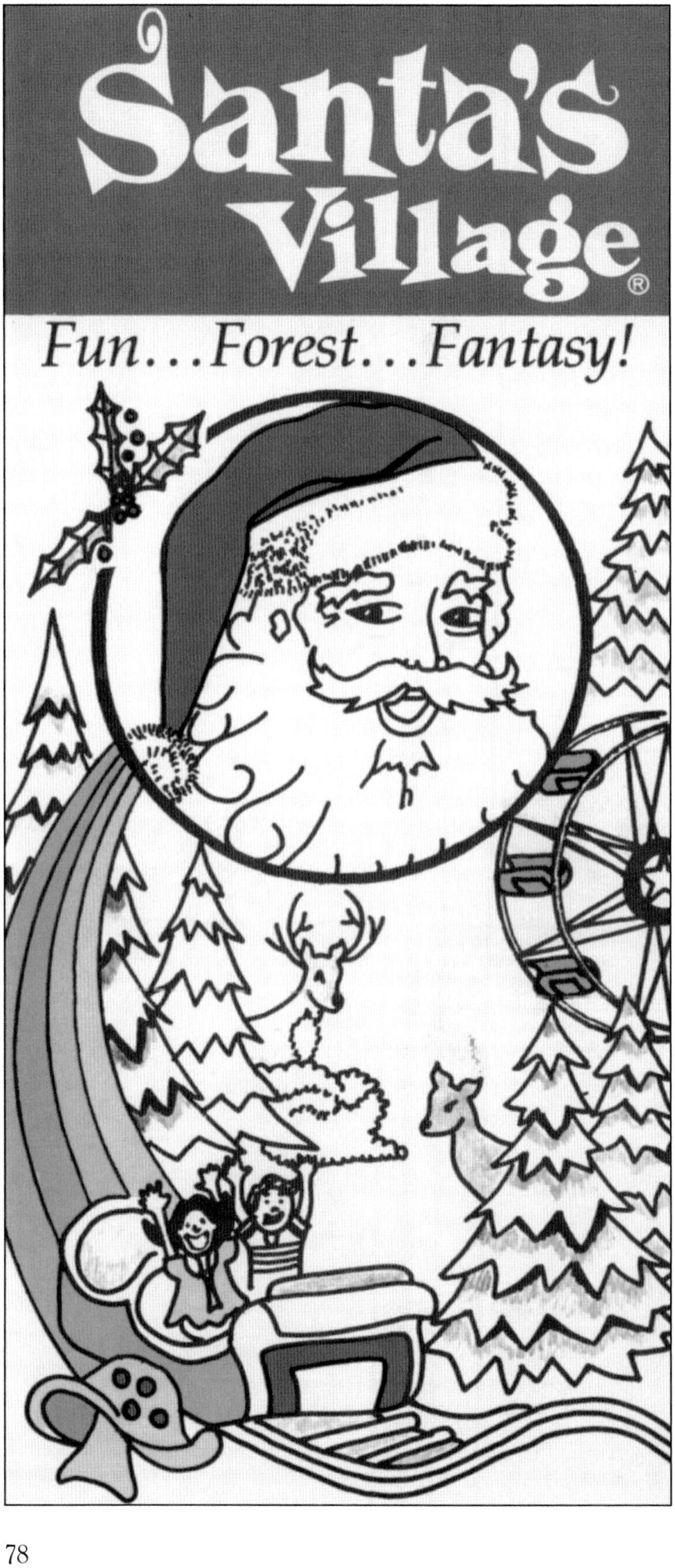

Santa's Village on Highway 18. The top of the page on the back of this 1990s brochure proudly proclaims "The Wonderland of Santa's Village . . . Only 30 Minutes from San Bernardino on Highway 18!" Detailed instructions are given from San Bernardino, and directions to San Bernardino are provided from Los Angeles, Orange County, San Diego, Palm Springs, and Barstow. Virtually the entire back of the brochure is covered by road and highway transportation information. Santa's Village was something of a trailblazing enterprise. Although extremely compact, it had a large selection of rides and special places. In an ironic historical twist, children could ride Santa's burros along a winding trail in the theme park. Eighty years before, burros and mules were a preferred and daily means of travel on the Rim of the World Drive. It seems that everything had changed since 1910 and yet nothing had changed at all. At Santa's Village, the past had been remarkably carried into the present.

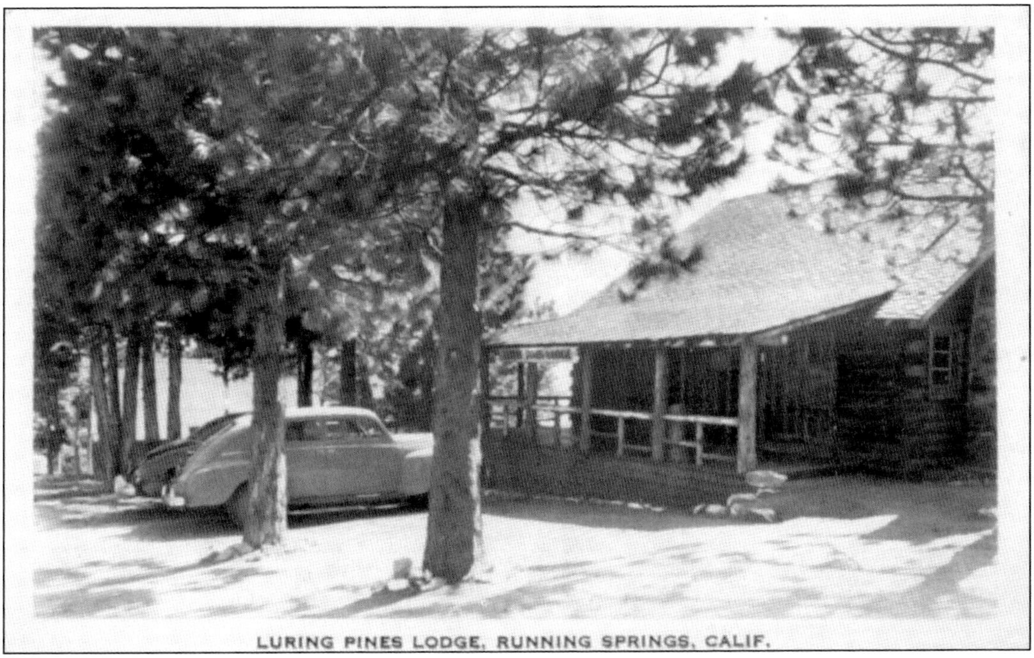

LURING PINES LODGE. Raymond Luring built the lodge shown here on the Rim of the World Drive in the early 1930s as part of his grand Running Springs development scheme, which included a lake, residential tracts, and the Luring Pines Mountain Club. The key to it all was transportation, and his many advertisements continually mention the Rim of the World Drive. (LD.)

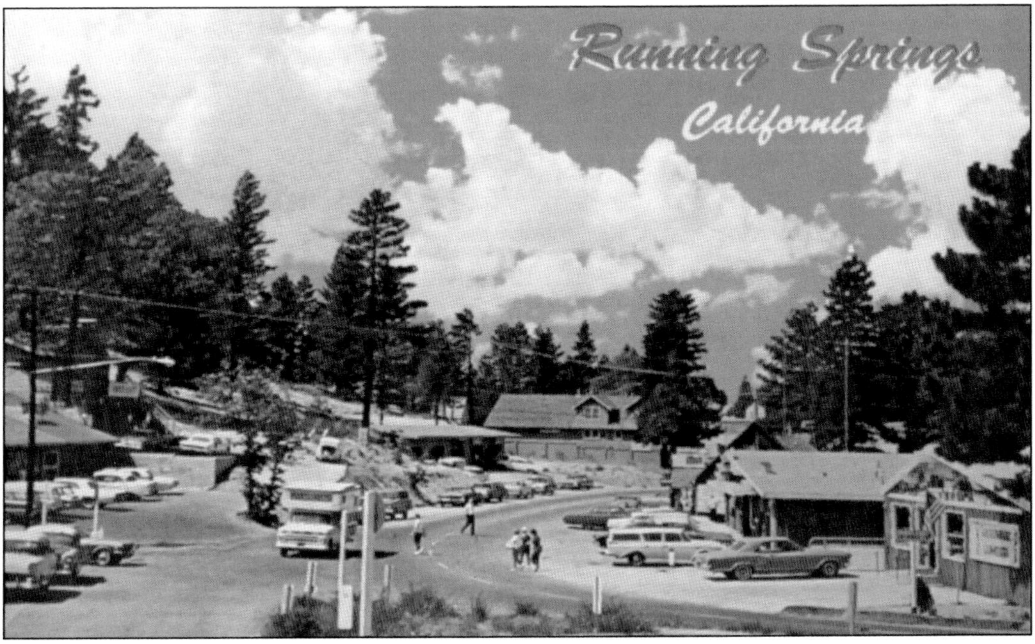

RUNNING SPRINGS, 1960S. The back of this postcard reads, "This popular vacation spot is picturesquely situated among pines at the summit of the City Creek Highway. It is in reality the gateway to . . . the San Bernardino Mountains." Truer words were never written. Here traffic on the Rim of the World Drive met that of City Creek Highway, and a community was born. (FHS.)

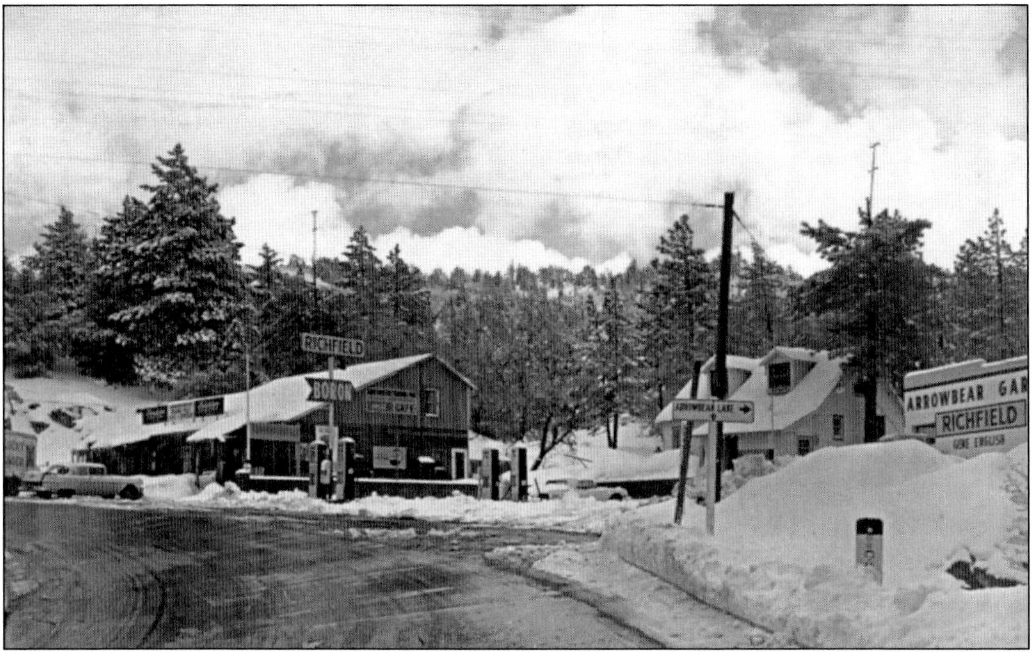

WINTER AT ARROWBEAR. The back of this 1963 postcard reads as follows: "On Highway 18, (Rim o' the World Drive) and City Creek Canyon Road, Elevation 6,000 Feet. 30 Miles from San Bernardino. Between Lake Arrowhead and Big Bear Lake and Valley. U.S. Post Office." Arrowbear Lake was built in the mid-1920s just off the Rim of the World Drive. (R.)

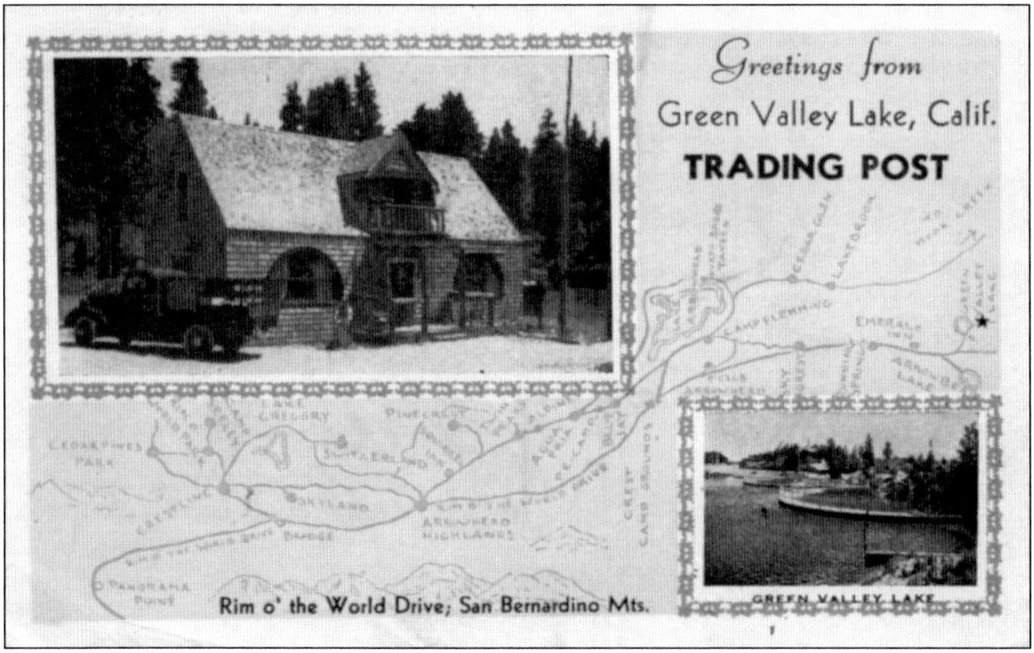

GREEN VALLEY LAKE RIM MAP. Originally the location of a tollhouse, Green Valley became an instant supply point on the original Rim of the World Drive in 1915. George Tillitt, the displaced toll gatekeeper, transitioned into a new life selling gas and as a real estate developer following completion of the dam and lake in 1926.

SNOW VALLEY LIFT AND CARS, 1950S. This card reads, "SNOW VALLEY—Rim of the World Highway. The chairlift is 5130 feet long with a Puma Lift that is 1500 feet long. There are eleven rope tows here. . . . It is one of Southern California's most popular ski areas." The key point here is that on the back of this postcard, the Rim of the World Drive is mentioned first and foremost. (CW.)

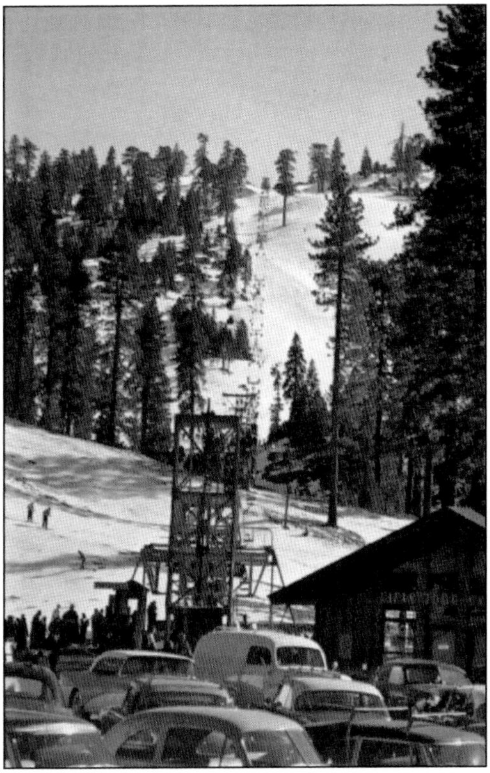

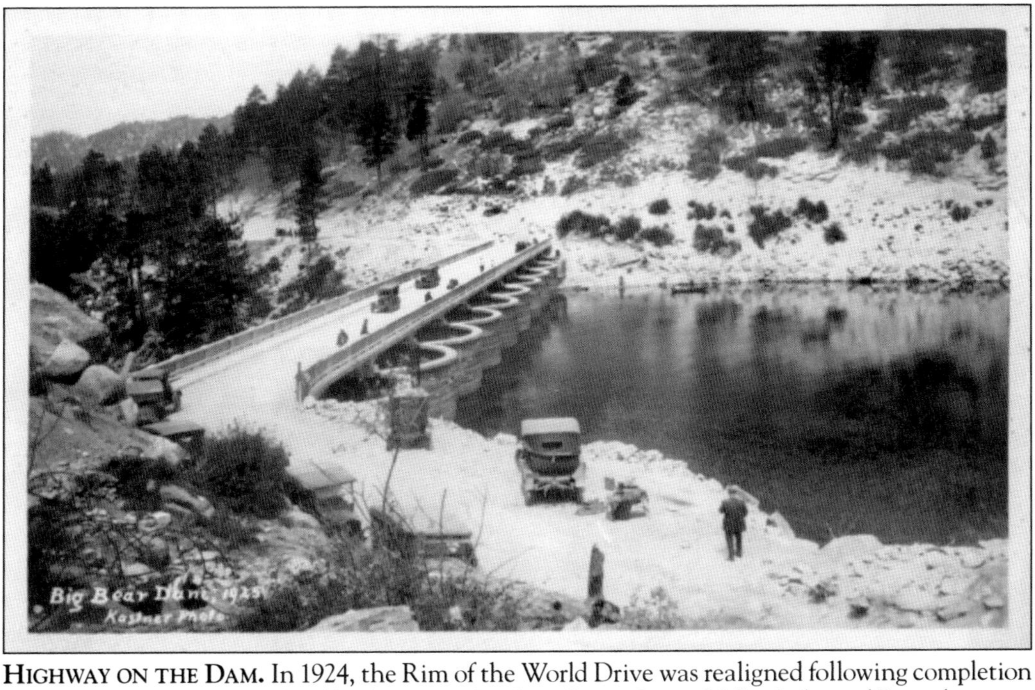

HIGHWAY ON THE DAM. In 1924, the Rim of the World Drive was realigned following completion of the Deep Creek Cut-Off and bridge across Big Bear Dam. Green Valley Lake and Fawnskin were instantaneously bypassed, much like thousands of communities nationwide during construction of the interstate highway system.

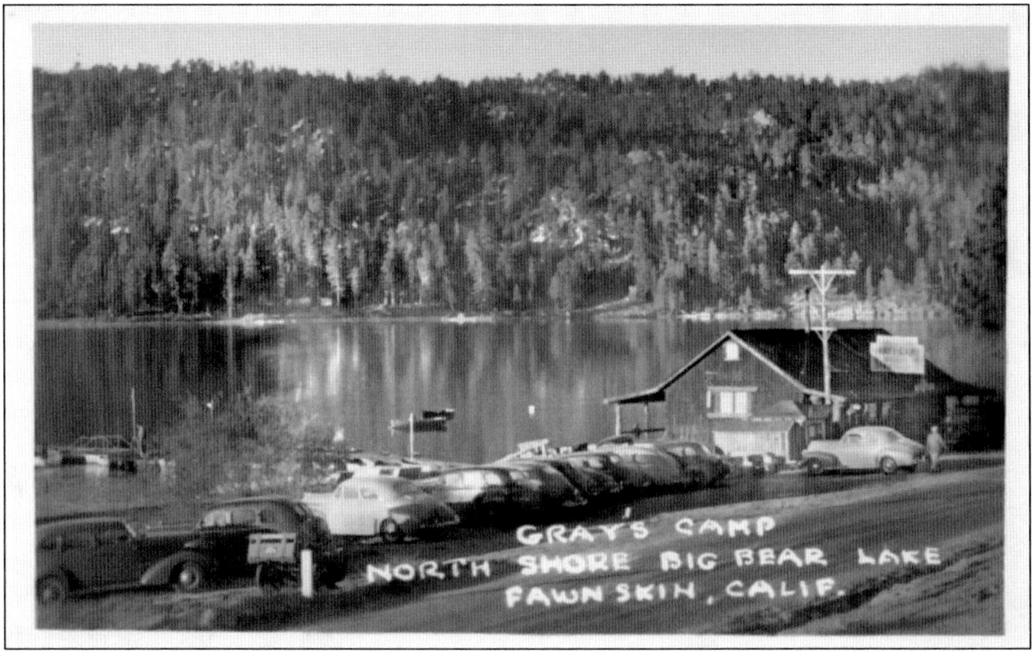

GRAY'S CAMP. In the mid-1920s, Gray's Camp offered the "best café on Big Bear Lake." One brochure notes, "The drive alone over the new Deep Creek cut-off is well worth a trip." The new Rim of the World Drive alignment was clearly viewed by the owners as promoting business at Gray's.

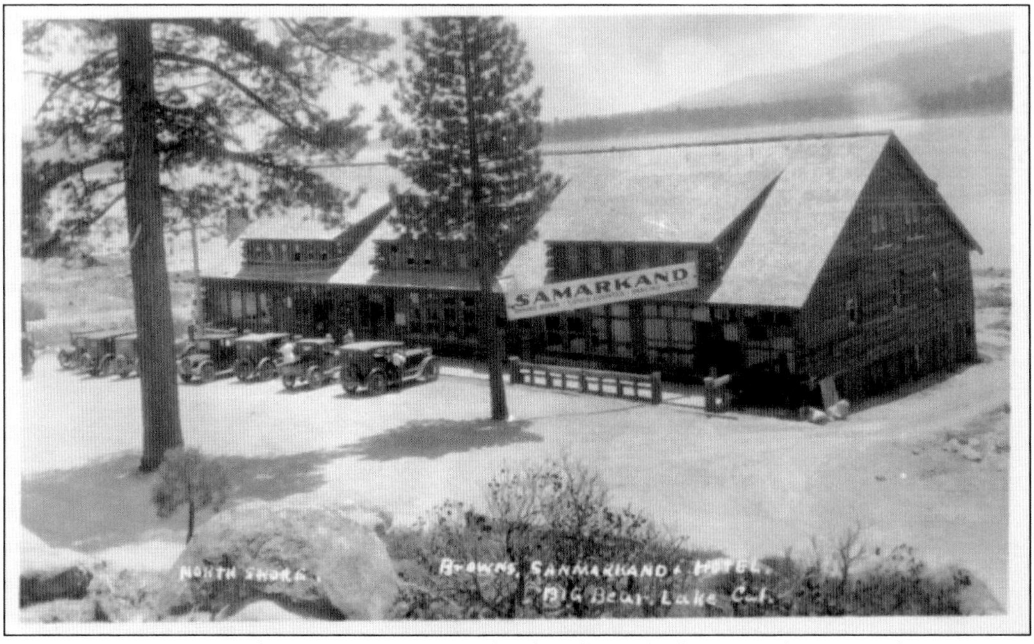

SAMARKAND HOTEL. This one-time Big Bear landmark was built in 1927 by Coy and Lex Brown. The completion of the Deep Creek Cut-Off on the Rim of the World Drive increased traffic to, from, and around Big Bear Lake. Samarkand was built to capture some of the trade.

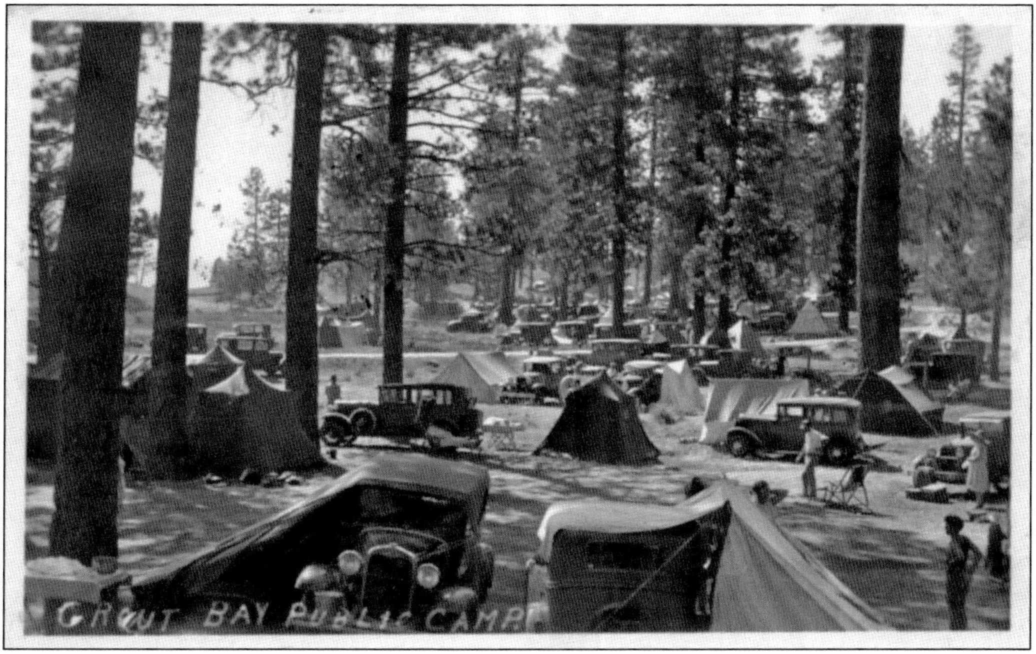

PUBLIC CAMP. The free government camp at Grout Bay was always crowded. The back of this 1928 postcard reads, "I am fine—got here Sunday at 9:30—had a perfect trip no trouble at all. . . . slept in the car & slept fine. Mama." Postmarked Crestline, "Mama" must have continued her trip along the famous Rim of the World Drive to the west.

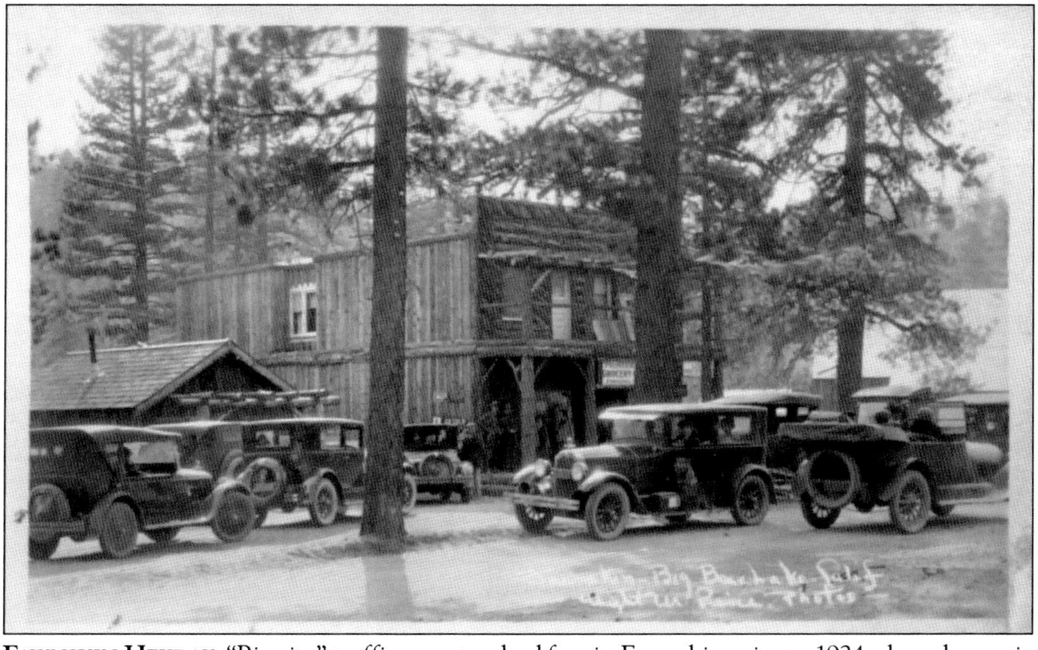

FAWNSKIN HEYDAY. "Big city" traffic was standard fare in Fawnskin prior to 1924 when the rustic lake community was located directly on the Rim of the World Drive. The Pioneer Grocery in the background exhibits typical early Bear Valley design themes with natural wood columns and rustic architectural accents. (WMP.)

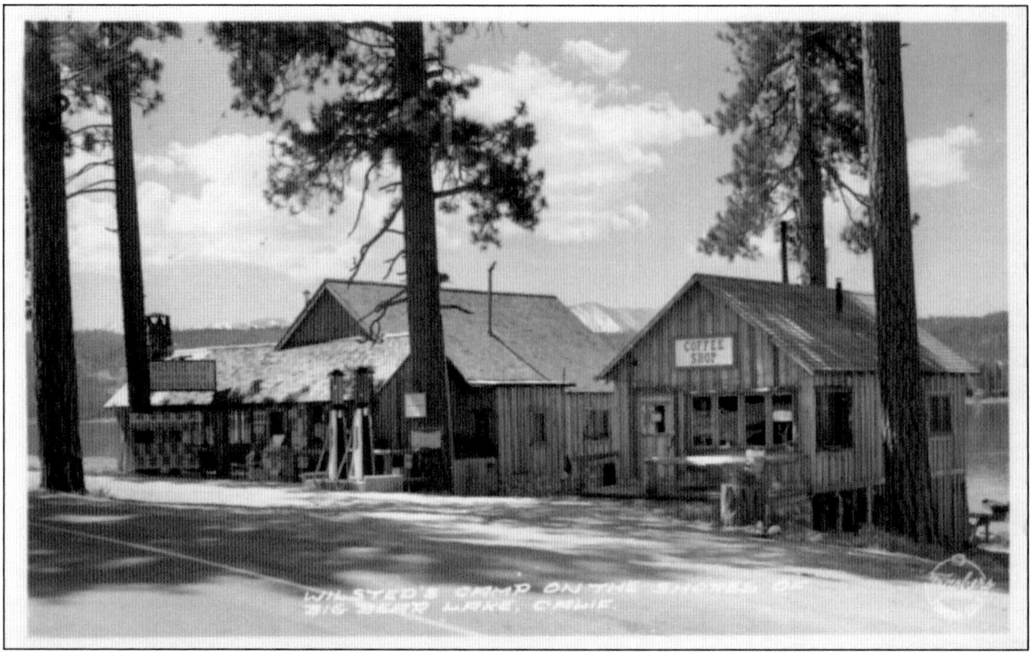

Wilsted's Camp. This small camp, near Fawnskin, was a popular lakefront location. The survival of this small resort was entirely dependent on automobiles reaching Big Bear on the Rim of the World Drive. A key element was the availability of gasoline immediately adjacent to the roadway. (FI.)

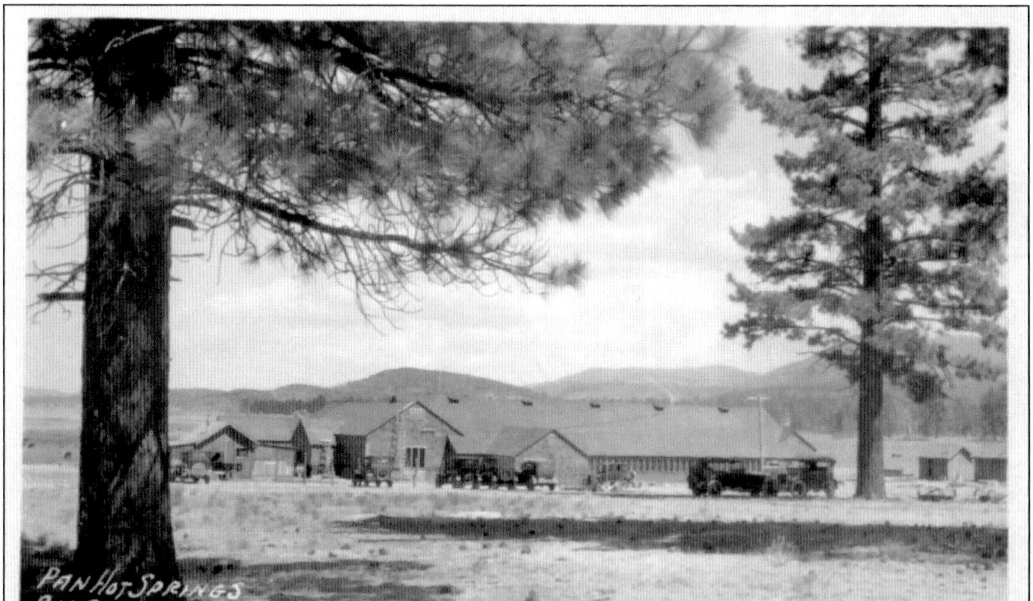

Pan Hot Springs. Built in 1924 by Emile Jessup, Pan Hot Springs was a sprawling complex consisting of a hotel, swimming pools, and spas. Although the hotel burned in 1933, the pools operated until the early 1990s. Pan Hot Springs was included in a 1931 *Los Angeles Times* article featuring mountain resorts located on the Rim of the World Drive.

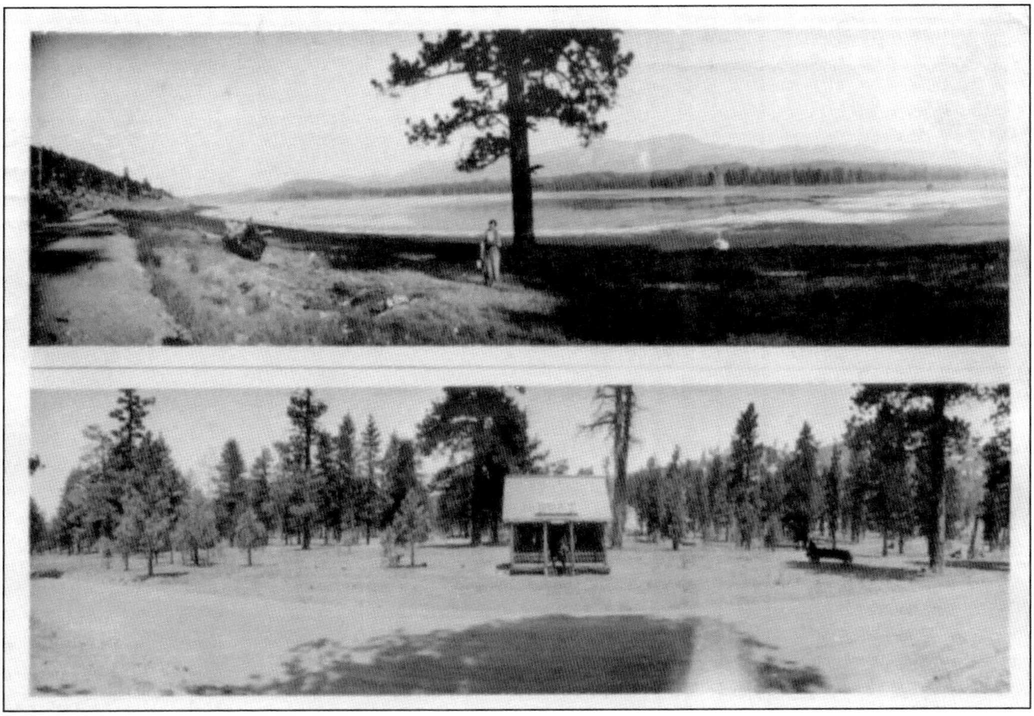

Baldwin Lake Real Estate Office. This mini-panorama shows the undeveloped shores of Baldwin Lake and the Baldwin Lake Tract real estate office. Subdivided by the Shay brothers, this development venture, like many others throughout Bear Valley beginning *c.* 1915, was in direct response to the arrival of the automobile and influence of the Rim of the World Drive.

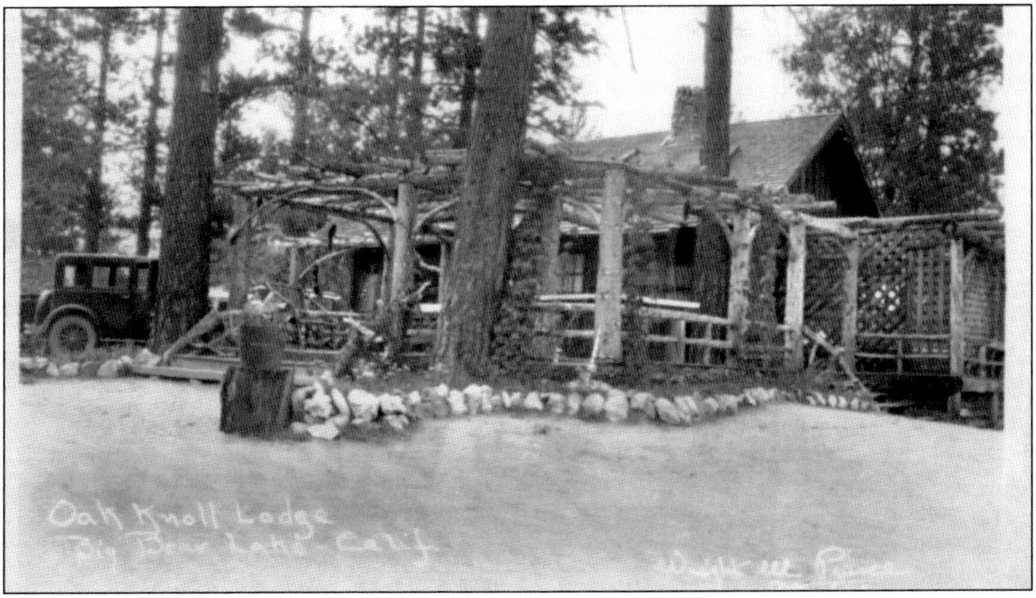

Oak Knoll Lodge. The historic Oak Knoll Lodge was the first Bear Valley camp reached by way of Mill Creek Road on the Rim of the World Drive. It offered "home cooking and home-like table" and cabins for two to eight people. Mid-1920s rates started at $15 per week per person (including meals).

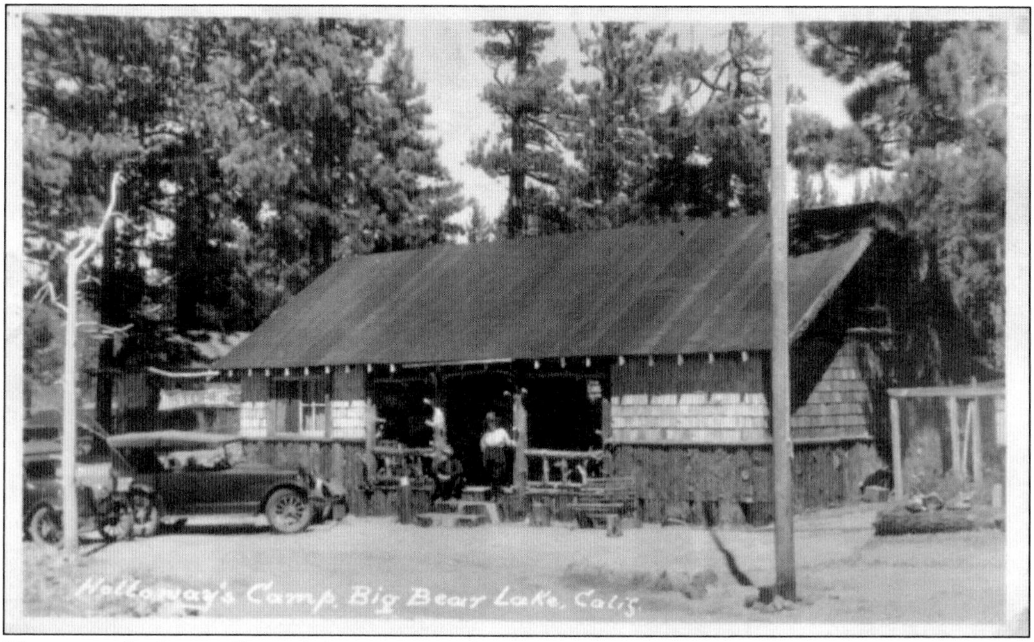

Holloway's Camp. One of the most popular Bear Valley resorts was Holloway's on the shore of Big Bear Lake. It was built during the development boom that hit Bear Valley following the 1915 opening of the Rim of the World Drive. Mid-1920s rates rented furnished cabins from $18 to $35 per week.

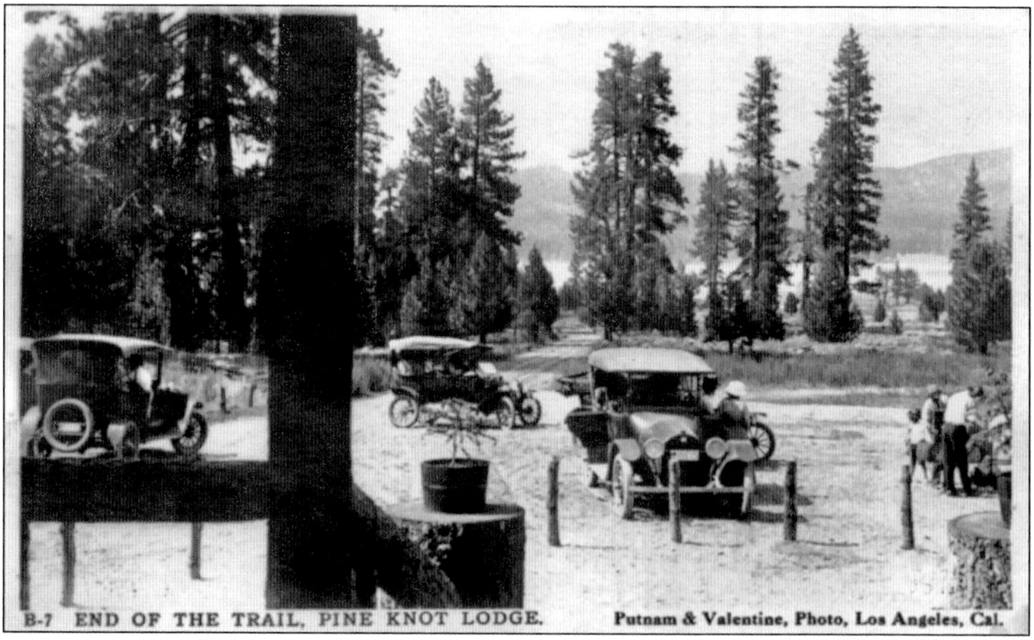

End of the Trail. Pine Knot Lodge was historically the end of the trail (it really was prior to 1892) and was advertised as such even after completion of the Rim of the World Drive. Log cabins with or without baths were available. American-plan rates were, per person with meals, $4.50 to $5.50 per day without bath, $7 to $8 per day with bath. Baths were clearly not for the bargain minded.

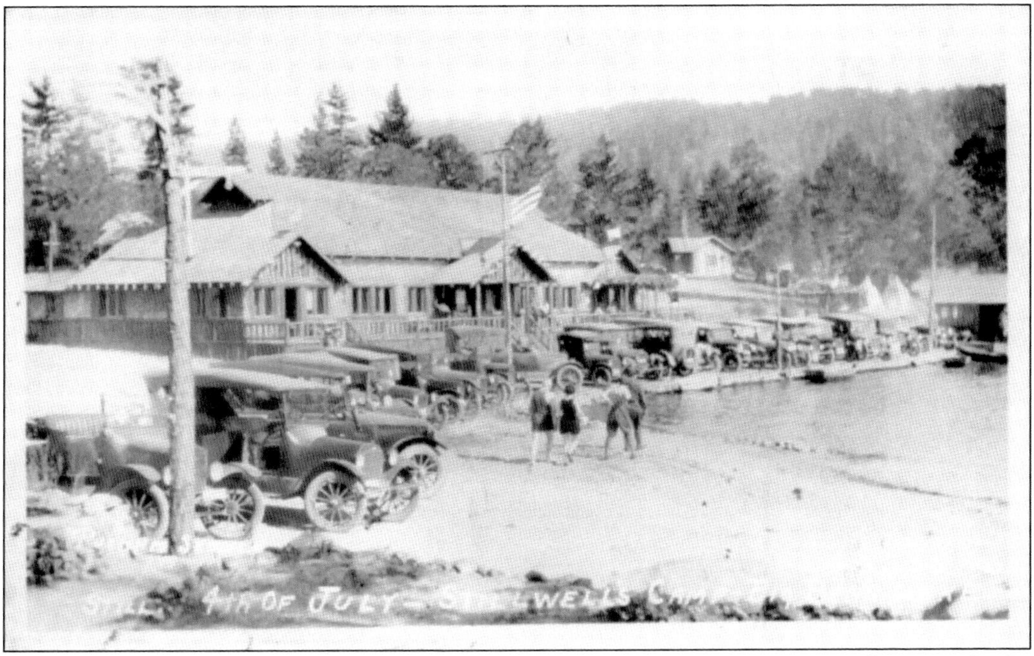

BEACH AT STILLWELL'S. The back of this mid-1920s card reads, "Dear Son, We have just had a dandy thunderstorm. Our week is almost up, wish we could stay longer. Think this must have been Ford day over here. Mother." Note the cars parked at the shoreline—Fords do appear to be the car of choice on the Fourth of July, the date that this photograph was taken.

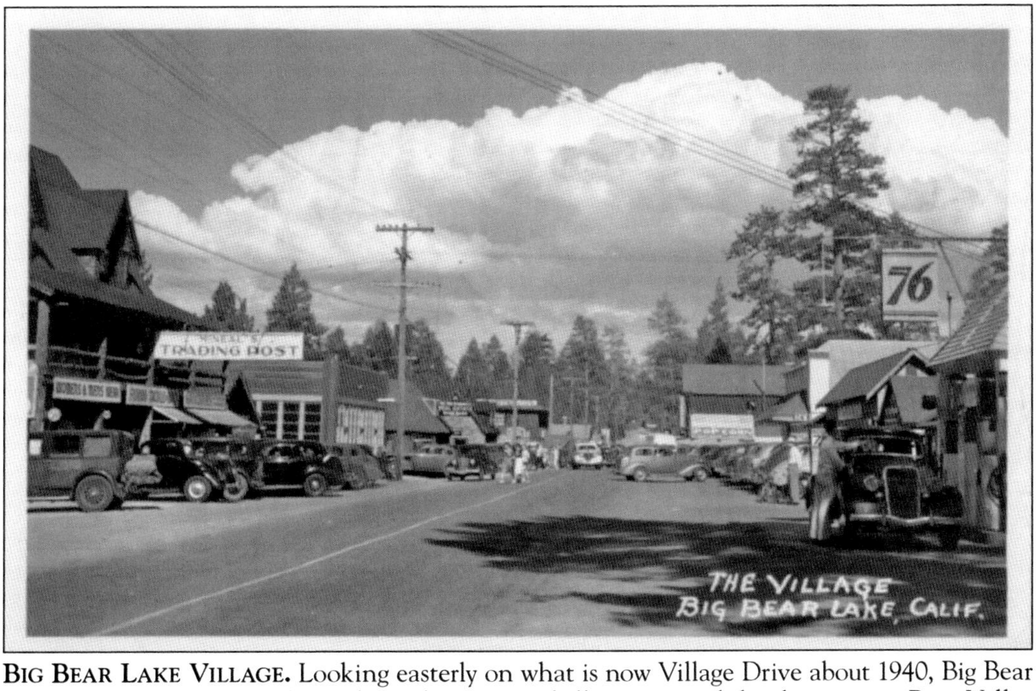

BIG BEAR LAKE VILLAGE. Looking easterly on what is now Village Drive about 1940, Big Bear Village was clearly a very busy place, the center of all commercial development in Bear Valley and the business district loop of the Rim of the World Drive. Pictured here are McNeal's Trading Post, Chad's Café, the Navajo Hotel, and the Grizzly Theater.

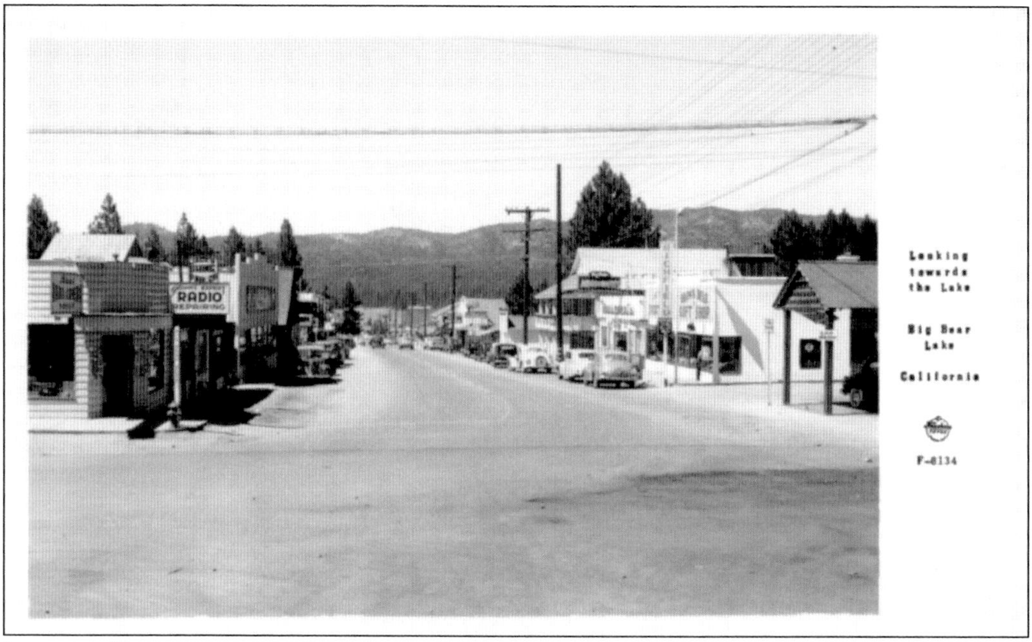

LOOKING TOWARDS THE LAKE. This mid-1940s view looks northerly along Pine Knot Boulevard. It tells quite a bit about postwar Big Bear. The speed limit was 25 miles per hour, a car wash was available at the gas station, a snooker and pool hall was there for the men, and gift shops abounded. (FI.)

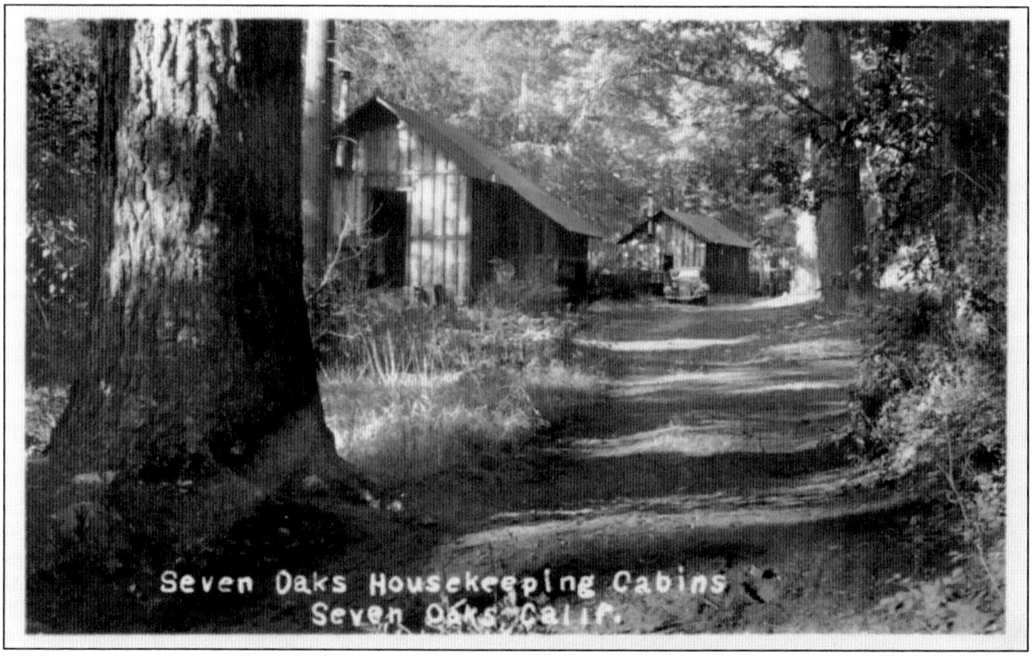

SEVEN OAKS CABINS. As the oldest continuously operating San Bernardino Mountain resort, Seven Oaks catered to families (note the car and cabin). On the banks of the Santa Ana River, alongside a prehistoric trail transformed into a mule path, it was only a mile and a half off of the Rim of the World Drive.

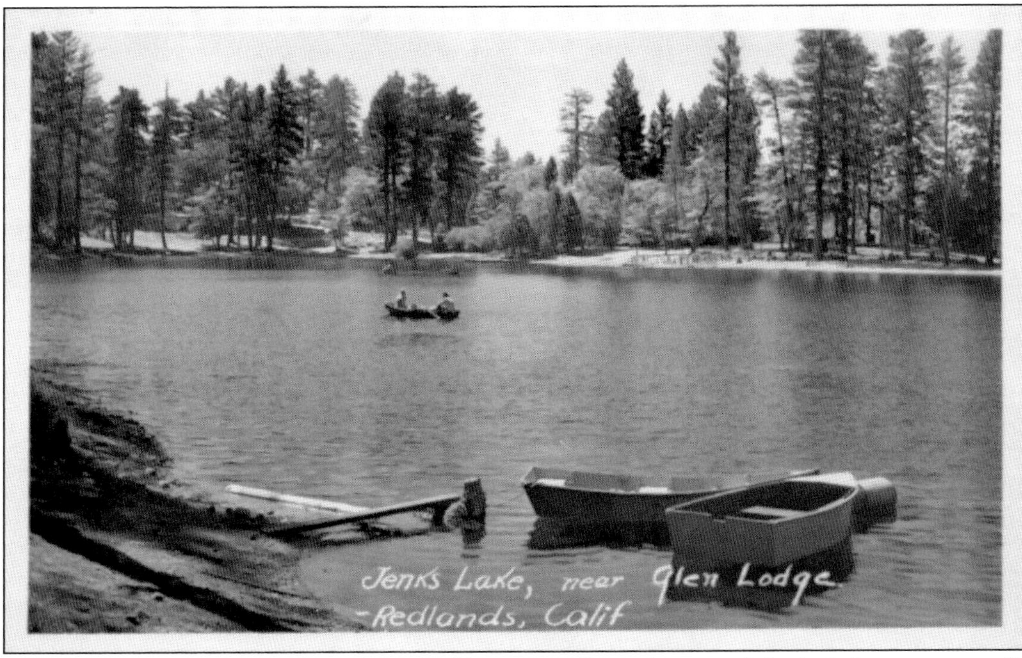

JENKS LAKE. Located just off Highway 38 (the present Rim alignment), Jenks Lake was originally built in the late 1920s on a branch road connecting to the Rim of the World Drive. It remains a popular destination point for weekend mountaineers.

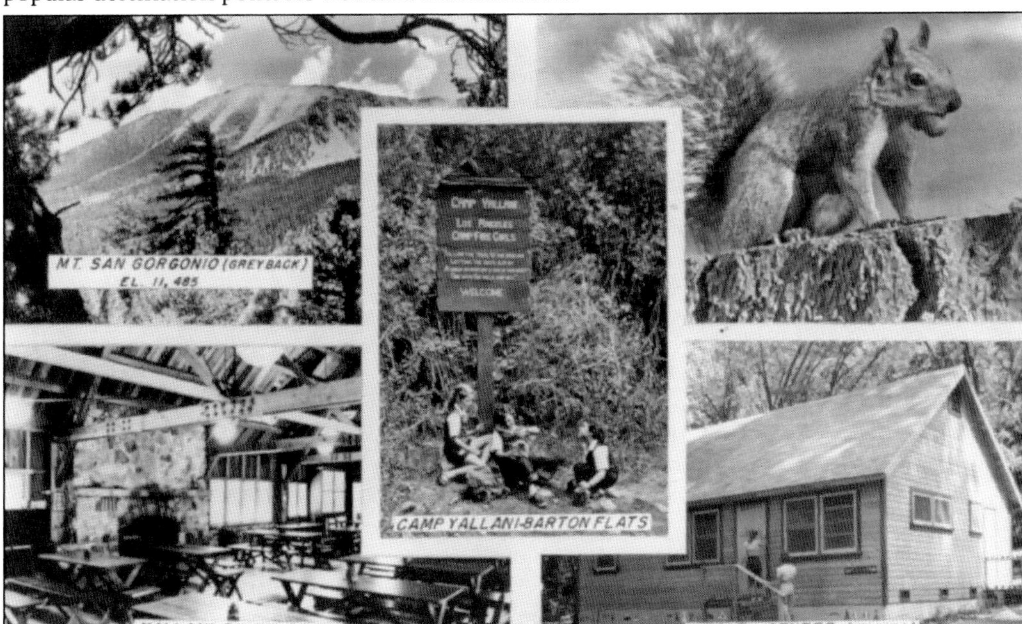

CAMP YALLANI. Since 1927, Camp Yallani (now Camp Metoche) has operated under a Forest Service Special Use Permit. Many older Barton Flats recreational camps still exist although in dwindling numbers. This card reads, "Paula got laringitis [*sic*] and had to go to Wakiya [isolation cabin]. . . . While she was there that nutty nurse left, even though flu and colds have been going around camp. . . . I've been having lots of fun."

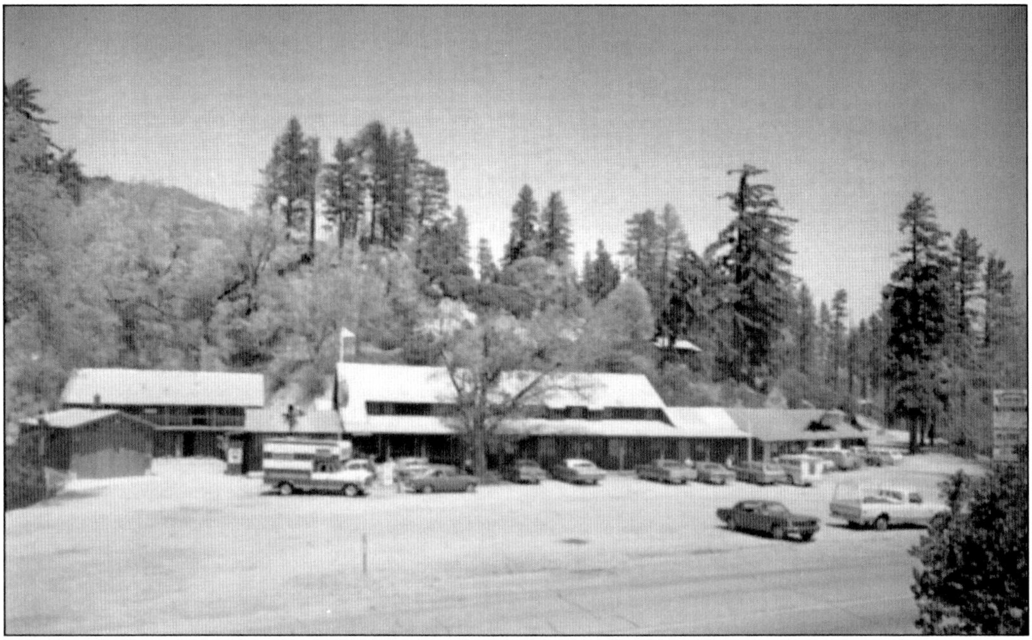

ANGELUS OAKS ON HIGHWAY 38. The back of this 1960s card reads, "Angelus Oaks is located on the old 101 Mile Drive that opens the San Bernardino Mountains to recreational activities. . . . This photographer remembers the control point at Igo's store where traffic would be held up for the cars coming down." (RP.)

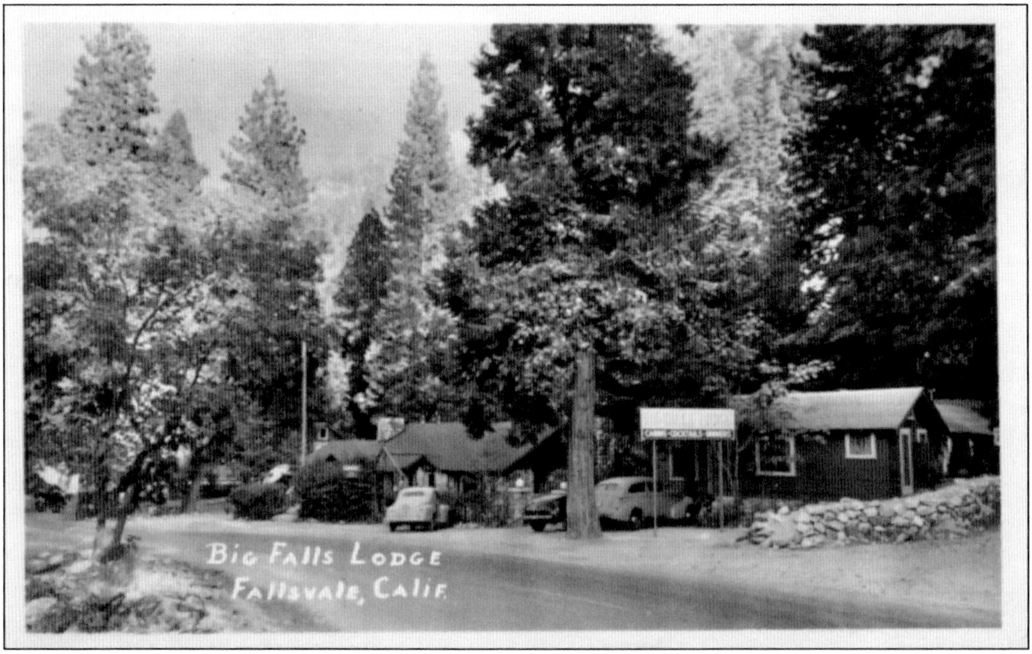

BIG FALLS LODGE. Once known as Valley of the Falls, then Fallsvale, and today as Forest Falls, Big Falls Lodge and store once offered "Lobster Sandwiches and Coffee" as an advertised specialty. Located just off the Rim of the World Drive, the lodge appears to have been photographed about 1945.

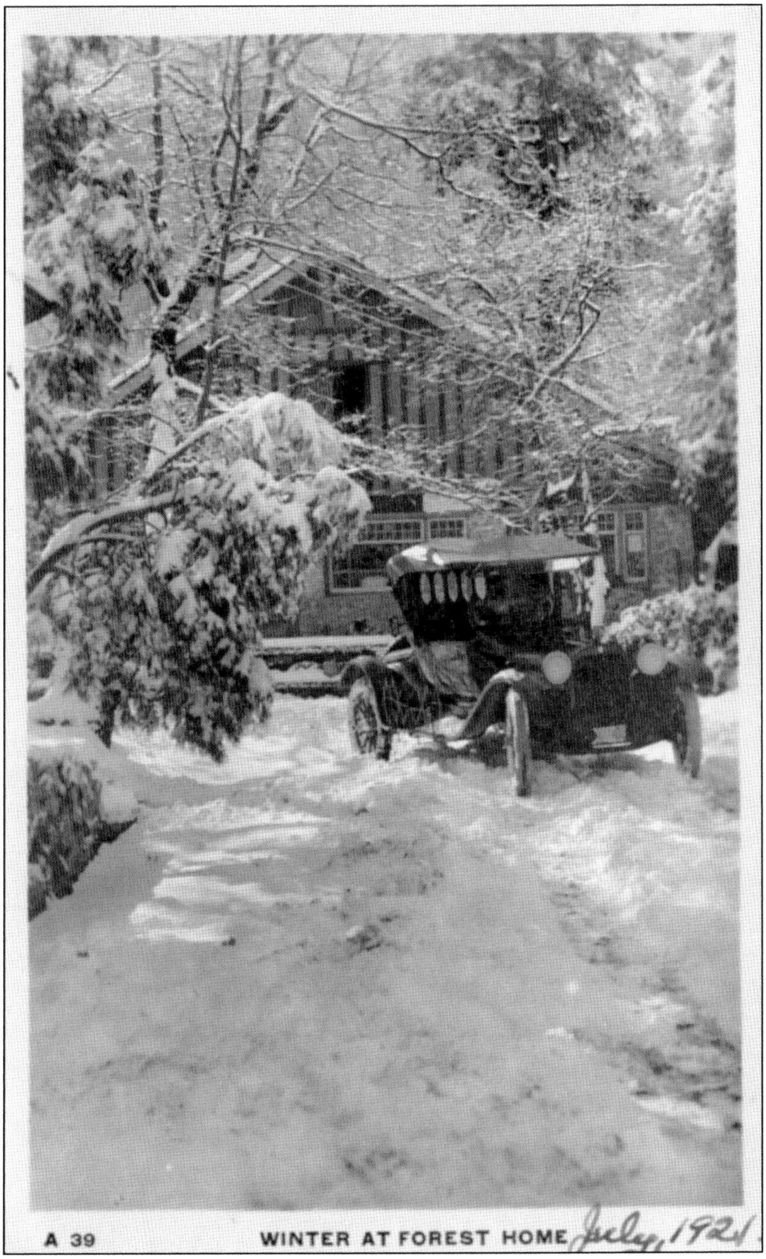

Forest Home Auto in Winter. A popular mountain resort location beginning in the late 1890s, by the early 1920s (this photograph was taken in 1921), Forest Home had transitioned from mules and wagons to automobiles (even in winter). According to a mid-1920s historic brochure, a particular advantage was that it was only 16 miles from Redlands. The brochure continues as follows: "Modern hotel and bungalows or housekeeping cabins. Hotel service if desired. Close to store, post office, and amusement center. Exclusive . . . with all modern conveniences. Reached via Pacific Electric railway to Redlands thence via mountain auto line." Appearing in many Rim of the World Drive brochures, Forest Home is also featured on historic maps "Showing Location of Resorts and Roads on Rim of World." Forest Home, clearly a part of the Rim identity, is the last mountain stop on this historic tour through time on the Rim of the World Drive.

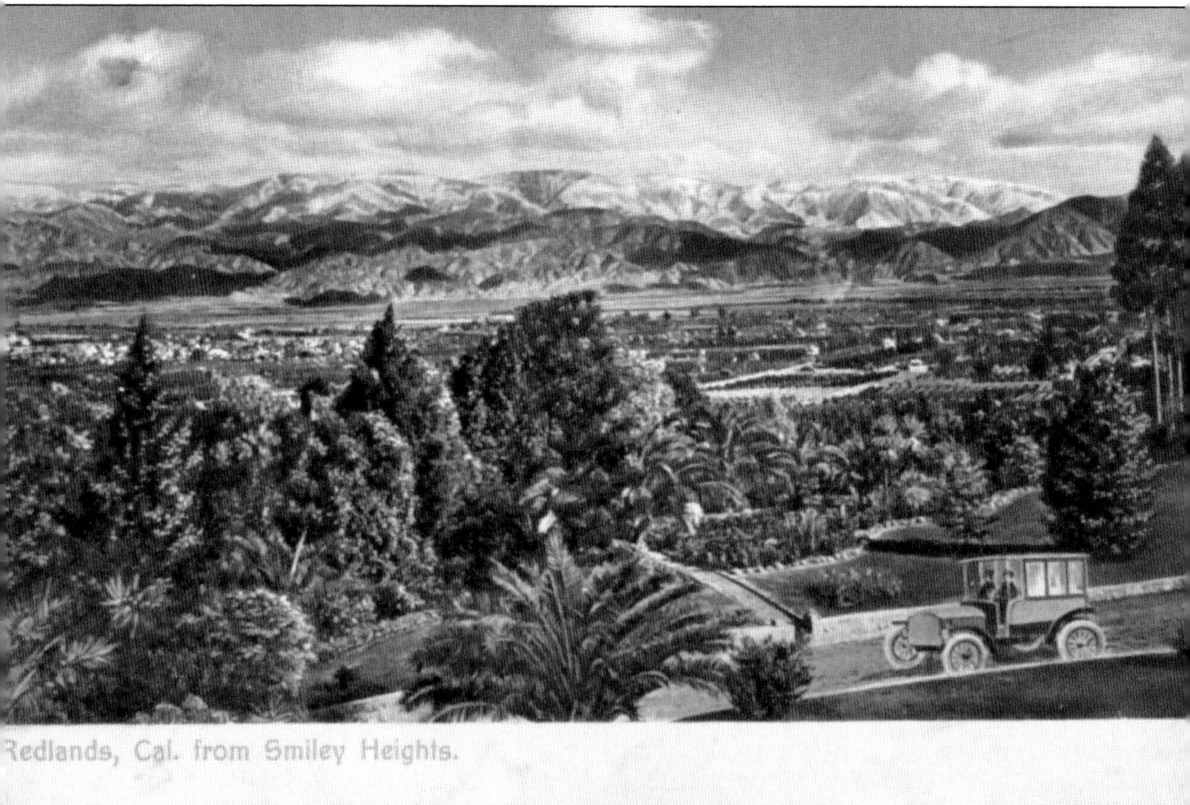

REDLANDS END OF THE LINE. The image on page two of this book shows the San Bernardino Mountains as viewed from San Bernardino. The image here, taken at about the same time, shows the mountains as viewed from Redlands. Both cities served as historic departure points for mountain-bound travelers. During the age of wagons and buggies, Redlands predominated. By 1915, San Bernardino had replaced Redlands as the primary mountain departure point. Every major mountain auto stage line had opened for business in San Bernardino, and the original 1915 alignment of the Rim of the World Drive through lower Santa Ana Canyon headed straight for San Bernardino. Redlands, however, didn't give up without a fight, and when the Rim of the World Drive was realigned up Mill Creek in 1916 (with pressure from Redlands businessmen), this wonderfully picturesque community was once again regarded as a springboard to the mountains. Today one can wake up in Las Vegas and have lunch in the San Bernardino Mountains; there are no fixed departure points to the Rim of the World Drive.

Four

Then and Now on the Rim

The Rim of the World Drive then is a world away from what it is now. Only a very small portion of the Highway 18 and Highway 38 route driven today represents the alignment dedicated on July 18, 1915. Yet the Rim of the World Drive still encircles and connects all major mountain communities in exactly the same manner that it did in 1915. On a macro scale, the function of this historic roadway remains surprisingly unchanged. On a micro scale, the changes between then and now become photographically intriguing.

This chapter targets a balanced mix of locations along the historic Rim of the World Drive that have changed to a greater or lesser degree. All are readily accessible to Rim visitors today. One of the chief drawbacks of "Then and Now" books has hopefully been eliminated whereby readers are perpetually horrified by the pictorial comparison between past and present caused by demolition of historical landmarks and other marked changes. On the other hand, the selected images are intentionally significantly different in order to provide food for thought.

Most importantly, each image tells a story directly related to the historical growth and development of the Rim of the World Drive. Each historical image reflects a specific point in time, and each modern image helps carry the past into the present. Finally, each selection clearly illustrates how the Rim of the World Drive has changed everyday life in the San Bernardino Mountains.

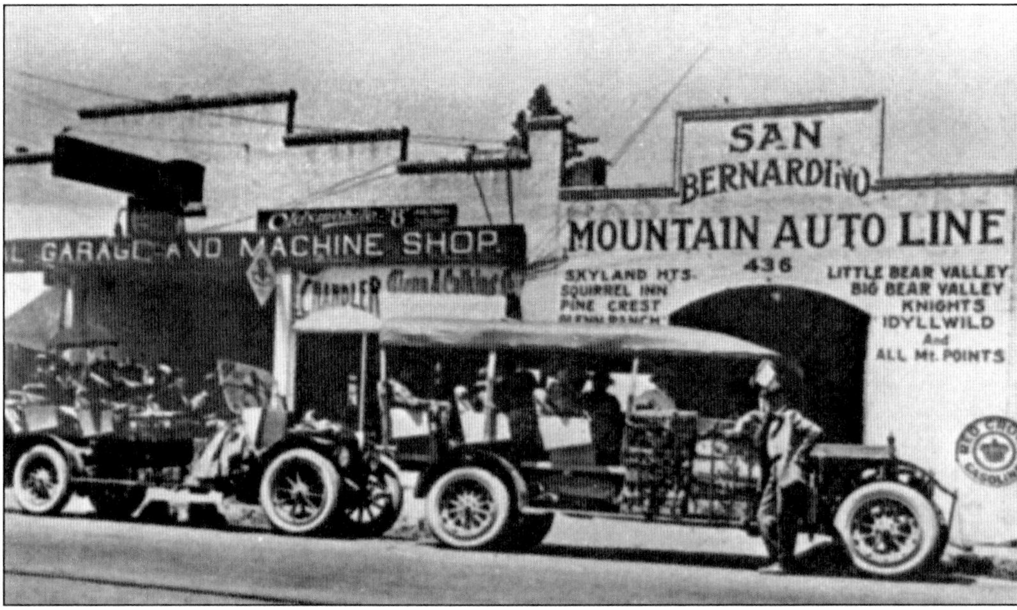

AUTO STAGE HEADQUARTERS THEN AND NOW. The above *c.* 1913 photograph depicts the location of the San Bernardino Mountain Auto Line headquarters. The business established San Bernardino as the primary departure point for mountain tourists. Today the location is a parking lot (see palm trees below for the approximate location of the original building) adjacent to the county law library. Ironically, mountain-related transportation activities are still occurring here, as the tall building to the extreme left of the modern image below is today's Caltrans District 8 Headquarters, and State Highways 18 and 38 (the present Rim of the World Drive alignment) are managed by Caltrans from this location.

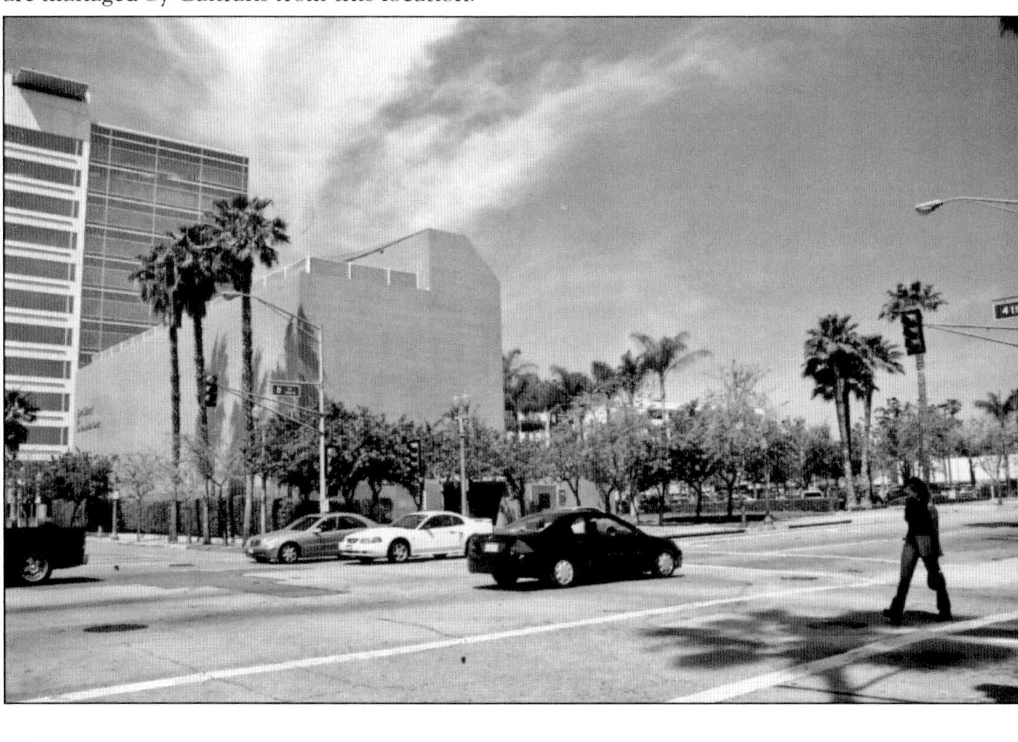

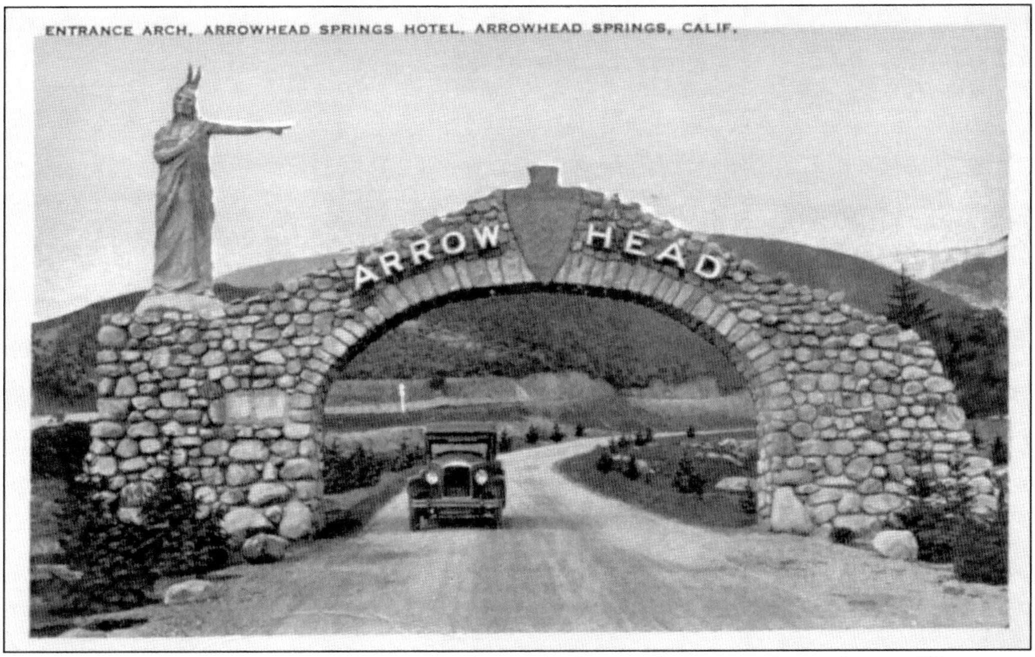

ARROWHEAD SPRINGS GATEWAY THEN. This arched entry first greeted travelers up Waterman Canyon on the Rim of the World Drive in 1925. When tourists and residents alike passed this location, they knew they were officially in the San Bernardino Mountains. (BRM.)

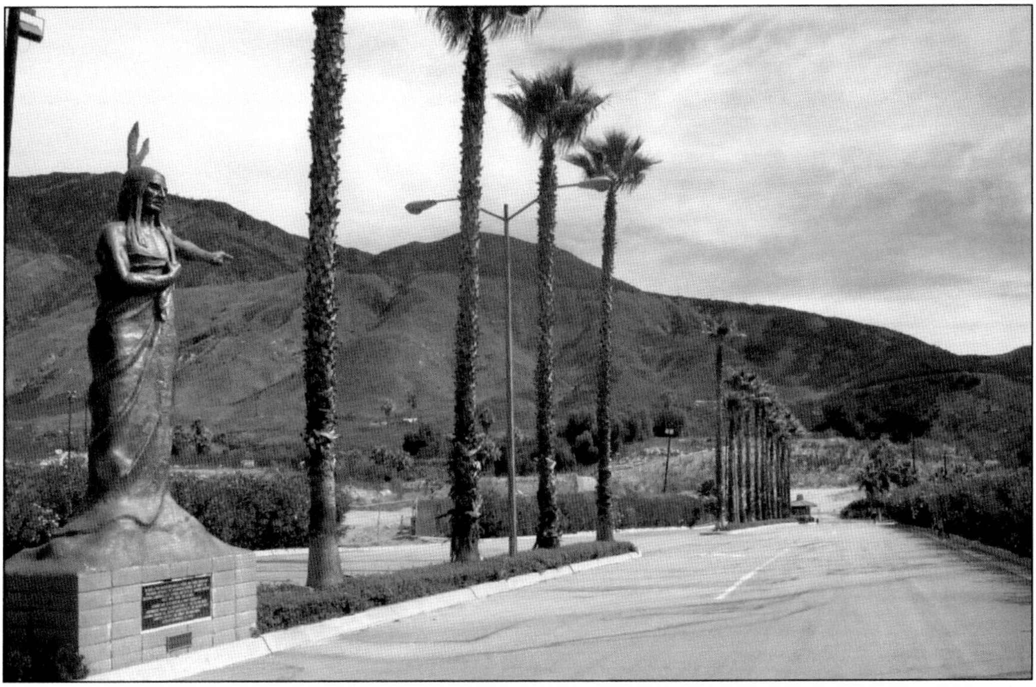

ARROWHEAD SENTINEL NOW. When Highway 18 was widened to four lanes in the 1960s, the original stone arch was demolished. In 1976, the Native Sons and Daughters of the Golden West, together with the new owners of the hotel, re-erected the statue. Sadly, the Arrowhead Hot Springs Hotel is no longer open, but the silent sentinel survives as a touchstone to times past.

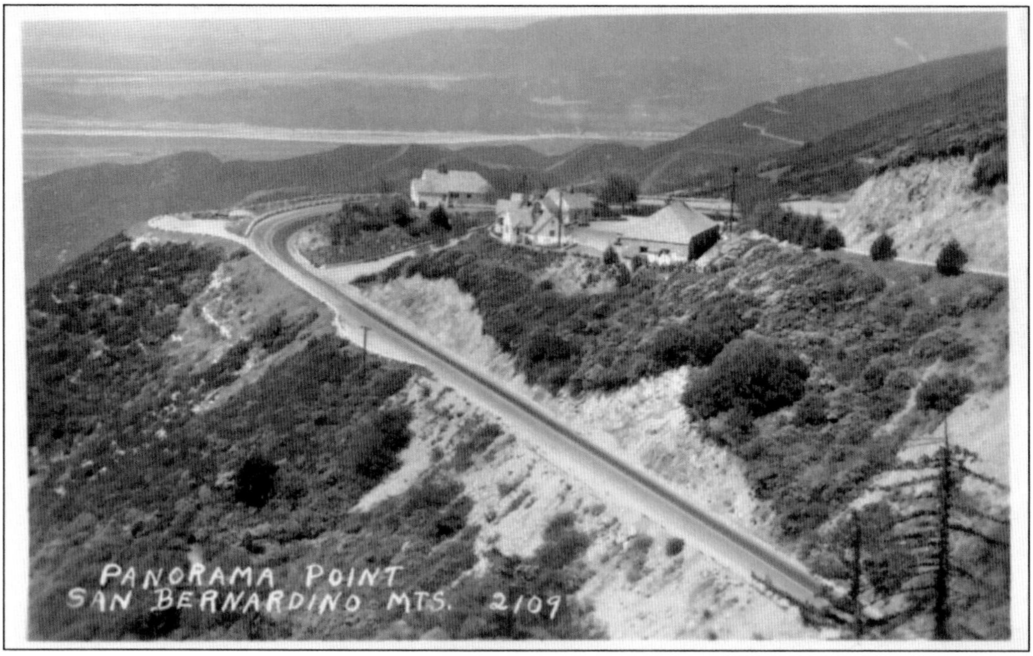

PANORAMA POINT THEN AND NOW. In 1928, the State of California developed Panorama Point as a maintenance facility and a "park for the traveling public" on the Rim of the World Drive. The mid-1930s photograph (above) shows the site in its heyday, including worker housing, drinking fountains, and maintenance buildings. In the 1960s, the once-popular turnout was altered by construction of the four-lane Highway 18. The modern image (below) shows Panorama Point after having been totally destroyed in 2003 by a forest fire. Only a few stone walls remain. Incredibly, today's image is remarkably similar to the historic pre-automobile view on the opposite page, when Panorama Point was a just sharp turn in the road.

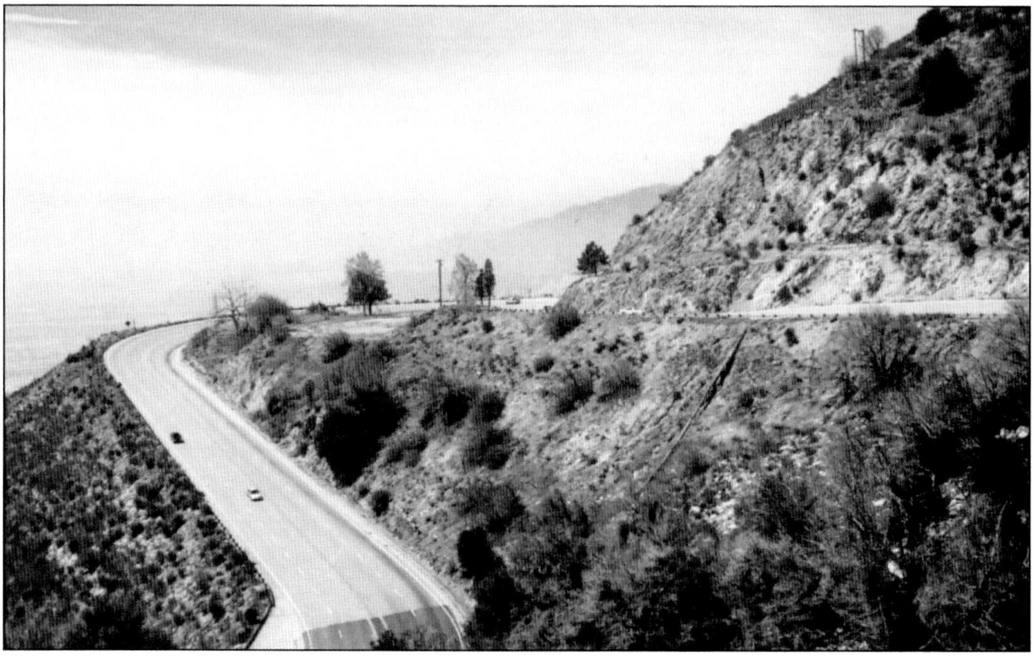

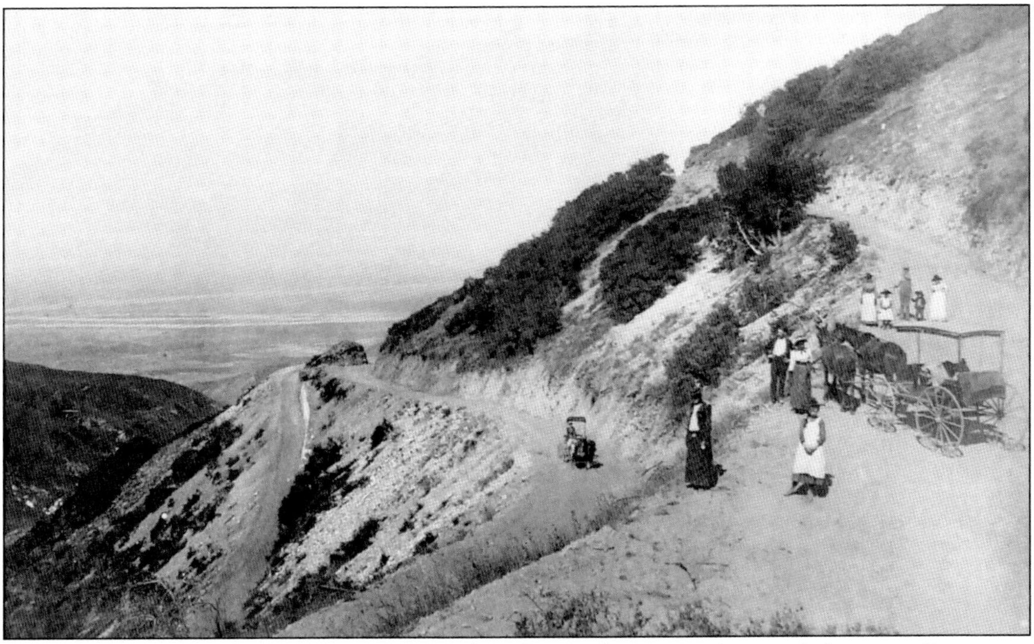

BEFORE AND AFTER THE AUTOMOBILE. Perhaps better than any other single location, Panorama Point reflects the history of the Rim of the World Drive. In one form or another, Panorama Point has always been a transportation landmark on the way up the hill. Here, on the Arrowhead Toll Road or later on the free county road, one could rest the horses and gaze across an unspoiled panoramic view (above) of the entire San Bernardino Valley. By 1920, a Richfield gas station and restaurant (below) was built to better accommodate the modern age of the automobile. Panorama House was demolished during late-1920s high-gear road construction improvements on the Rim of the World Drive.

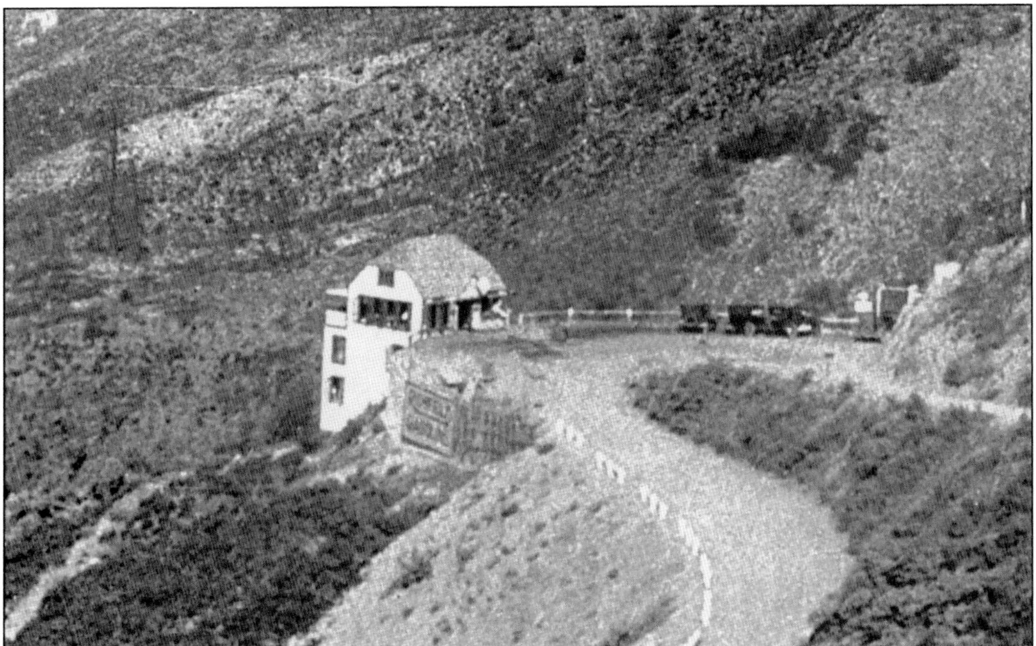

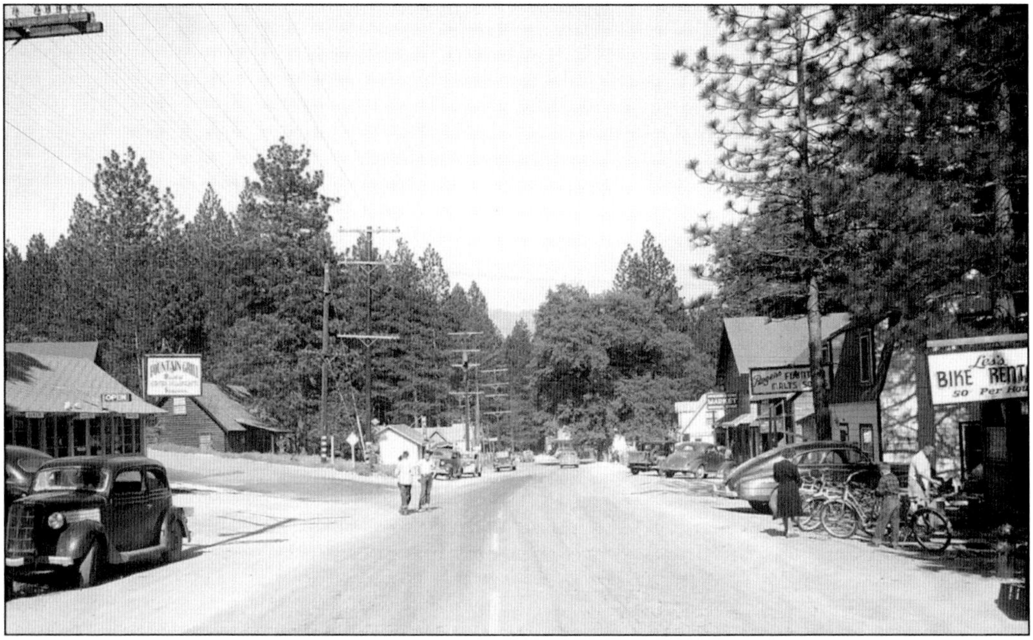

LAKE DRIVE, CRESTLINE, THEN. Taken in 1948 at the intersection of present-day Lake Drive (originally Huston Flats Road) and Thousand Pines Road in Crestline, everything about this photograph defines postwar America, especially the young man renting a bike with plaid shirt and jeans rolled up above his shoes.

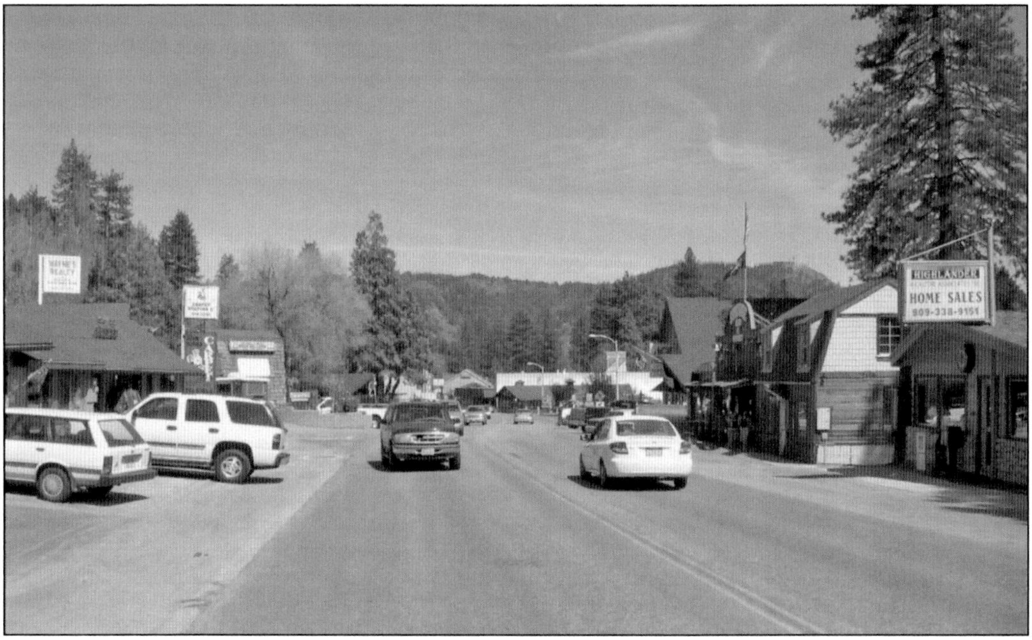

LAKE DRIVE, CRESTLINE, NOW. At first glance, downtown Crestline today appears much the same as it did nearly 60 years ago. The original Goodwin's Market building still stands, for example, as Lake Drive Hardware, and the remodeled malt shop building also survives. Yet the one-time vacation community is now a bedroom commuter suburb, and year-round residents have replaced summer tourists. Traffic (note the cars) even at off-peak hours is amazing.

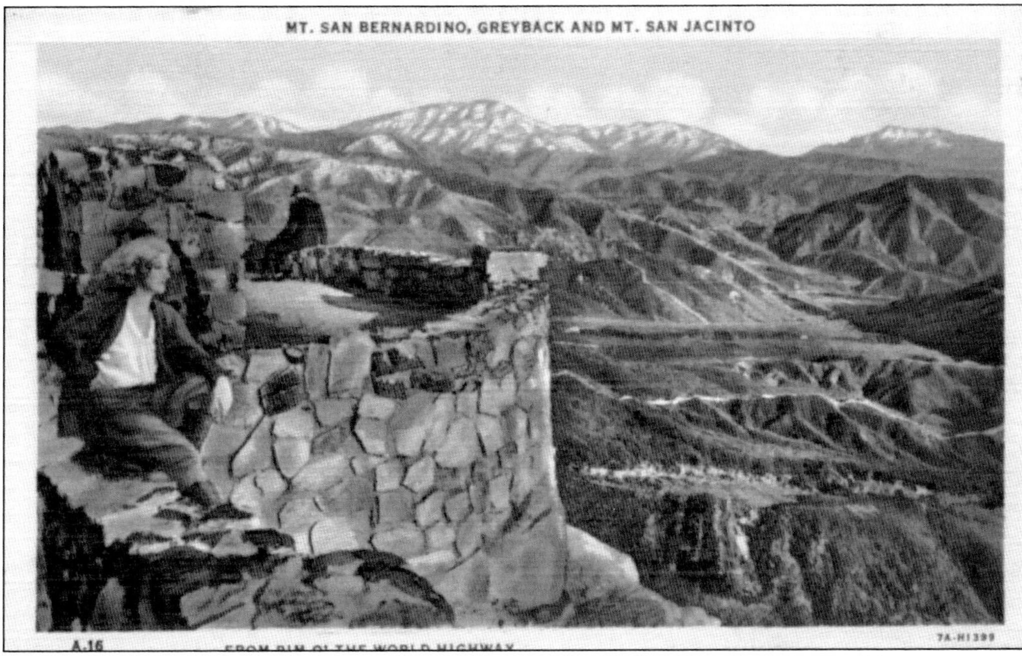

RED ROCK WALL THEN. Printed in the mid-1930s, the back of this highly posed linen postcard reads, "This glorious scenic drive over the high gear state highway leads quickly and easily to the beautiful land of sky-blue waters in the San Bernardino Mountains. Wide panoramas of the whole countryside spread below in colorful splendor." (CC.)

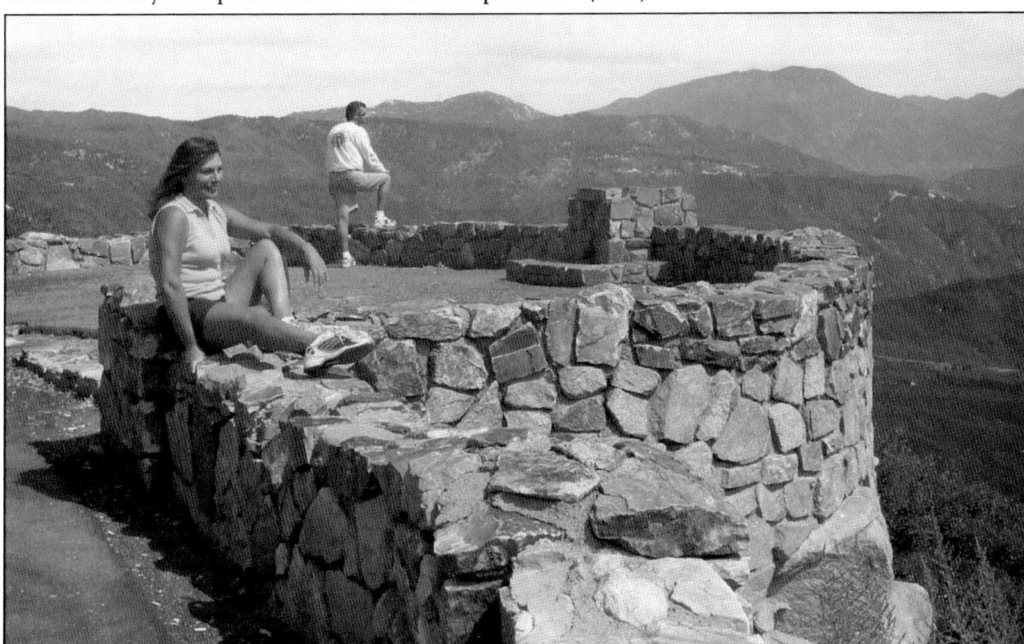

RED ROCK WALL NOW. This equally posed view was taken with the permission of an impromptu model traveling along the Rim of the World Drive while on vacation. This good-natured couple (note the gentleman in the background) stopped to appreciate the same panoramic views that have captivated Rim of the World drivers for more than 70 years.

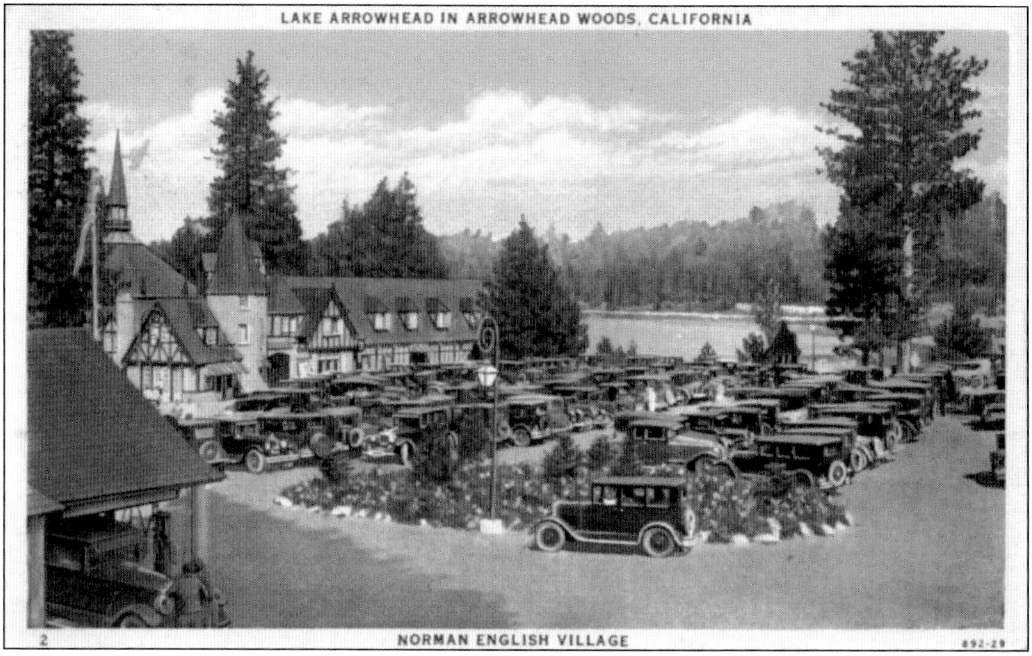

LAKE ARROWHEAD VILLAGE THEN. Lake Arrowhead Village—consisting of a stage depot, post office, hardware store, tackle shop, market, drugstore, art shop, cafeteria, gas station, offices, and a dance pavilion—opened on Saturday, June 24, 1922. By the late 1920s, astronomical increases in automobile tourism caused parking nightmares on holiday weekends. The Rim of the World Drive was really doing its job. (PS.)

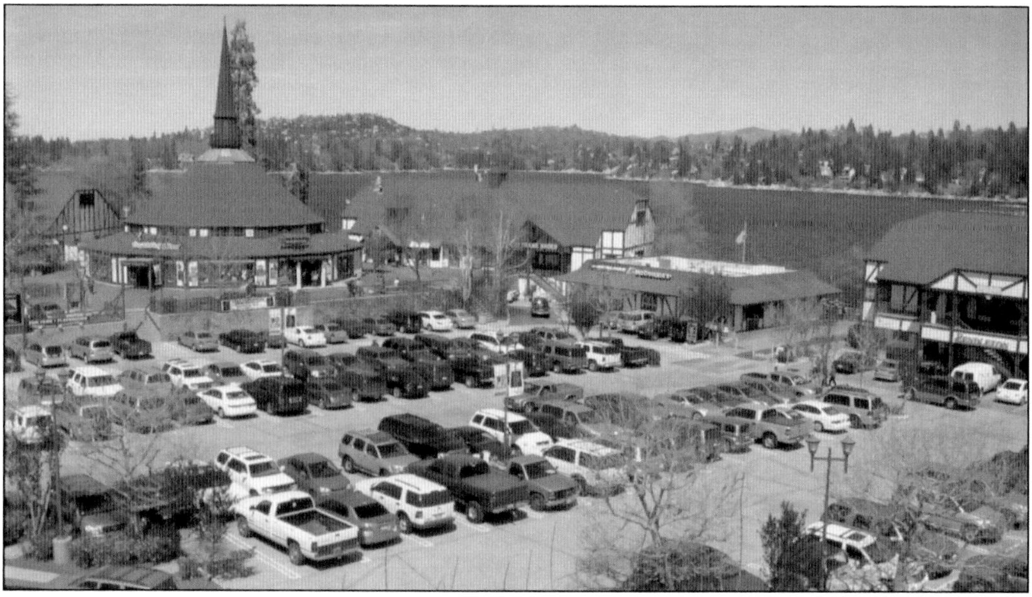

LAKE ARROWHEAD VILLAGE NOW. The Casino (see the steeple) is the sole remaining vestige of the original village. The old village was razed, in a "burn-to-learn" exercise in April 1979, following a decision by owners to construct new buildings rather than fix the deteriorated historic ones. Although most of what is seen here is new, the overall sense of place is surprisingly the same today as it was then.

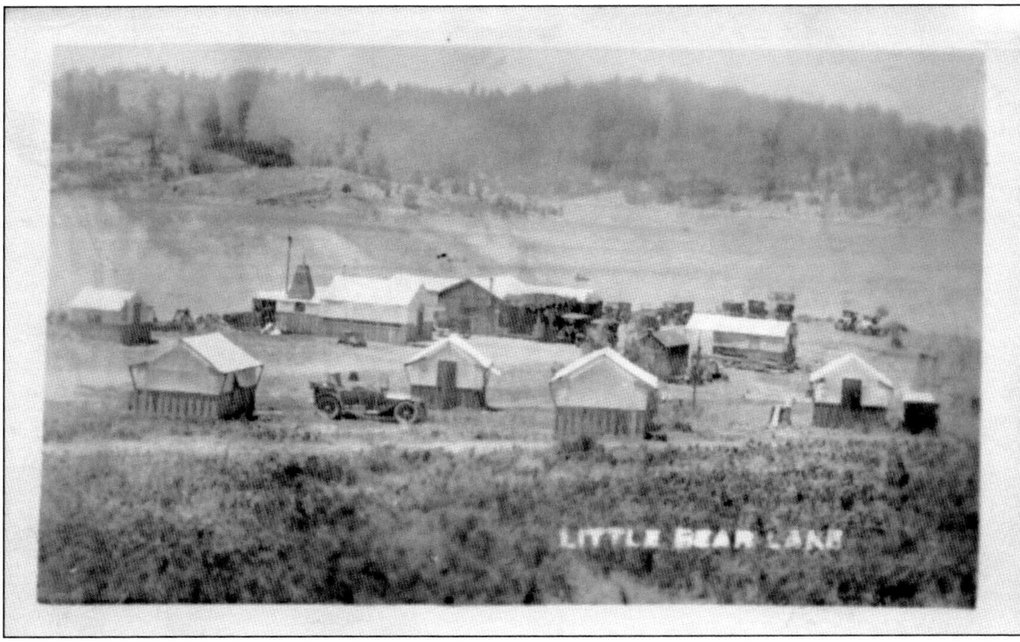

AUTOMOBILES AND LAKE ARROWHEAD TOURISM. The *c.* 1918 image (above) provides an overview of the resort area on the southern peninsula of Little Bear Lake at the beginning of the age of the automobile. Note the haphazard and entirely impromptu parking arrangement. In 1915, sportsmen began to arrive in record numbers thanks to the newly dedicated Rim of the World Drive, and by the late 1920s, a special "blue line" route from Los Angeles to Lake Arrowhead was advertised (below). This map (look closely) also shows the Rim of the World Drive leading from Lake Arrowhead to Big Bear. (Below BRM.)

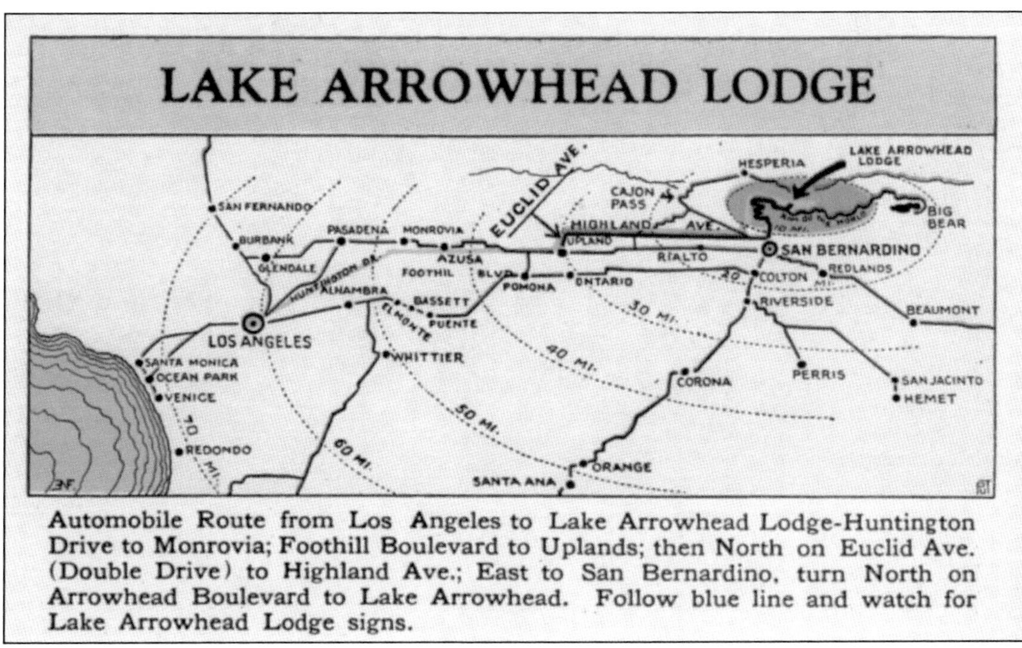

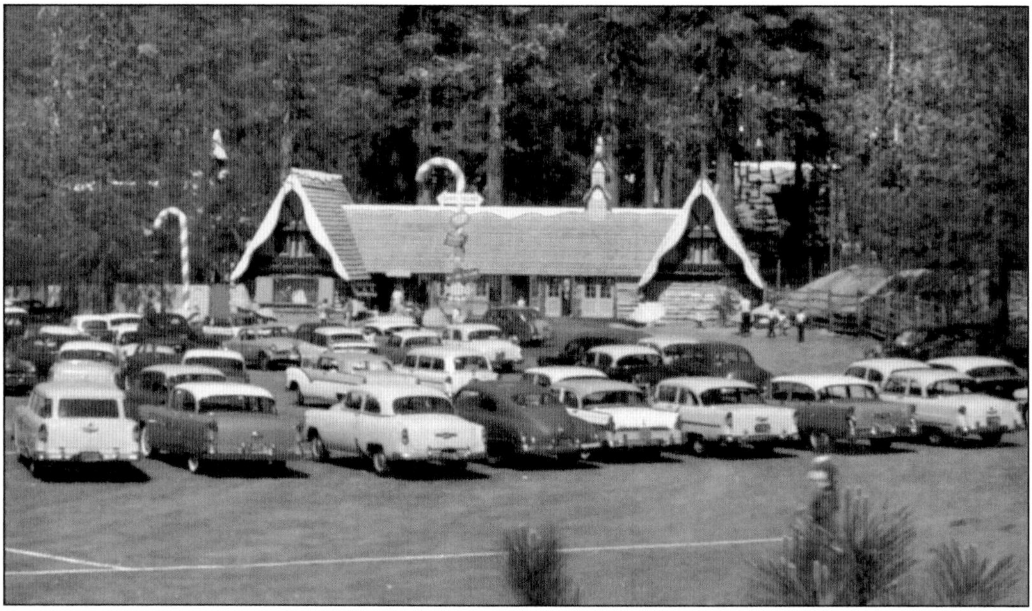

SANTA'S VILLAGE THEN. Built on Highway 18, Santa's Village operated from the mid-1950s to 1998 and was advertised as "The Funnest Place in the Mountains." The popular theme park was open daily (summers and winters) and on weekends year-round. Popular features included a magic train ride, antique auto ride, burro ride, monorail, bobsled run, and, of course, a visit with Santa. (SV.)

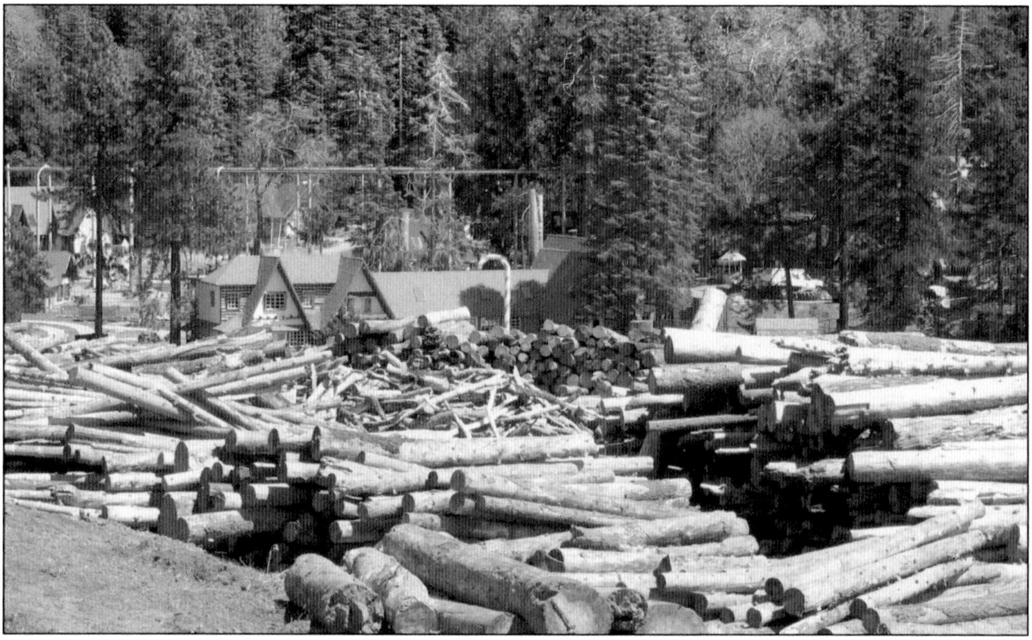

SANTA'S VILLAGE NOW. Santa's Village was sold by the original builders and owners in 1998 to an optimistic investor. Various plans were developed to convert the theme park to a village of shops directly adjacent to the Rim of the World Drive (Highway 18). A devastating bark beetle infestation changed everything, and today the parking lot is filled with fallen trees rather than cars filled with children.

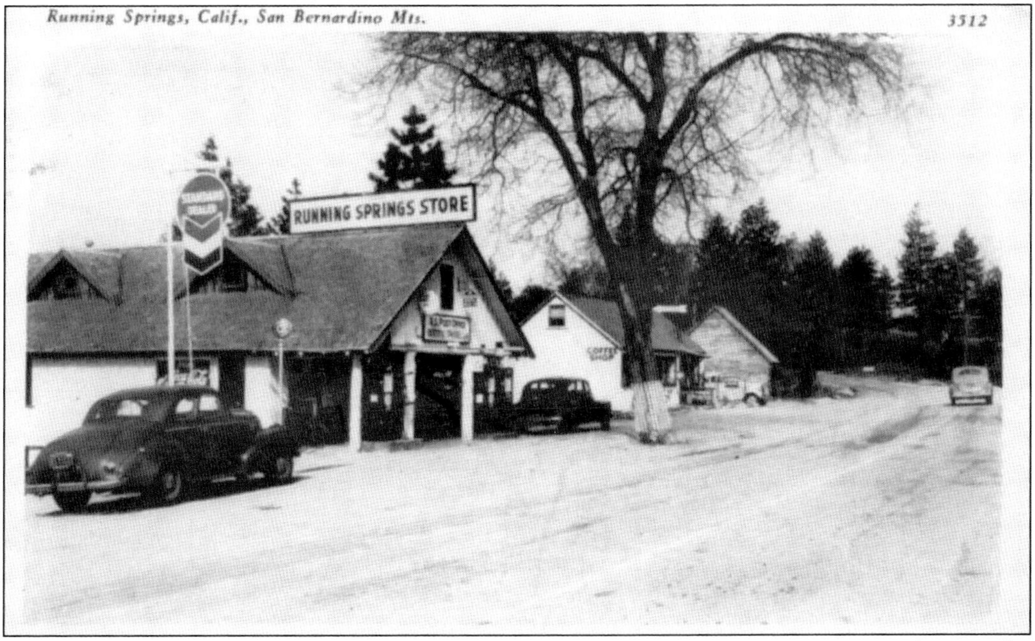

RUNNING SPRINGS THEN AND NOW. This 1940s view of downtown Running Springs features the Running Springs Store and Post Office. Development of the Running Springs business district is linked directly to the Rim of the World Drive and the completion of a rebuilt City Creek Road. Intersecting at Running Springs, the two roadway alignments were a natural location for business development beginning in the mid-1920s. The current image below is taken from almost the exact location as the historic image. Running Springs has clearly expanded in response to increased highway traffic on Highway 18 (Rim of the World Drive) and Highway 330 (City Creek Road). The old store is now a Mexican restaurant. (Above R.)

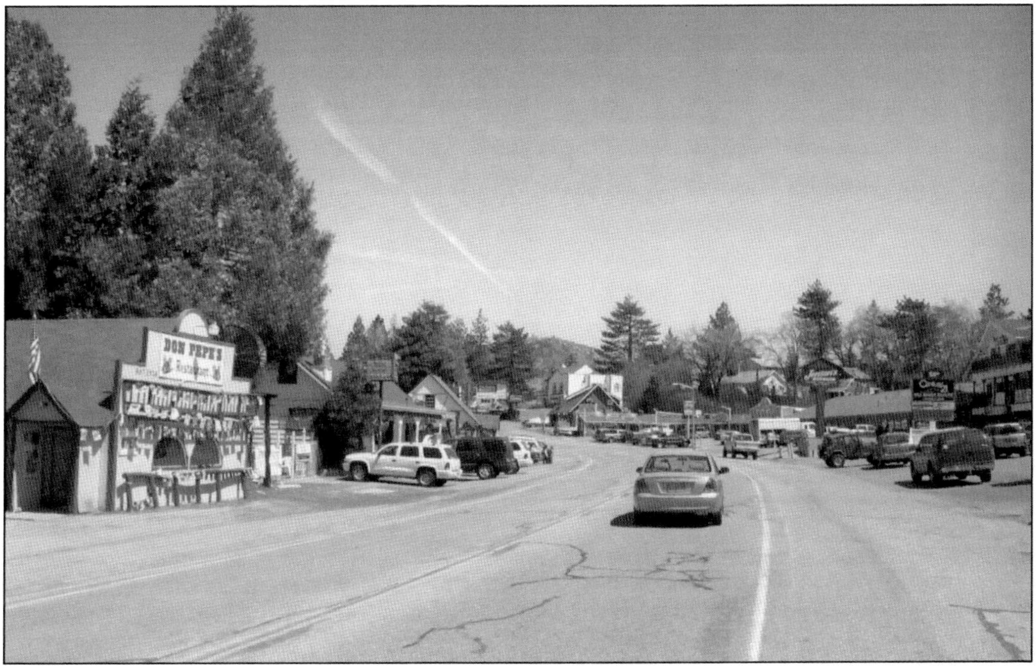

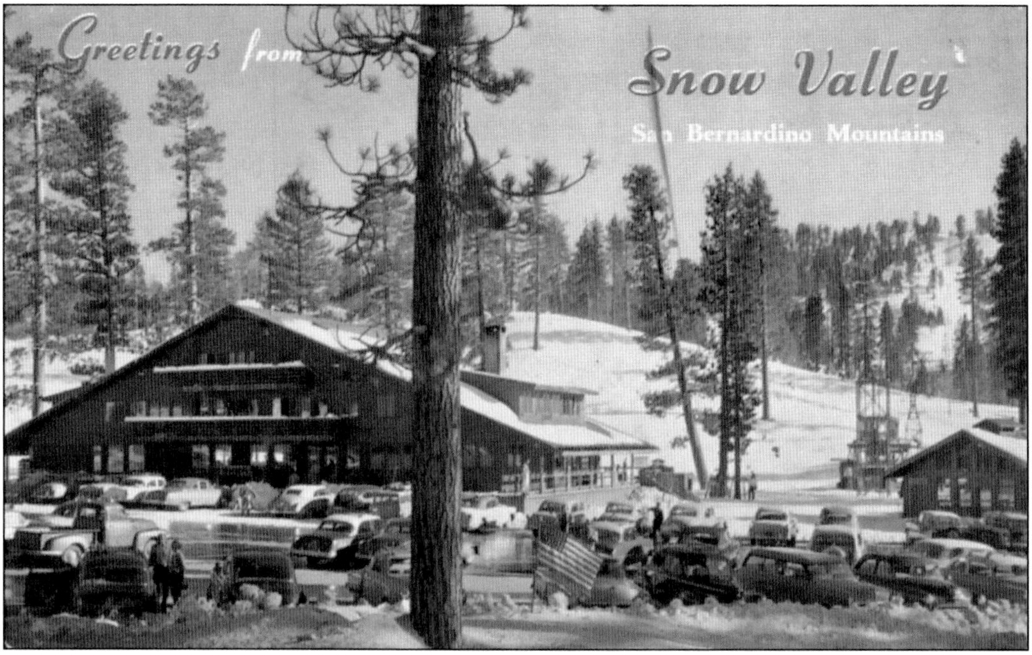

SNOW VALLEY THEN AND NOW. In 1941, ski jump champion John Elvrum purchased a small ski resort east of Running Springs on the Rim of the World Drive. After the end of World War II, he created a popular winter sports destination. The back of the 1950s postcard above reads, "Southern California's favorite ski resort, only 85 miles from Los Angeles on an all-year highway." As seen in the modern image below, Elvrum's dream still operates as a hugely expanded enterprise. Buildings, lifts, runs, and parking facilities have been added to accommodate a massive seasonal influx of snowboarders and skiers from across Southern California. Snow Valley and the Rim of the World Drive (Highway 18) remain as closely linked today as when it first opened. (Above FHS.)

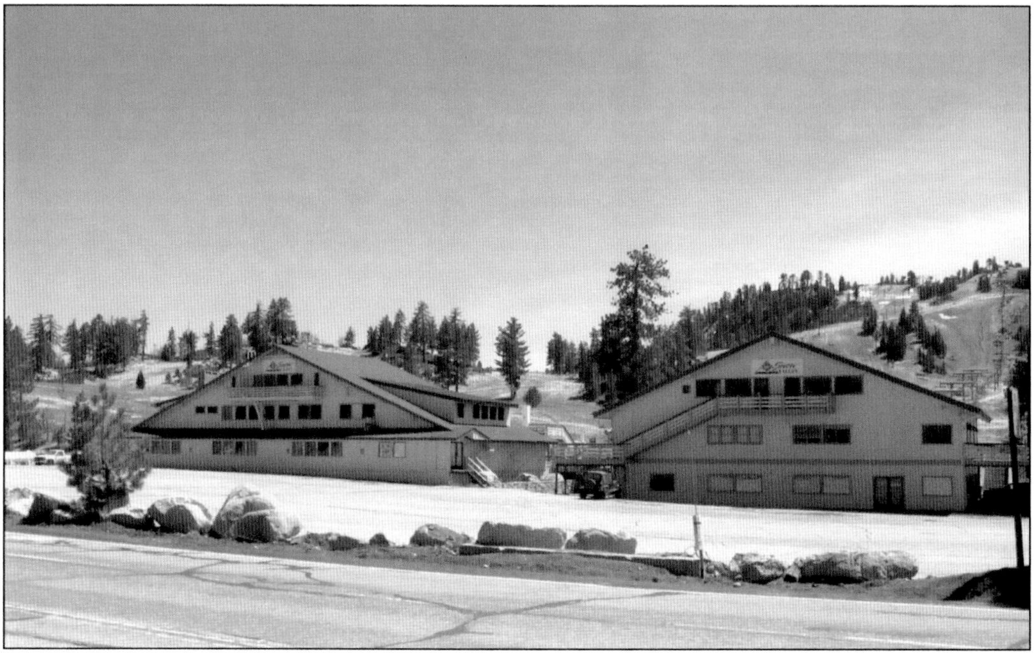

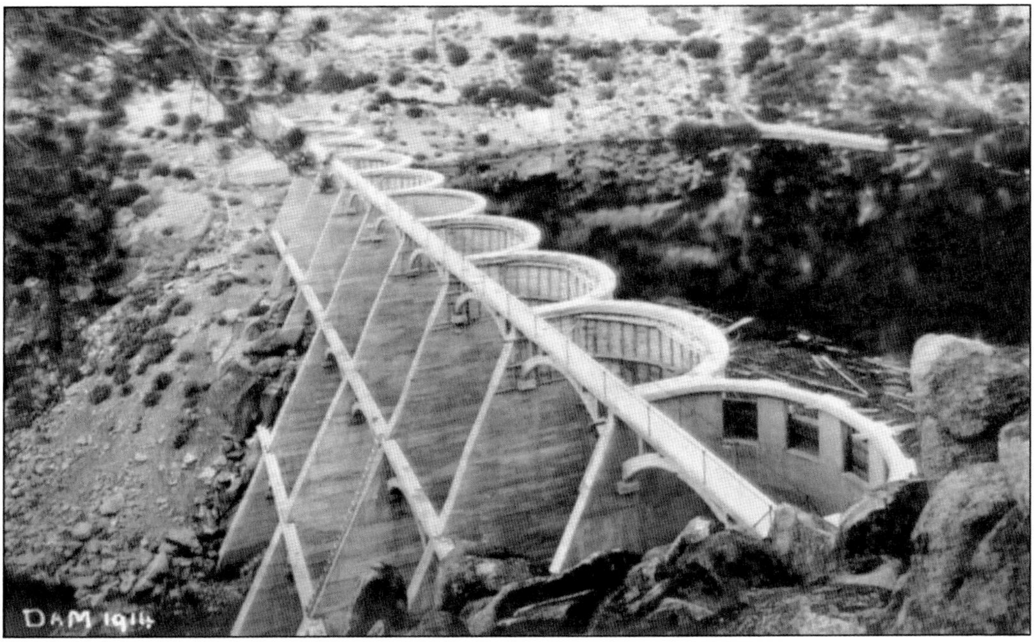

BIG BEAR DAM THEN. Completed in 1912, the Big Bear Dam seen in this 1914 image was built to increase water supplies to Redlands/Highlands–based agricultural interests in the San Bernardino Valley. Designed by John S. Eastwood, many could not believe that such a fragile-looking structure could hold back so much water. (BS.)

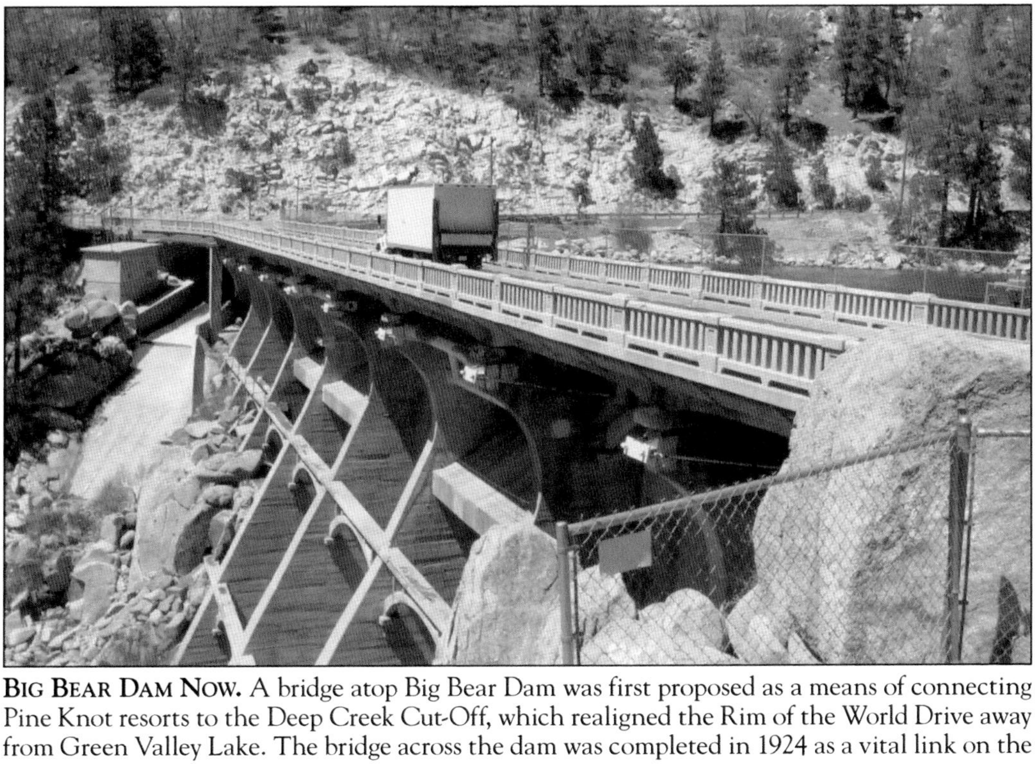

BIG BEAR DAM NOW. A bridge atop Big Bear Dam was first proposed as a means of connecting Pine Knot resorts to the Deep Creek Cut-Off, which realigned the Rim of the World Drive away from Green Valley Lake. The bridge across the dam was completed in 1924 as a vital link on the Rim of the World Drive.

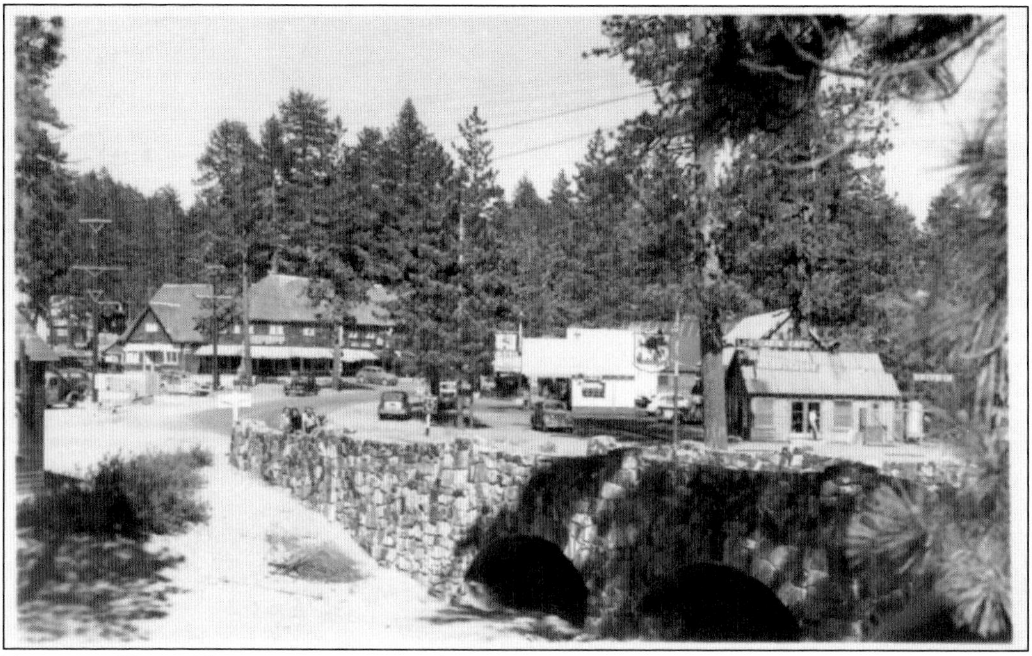

FAWNSKIN THEN. This quaint 1940s view depicts the approach to Fawnskin looking across a historic bridge. This bridge, like many rock roadway features along the length of the Rim of the World Drive in the San Bernardino Mountains, was built in the mid-1930s utilizing WPA assistance.

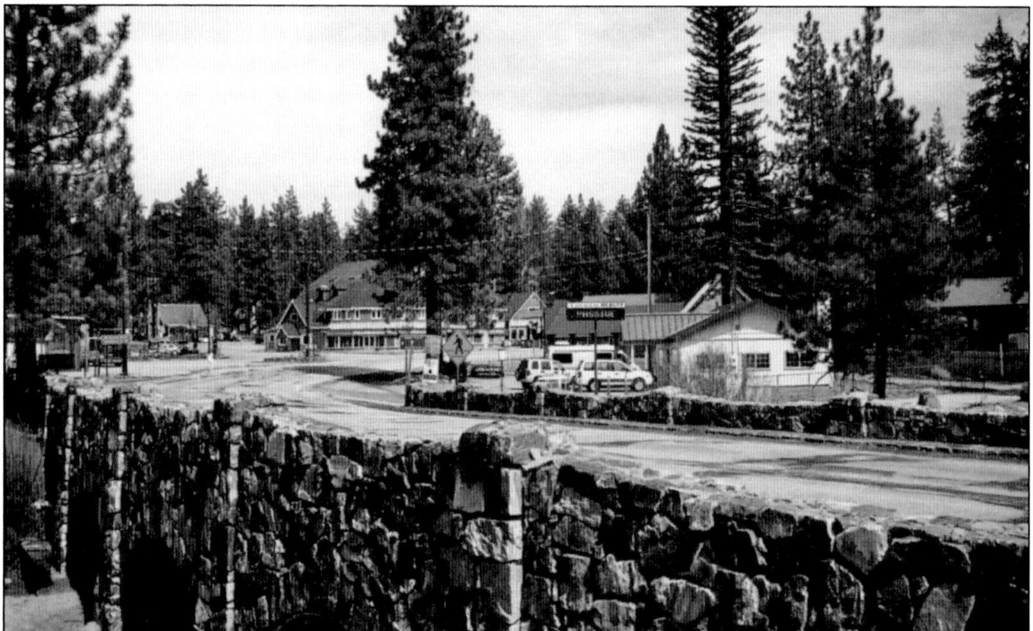

FAWNSKIN NOW. Today's view is remarkably similar to the historic view above, demonstrating that Fawnskin is one of the least-changed mountain communities. Once serving as a vital link on the Rim of the World Drive, Fawnskin was bypassed in 1924 with the completion of the bridge atop Big Bear Dam.

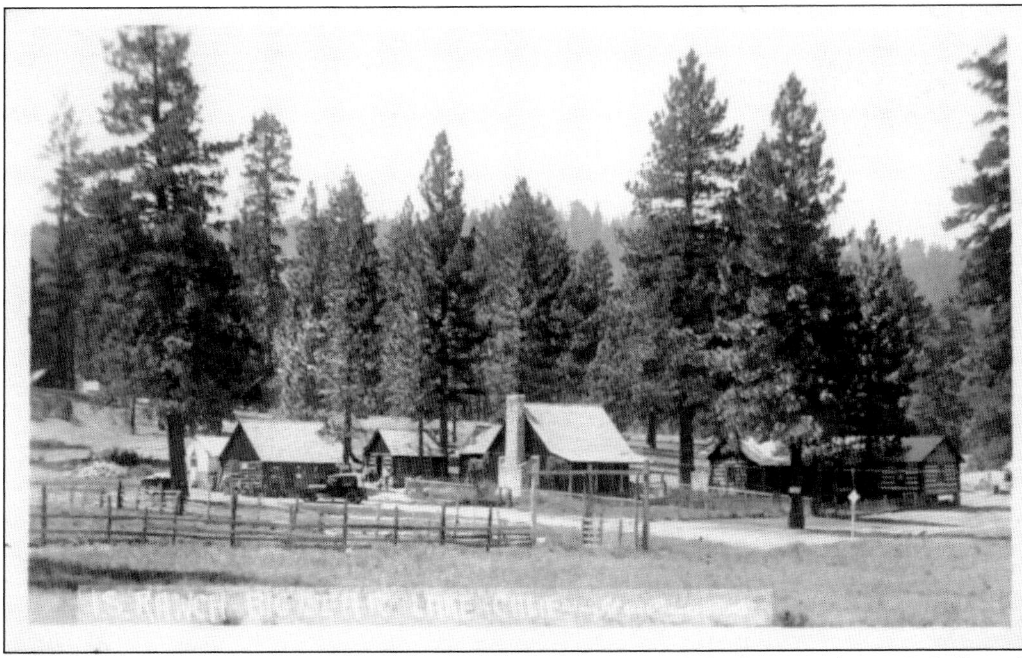

I. S. Ranch Then and Now. The *c.* 1917 view (above) of the historic lower I. S. Ranch headquarters shows the Metcalf Ranch House and Will and John Talmadge homes. The building behind the automobile is Warren's Store, where fresh beef was frequently available. Located west of Pine Knot on the south shore of Big Bear Lake, this was one of the most historic cattle ranches in all of Bear Valley. Today's view (below) shows an existing historic barn, the only known building survivor that can be linked to the once prominent cattle industry in Bear Valley. Visible from Highway 18 (Rim of the World Drive), the vertical log siding is an unusually photogenic architectural feature. (This is private property so please respect all rights of privacy.) (Above WMP.)

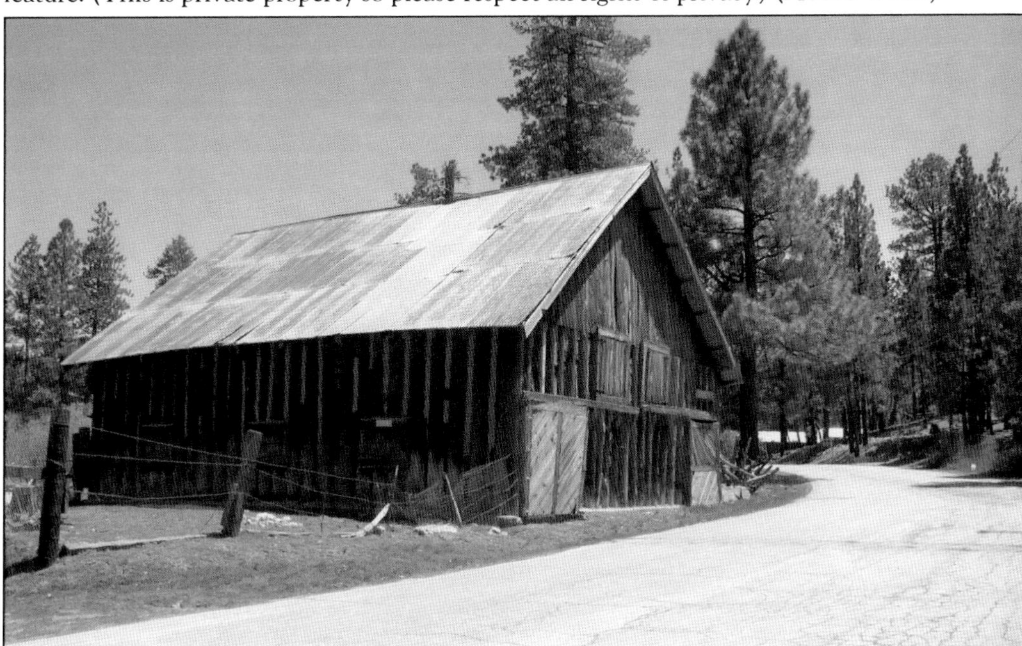

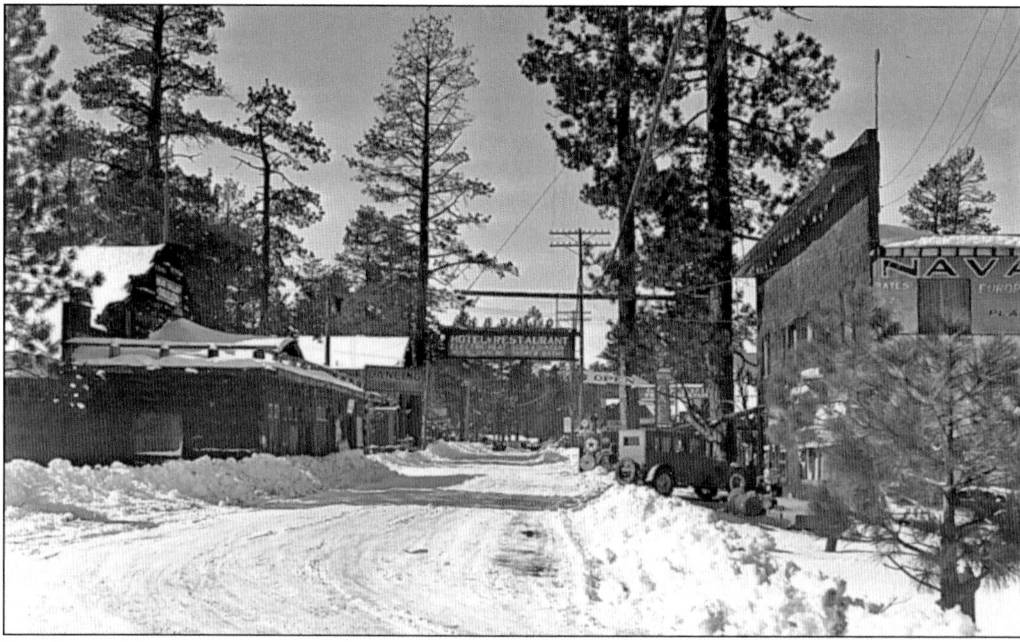

Big Bear Then and Now. The 1924 view (above) looks westerly along the main street in Pine Knot, depicting the historic Navajo Hotel on the right. Built about 1919, the hotel offered "Modern Electric Heat" and a European plan. The Big Bear Pavilion was across the street, and the Grizzly Theatre was the last building down the block on the left-hand side. Pine Knot in the early 1920s was, despite rustic outward appearances, an amazingly cosmopolitan place. The current view (below) is taken at exactly the same location as the historic view. The Navajo Hotel still stands as the heavily remodeled building with a corner tower on the extreme right of the photograph, and a Jack in the Box stands on the site of the Grizzly Theatre in the background on the extreme left.

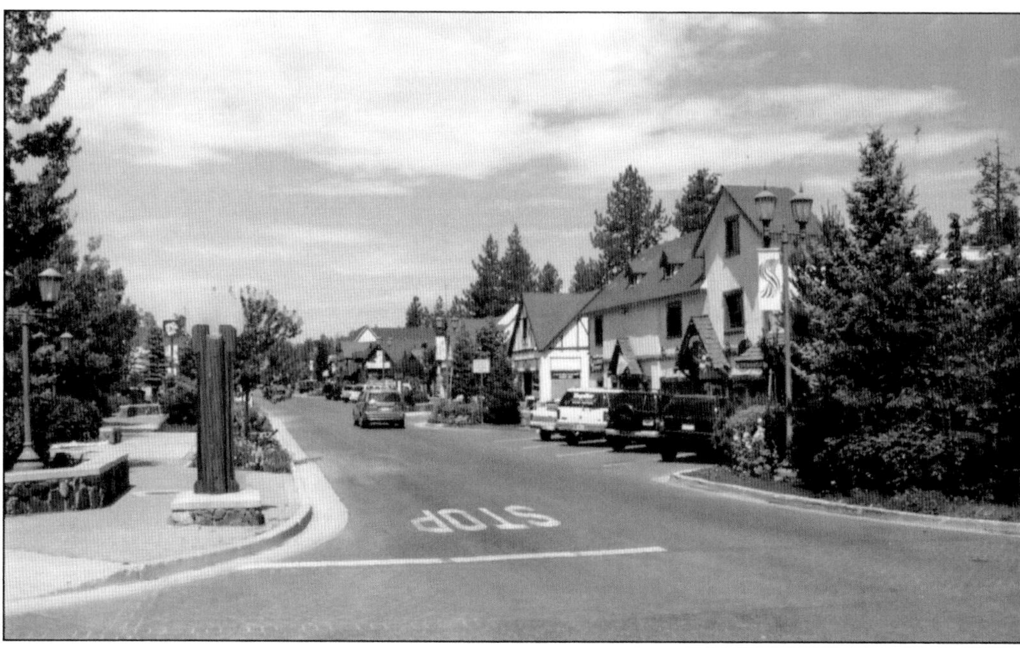

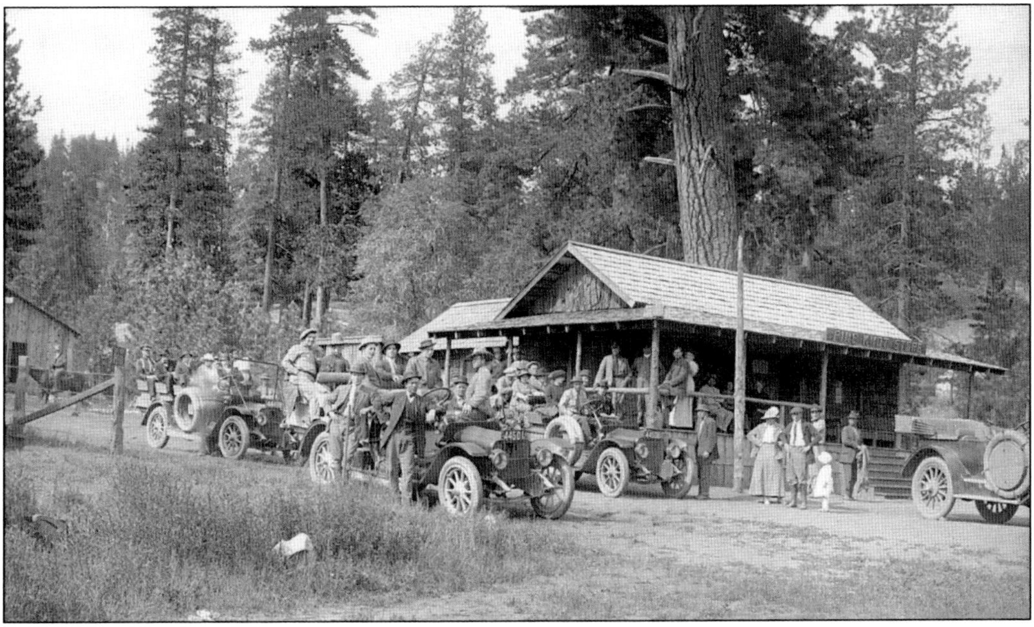

AUTOMOBILES CHANGE BIG BEAR. The 1914 view (above) shows several passenger trucks known as auto stages at the Pine Knot Store. An expensive round-trip ticket from San Bernardino cost $10 in 1915, indicating that the travelers depicted here were not numbered among the masses. The Pine Knot Store was the largest in Bear Valley at this time and was the historic namesake for the community itself. Increased automobile travel to and from Bear Valley would dramatically change Pine Knot in much the same way that it changed all other mountain communities. The 1940s view below clearly demonstrates the transition from rustic resort to modern mountain retreat. The Rim of the World Drive was the primary reason for this explosive development.

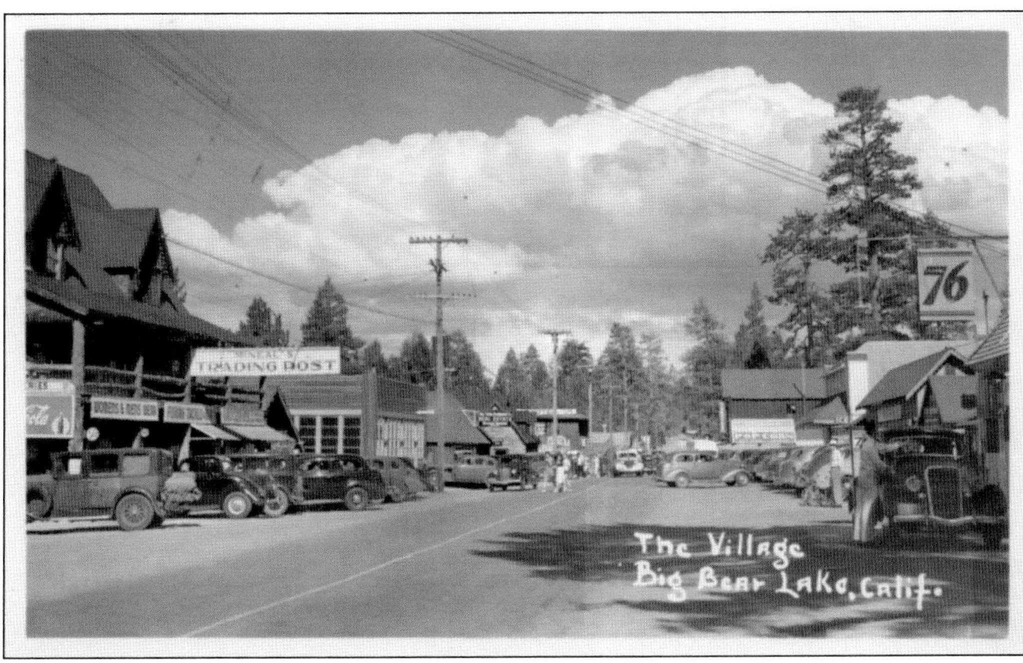

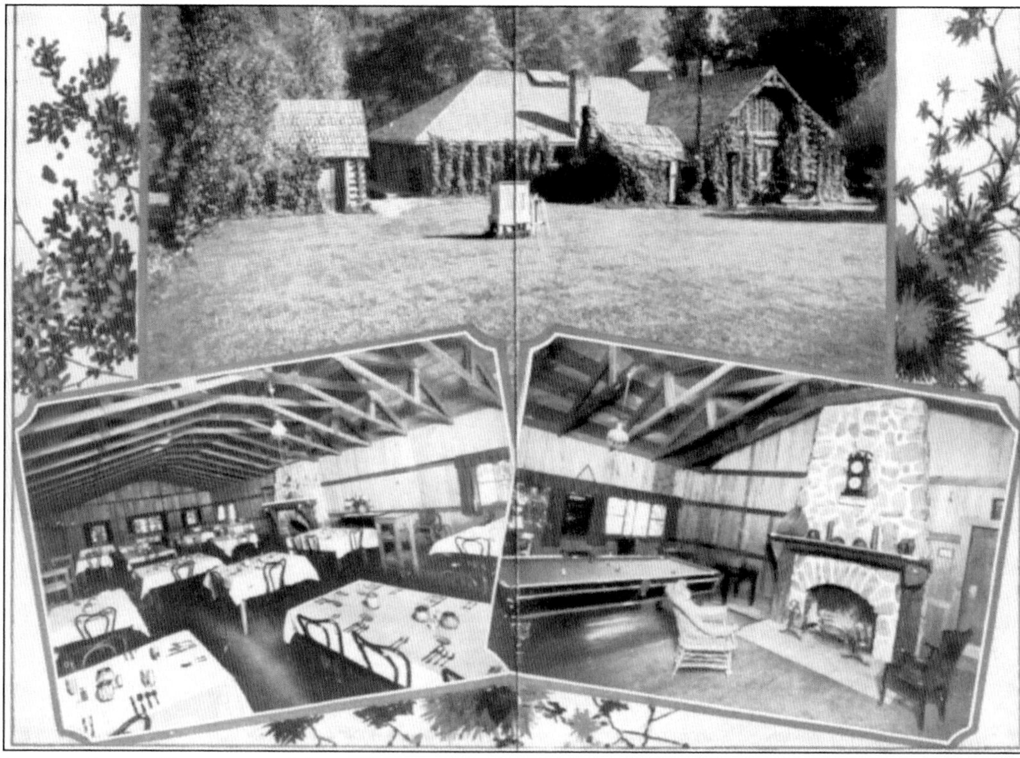

SEVEN OAKS THEN AND NOW. First serving as a primitive camp in the late 1880s, by 1924, the newly luxurious Seven Oaks Mountain Resort was depicted in the image above. Detailed instructions are provided to reach the resort from Los Angeles via automobile, the Pacific Electric, or by Motor Transit connecting with an auto stage at Redlands. The brochure also notes the trip from Los Angeles is an "easy ride of about four hours." Incredibly, not much more than 15 years earlier, a stage/burro trip from Redlands to Seven Oaks took an entire day. Automobiles really did change life in the San Bernardino Mountains, and the Rim of the World Drive was the key to it all. Today's view (below) shows the same building somewhat remodeled. (Note that the older image is printed reversed.)

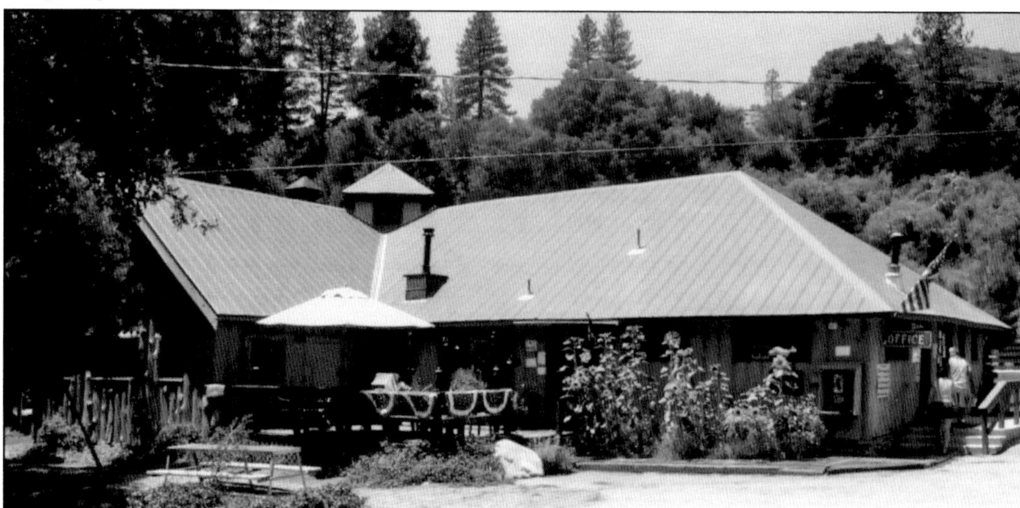

Five

Up Here on Top of the World

Postcards naturally distill the thoughts of the writer by providing limited space in which to write a message, generally producing uninspired greetings, but in very special instances, the thoughts, dreams, and reflections of those long-gone or long-forgotten bring the past to life.

In this chapter, each postcard is a story in and of itself, where the feelings of a Shakespearean cast of unknowns are laid bare. For all those interested in the personal side of life, these thoughts are of untold value, providing an incredible array of handwritten superlatives intimately describing San Bernardino Mountain communities, resorts, and landmarks found on or near the Rim of the World Drive. Writers complain of being "a trifle sore" after a day of mule or horseback riding at the dawn of the age of the automobile. Early automobile trips are recorded as "a wild drive," as "terribly hard work," or as "too close to the edge of high mountains." Following completion of the high-gear road in the mid-1930s, however, the term "a beautiful drive" is frequently applied.

Amazingly, with hundreds of postcards to choose from, tens of thousands were sent of relatively unexciting pictures of the road. Visitors would often send a postcard of the switchbacks, while describing Lake Arrowhead or other mountain communities on the back of the card as a "fairyland" or "a great place." Others might send a card postmarked Big Bear and yet write about nothing else but the road on the back. What does this mean? It appears to indicate that the trip up the hill on the Rim of the World Drive had become a major part of the mountain experience in and of itself.

Today the Rim of the World Drive is as much a part, albeit less dramatically, of the mountain experience as it was over 80 years ago when it truly defined the very identity of the San Bernardino Mountains. The following are more-or-less chronologically organized purloined postcard "peeks into the past" that drive home this point again and again.

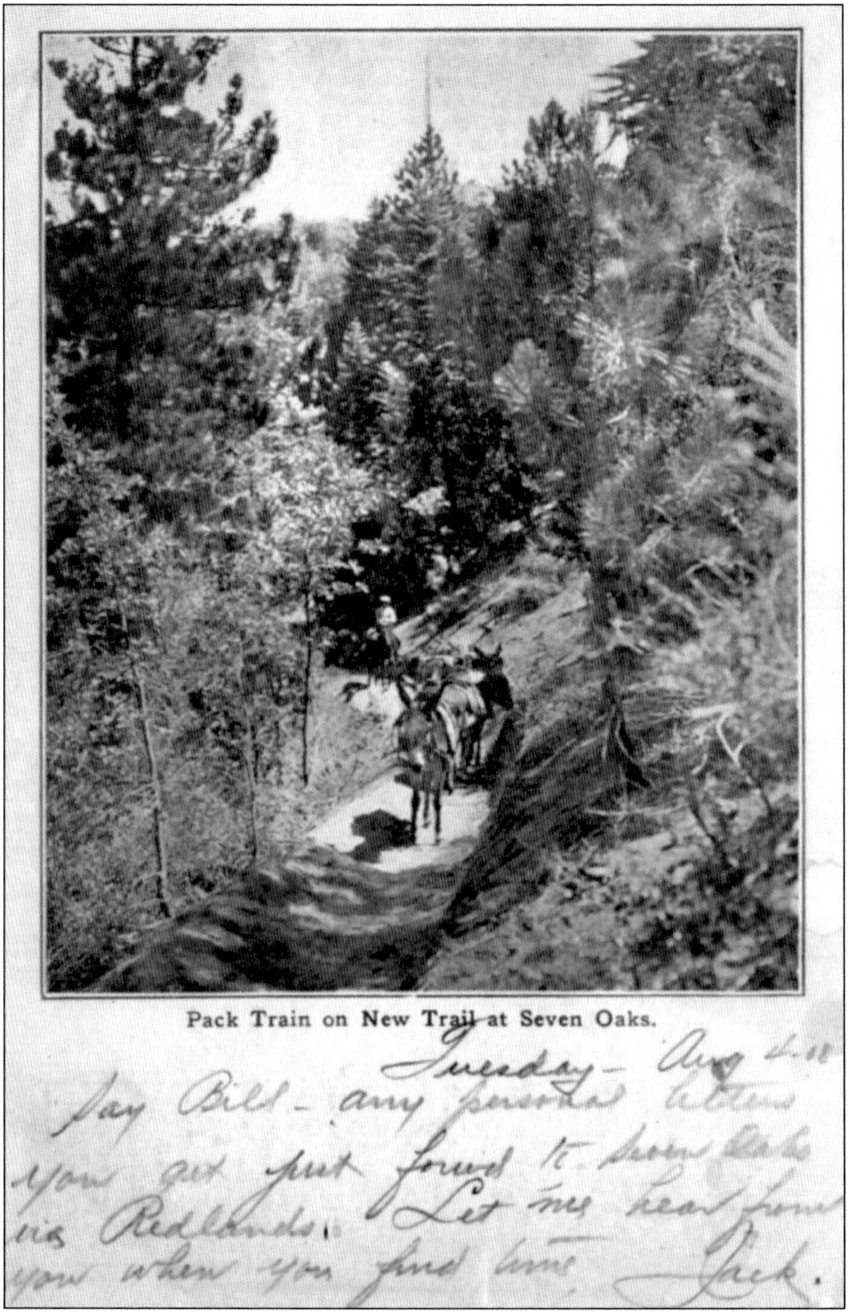

TWELVE MILES A DAY BY BURRO. This card, postmarked August 5, 1908, reads, "Hello Bill! This is certainly a beautiful spot here, and I do wish you were along. Made this trip to-day easily & caught largest trout of the party—12 inches. Have made 12 miles each day since Sunday. This place is too fine to leave. Shall stay another week & go up Greyback." The author continues on the front of the card, "Tuesday, August 4, 1908—Say Bill, Any personal letters you get just forward to Seven Oaks via Redlands. Let me hear from you when you find time. Jack." The writer here was clearly quite proud of his 12 miles a day. Travel today on the Rim of the World Drive frequently totals 12 miles in 12 minutes. (NC.)

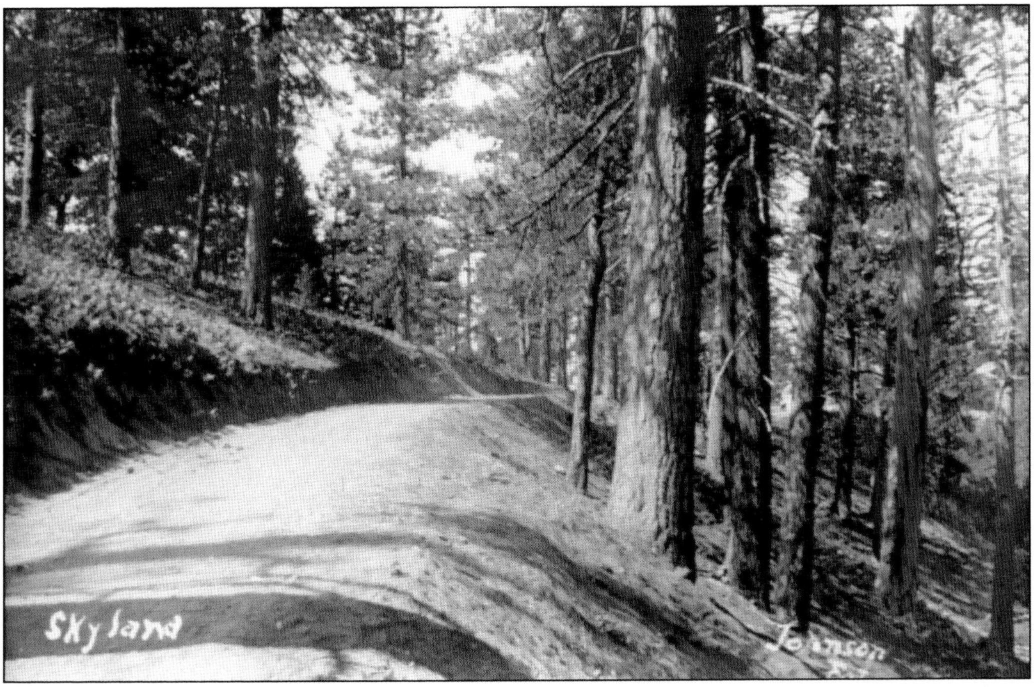

THIRTY-SEVEN MILES BY HORSEBACK. The author of this 1909 postcard sent from Incline (later Crestline Post Office) traveled a route that would soon become the Rim of the World Drive. He writes, "Dear Mrs. K.: Having a great time—we rode horseback to Big Bear Valley, 37 miles about killed us, so we stayed over till today. A hard trip but fine." (JF.)

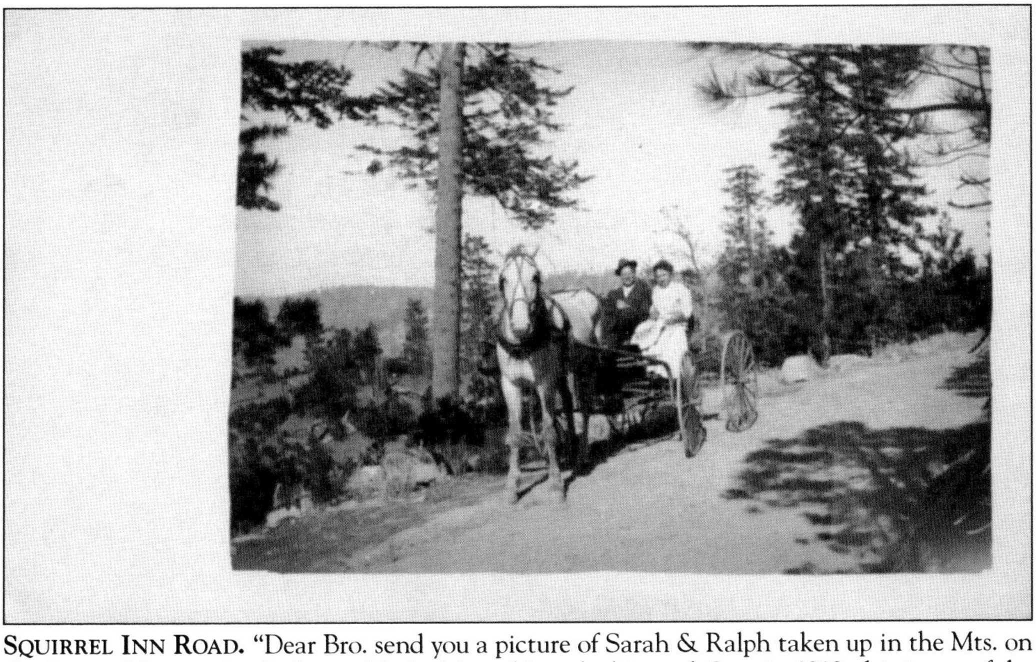

SQUIRREL INN ROAD. "Dear Bro. send you a picture of Sarah & Ralph taken up in the Mts. on the Squirrel Inn road, which is a delightful road," reads this card. Sent in 1910, this is one of the earliest real-photo postcards of travel along the free county road established in 1905 (later a part of the Rim of the World Drive) to San Bernardino Mountain resorts.

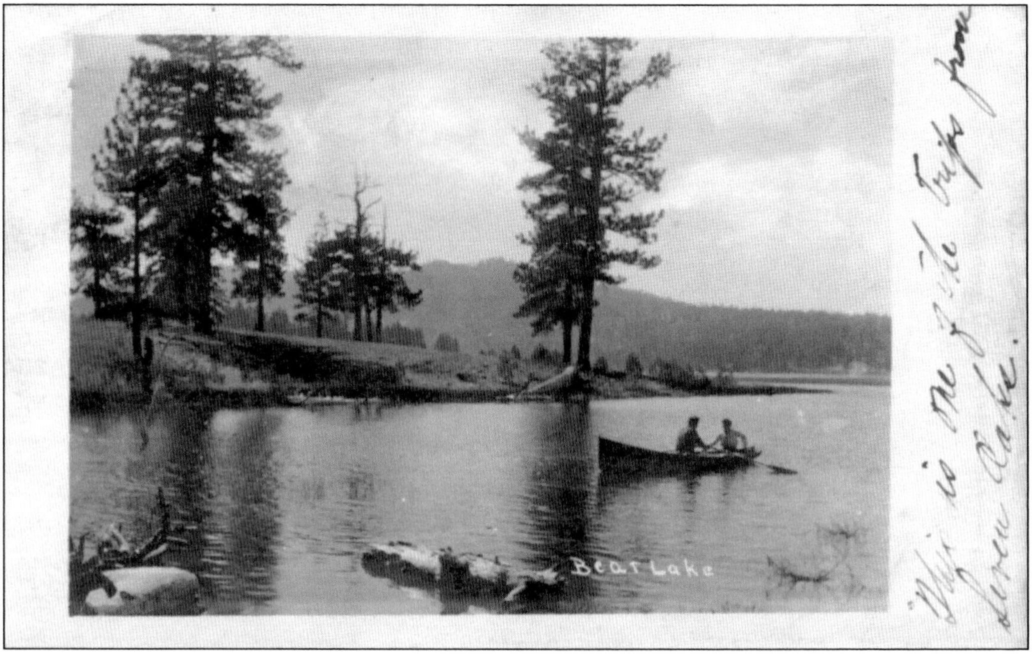

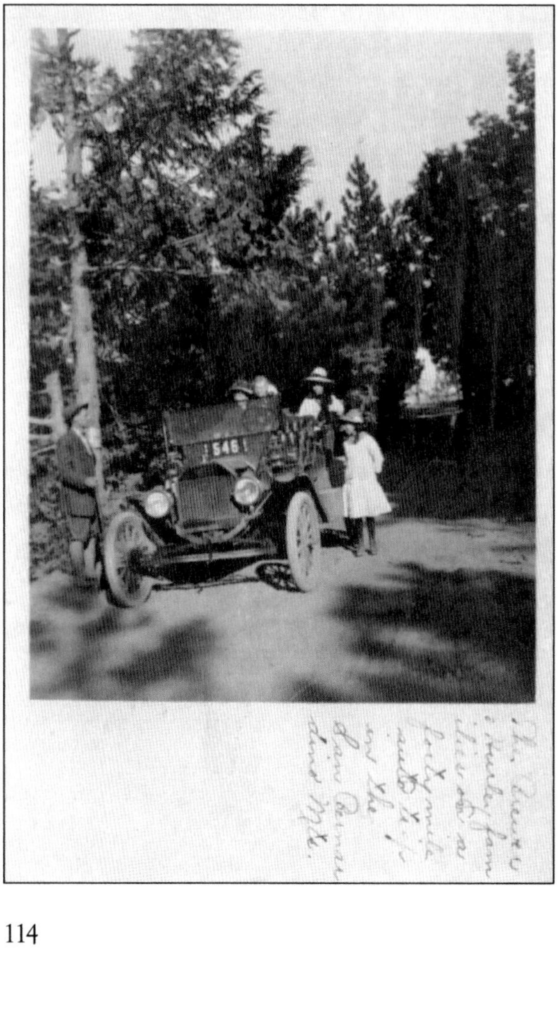

A Trifle Sore by Horseback. This card, postmarked July 18, 1912, reads, "It is grand up here. I'm still a trifle sore from the 12 mile horseback, but I guess that's because I can't ride. Lovingly, May." The author must have been one of the last to make the trip to Big Bear by horse (from Seven Oaks) as the auto stage was just getting underway. (PSC.)

A Mountain Auto Ride. The message on the front of this December 12, 1914, postcard sent to Milton, Wisconsin, reads, "The Brewer & Hurley families on a forty mile auto ride in the San Bernardino Mts." On the back, the author writes, "We would like to give you another auto ride." Many affluent American families, like the Hurleys, had already discovered the prestige and freedom that the automobile afforded.

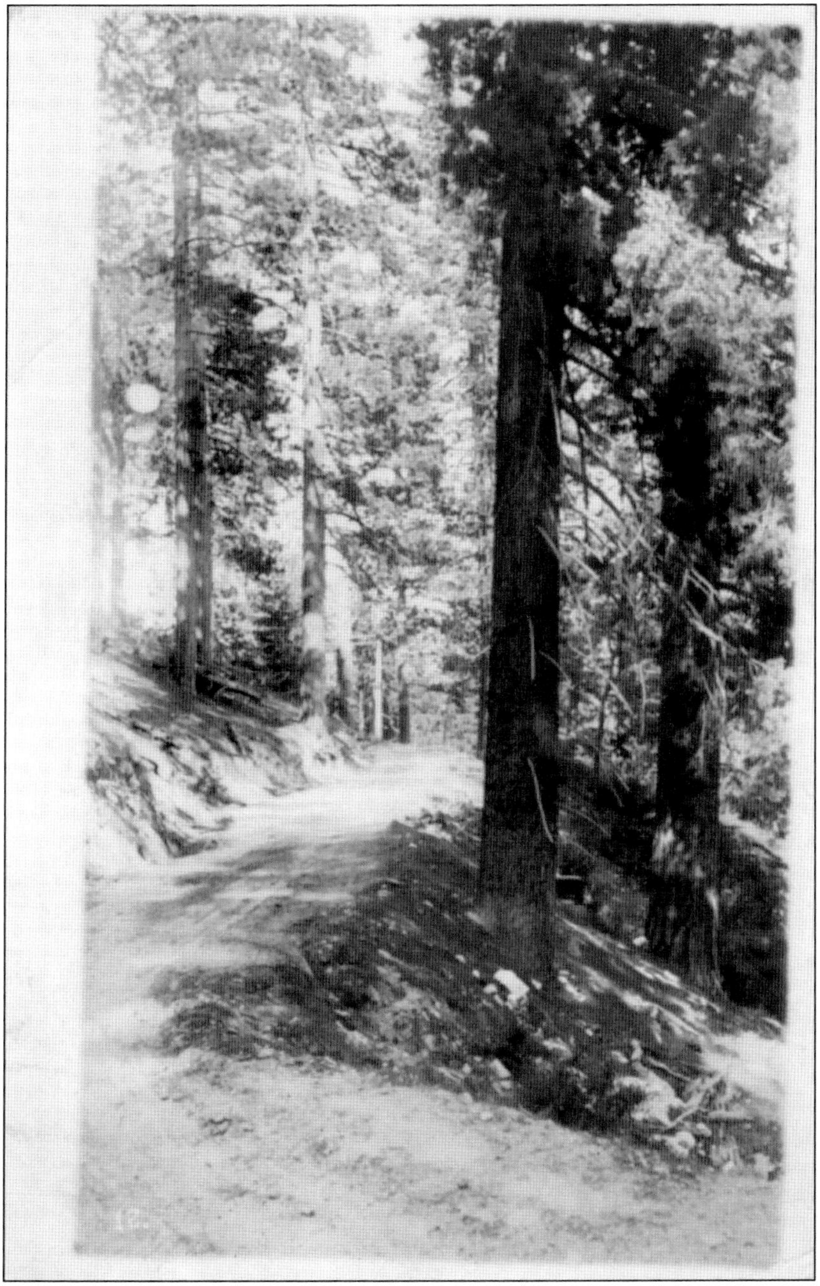

INTO BLUE JAY CANYON. Dated September 8, 1916, and mailed from Skyland Heights, this card reads: "On the road to Little Bear—Going into Blue Jay Canyon—We are having a splendid time—Love to my little 'golden head'—M." It was sent to a Mr. Covey Sr. in Riverside, California. Although the Rim of the World Drive had been dedicated the year before this card was sent, the various roads that crisscrossed the mountaintop were, by and large, still narrow, one-lane, dirt trails that led into dark canyons and across steep ravines. The image on this card is a perfect example. This is one route that fishermen took to Little Bear Lake beginning in 1915. By the 1950s, the community of Blue Jay had become the historic gateway to Lake Arrowhead and a major mountain business and commercial center.

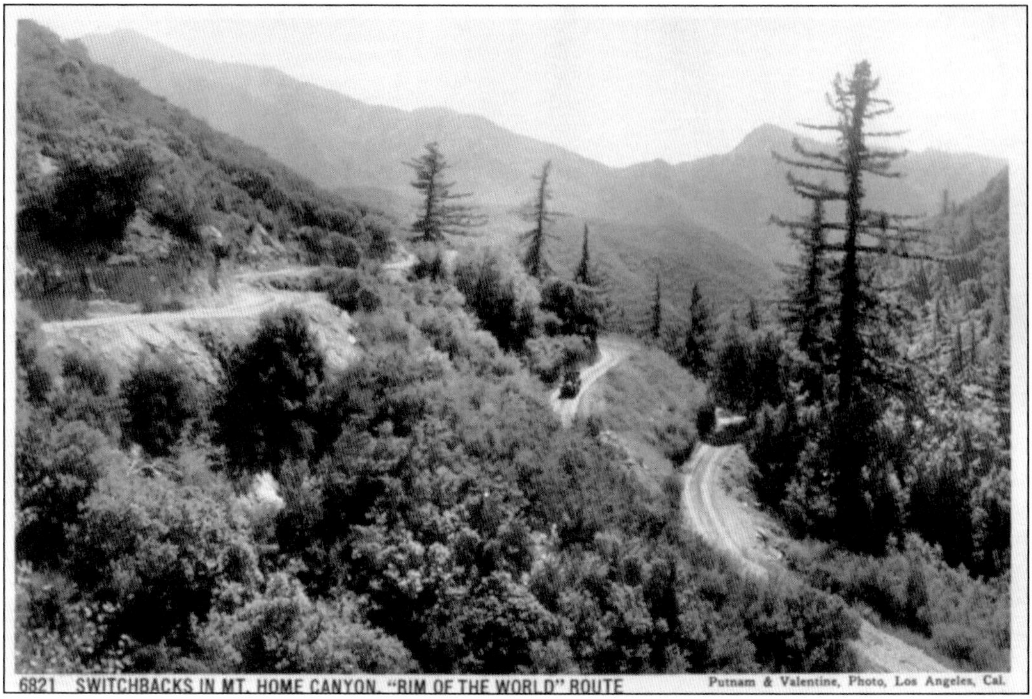

Some Trip Over the Rim. Sent from Pine Knot to Los Angeles, this July 19, 1918, card reads, "We are having a grand old lazy time up here. Some trip over the 'Rim of the World.' Emma." The switchbacks, a rite of passage on the Rim of the World Drive, were likely what Emma was referring to. (PVP.)

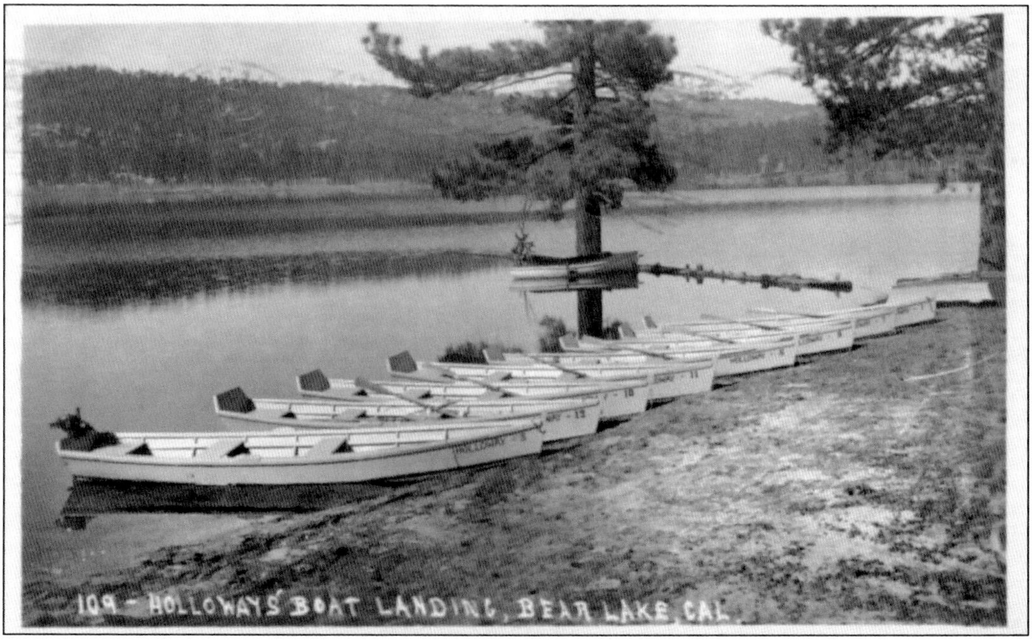

Wild Drive at Night. A "grand place, but a wild drive last night for a car," reads the message on this June 1919 postcard. A ride at night on Rim of the World Drive was truly an adventure. Even today, night fog can make a trip up the hill feel like a scene in a classic horror film. (BVP.)

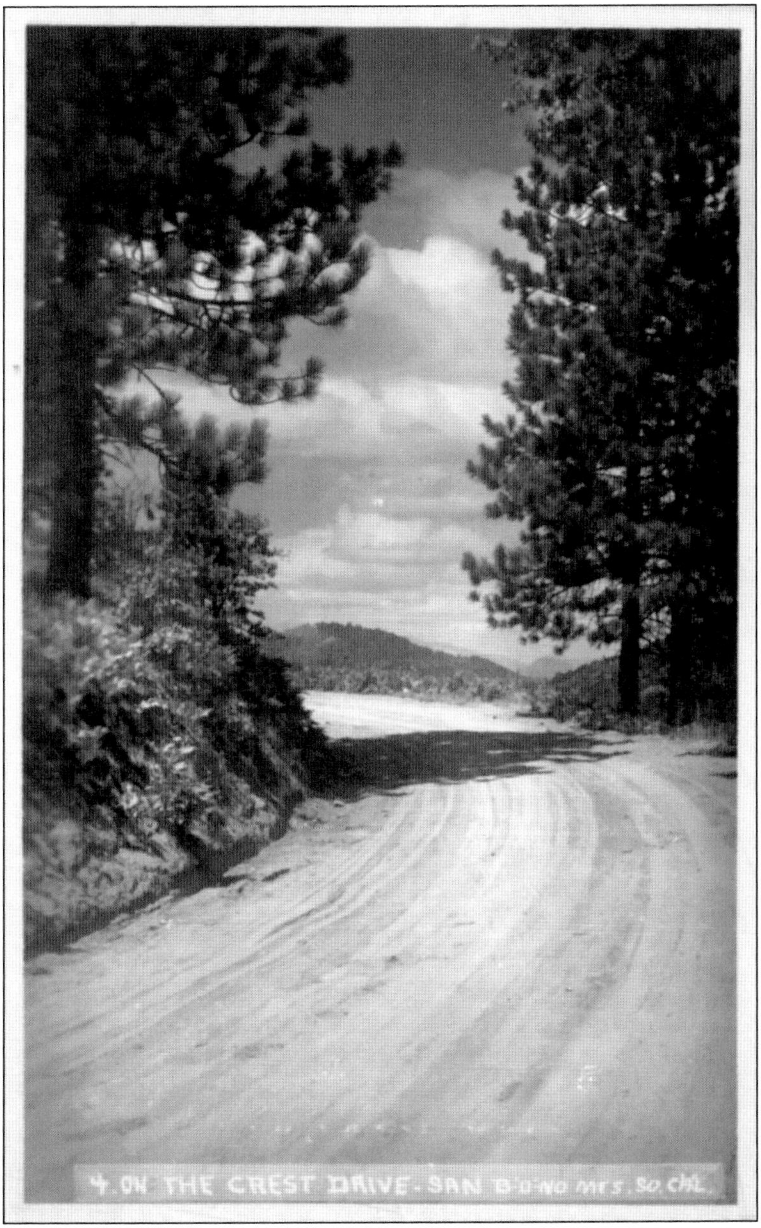

Hiker Follows Old Roads. This card reads as follows: "Left Camp Eureka about 6:30. Took 'cub' across lake to Gray's Camp. Got lift up first grade—about two miles. Nice walk over road to Green Valley—nine miles got there about 10:45. Beat stage. Saw White's on road and met Dr. Rhodes with his brother and family at Green Valley. Mrs. R. said we looked nice. Followed old wagon road for a little way from Green Valley to Ranger's cabin. Got lost, had to follow horse tracks. Hot walk. From rangers took road to trail to Fredalba. Had quite a talk with two men on road who wanted to know all about our trip—get information. Got into Fredalba about 5 o-clock—about 18 miles." This incredible narrative, sent from Camp Eureka in Big Bear on August 25, 1919, is actually a mini-history and contemporary time capsule of mountain roads. Following the old wagon roads off of the Rim of the World Drive apparently made for a particularly pleasant outing. (BVP.)

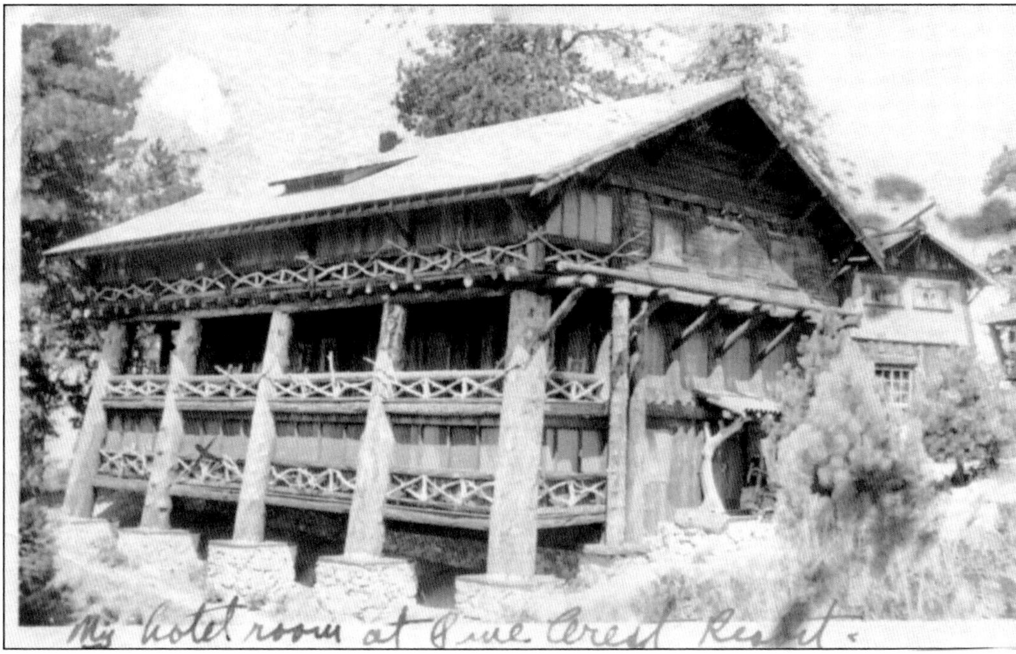

A Great 101-Mile-Drive Trip. This June 1920 card reads, "Pine Crest, San Bernardino Mountains. On a week end jaunt with So. Cal. Editorial Assoc. Great trip—101 mile mountain drive—about 75 editors in the party. George." It's hard to believe that 75 editors got along for an entire weekend, but it does underscore the growing recognition of the Rim of the World Drive.

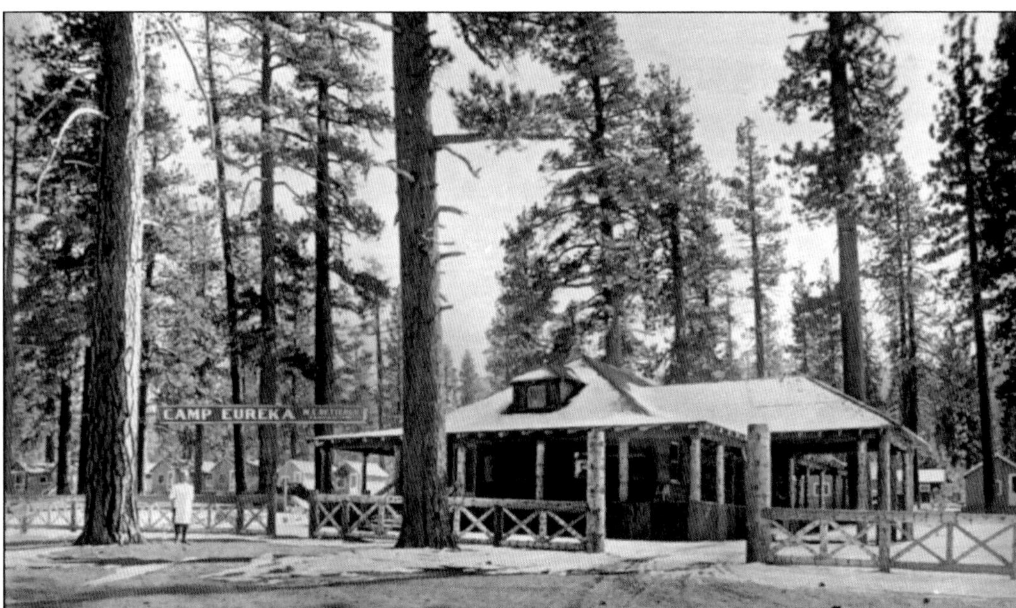

A Hard Time Coming Up. "This is how it looked the day before we got here. Had a hard time coming up. Too much load. And rain cats & dogs. George," reads a card mailed May 20, 1921, from Pine Knot (Big Bear) and sent to Los Angeles. At this time, there were controls on many mountain roads, and bad weather genuinely menaced travel.

Having a Slick Time. Another traveler writes, "Dear Leigh: Well how are you kiddo. Having a slick time and surely wish that you could be here. Thinking of you. Love, Louise." Dated 1921 and sent from Pine Knot Lodge, this card must have come from old stock at the lodge as the car is much older than the date sent. The road was, however, the subject selected to share with a friend.

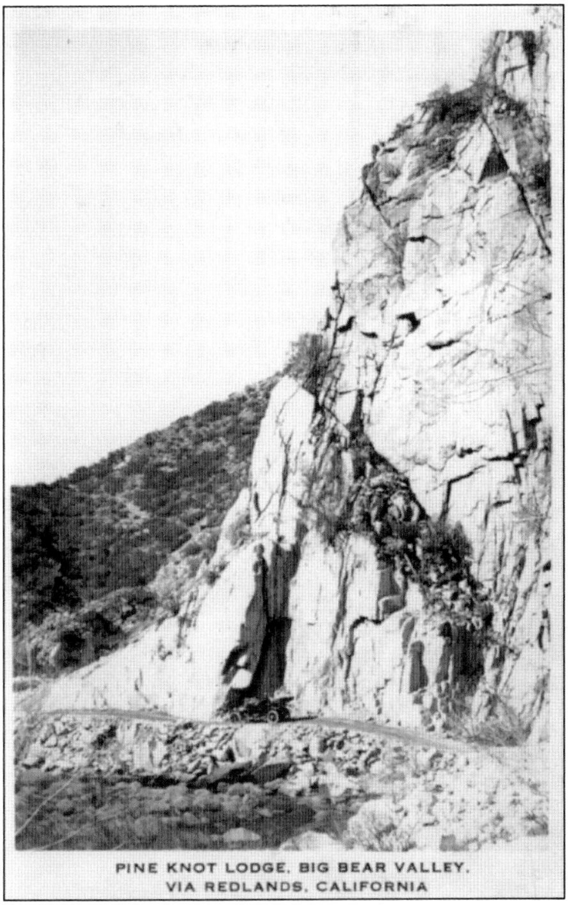

Rim Trip by Bus. Mountain travel was not for everyone. A fear of heights was often an obstacle for visitors. This August 1923 card reads, "Came up here, Mother, on the 'Rim of the World' stage [bus] from L.A. This is one trip I will <u>not</u> recommend to you as one rides too close to the edge of high mountains all the way up. Love Etta." (WMP.)

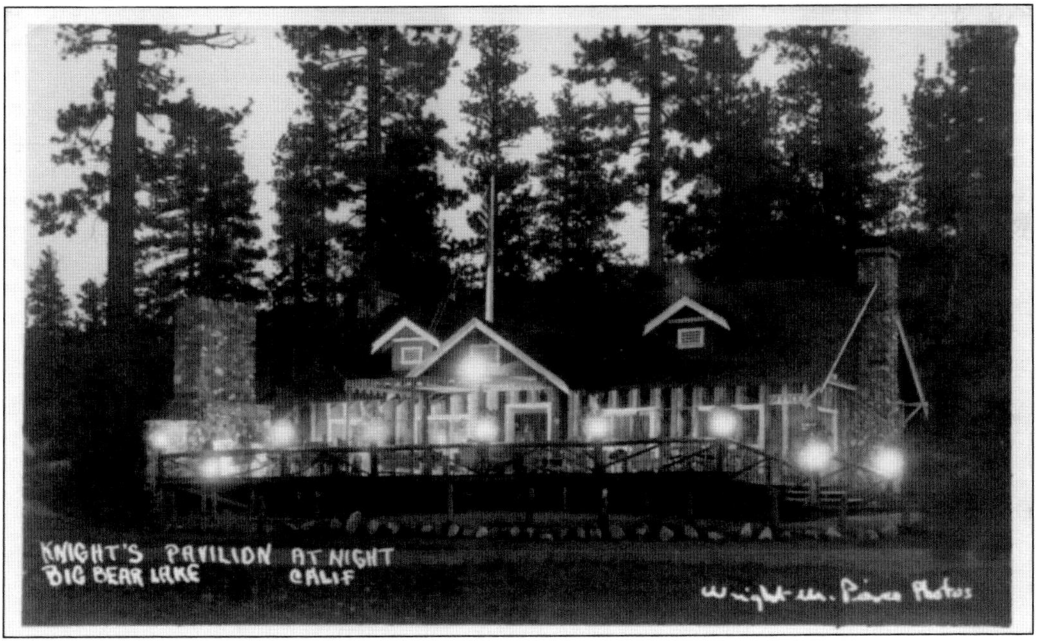

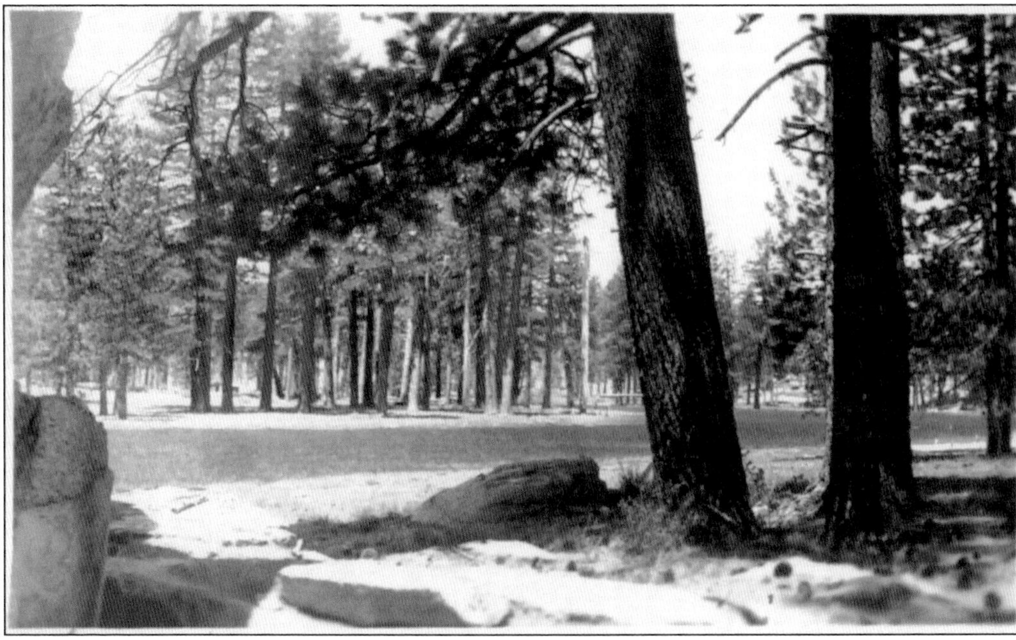

HARD WORK IN AN AUTO. This August 1924 Strawberry Flat postcard reads, "This is the sort of country that we camp in up here. Today we are trying to get enough energy to go to Arrowhead Lake, terribly hard work though—in an auto. Love Bud." Early travel on the Rim was not for the faint of heart, and it must have sounded adventurous to the recipient.

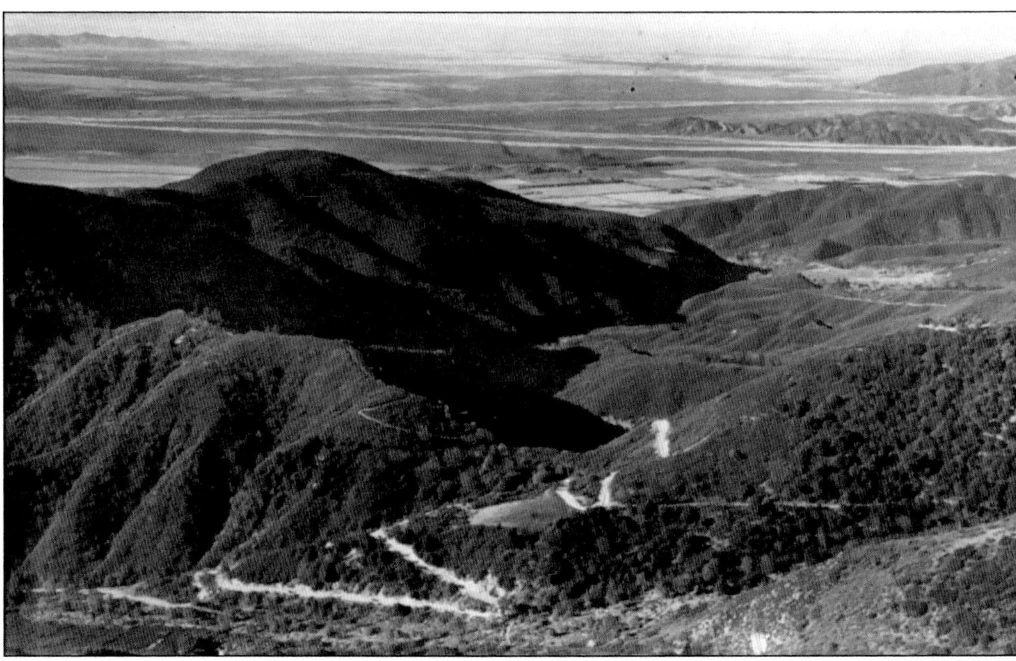

HAVING A GLORIOUS TIME. Postmarked Twin Peaks, this August 26, 1924, card reads, "Dear Sunshine: This is the road we came up a week ago. We expect to go to Big Bear Lake tomorrow. We are having a glorious time. Will be home Sept. 1st. Keep the kids straight. Love to all. Van." The Rim of the World Drive was, for some, the way to a glorious adventure.

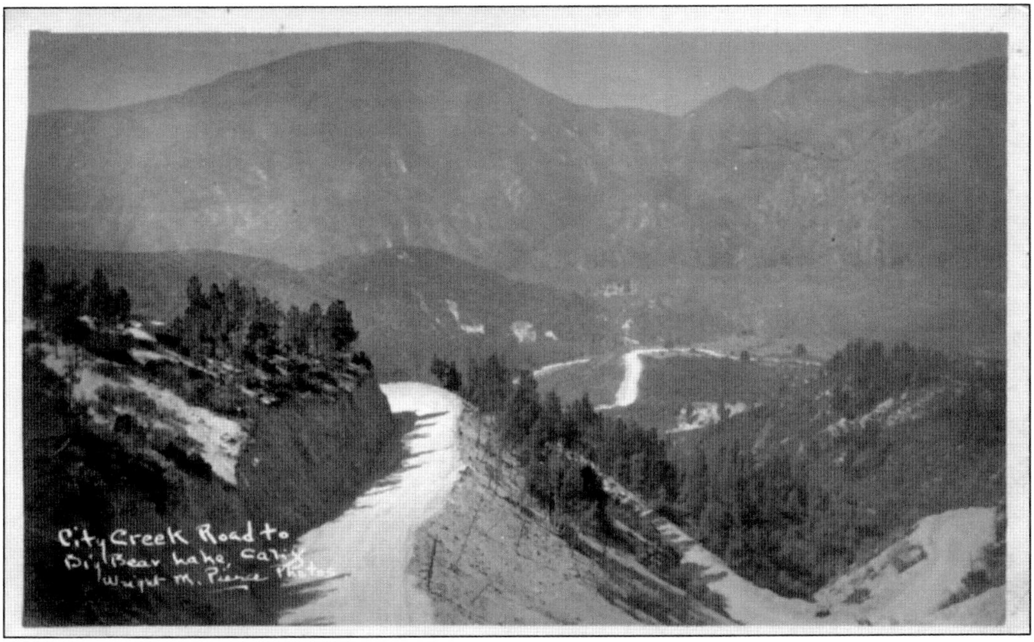

NOT A FAN OF THE ROAD. This card reads, "Dear Mama: We got here o.k. It's sure cold tonight. This is some of the road up here. It sure is awful. It's 32 miles starting up the grade. It's about 80 miles altogether. Bye Valeta & Leo." Dated July 2, 1927, and sent to San Jacinto, this card proves that not everyone was a fan of the Rim of the World Drive. (WMP.)

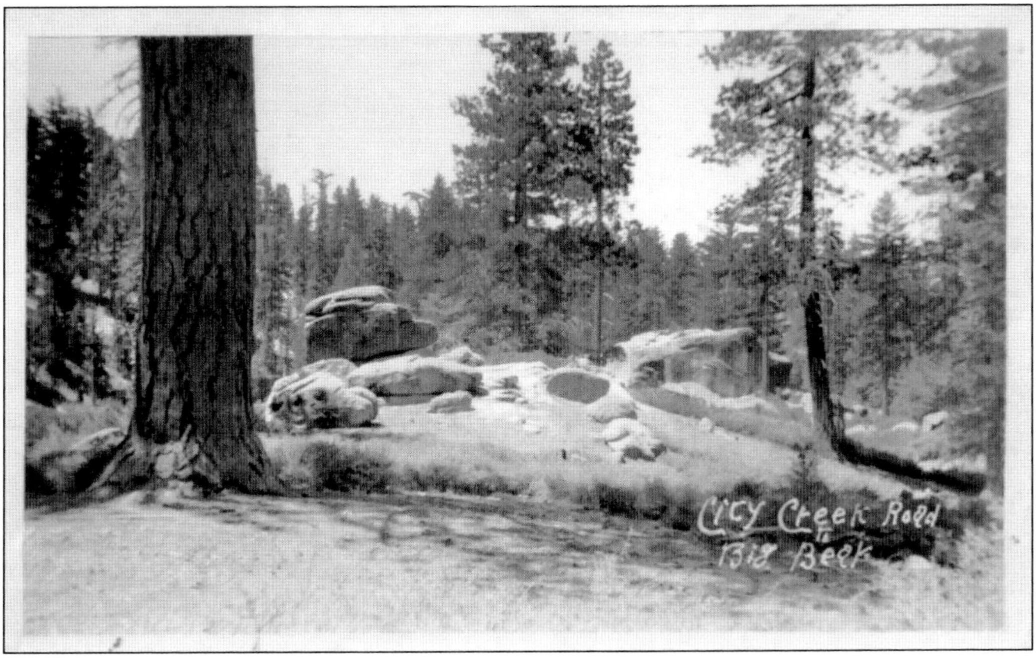

SUCH CURVES! Sent to Holly, Michigan, from Fawnskin, this August 1927 postcard reads, "Dears: We came up here yesterday. It is a glorious place. The pine trees are very 'smelly.' The ascent was very steep in places. We were climbing in low for 32 miles and such curves! Barbara." Even today, the Rim of the World Drive is a spectacularly curvy road.

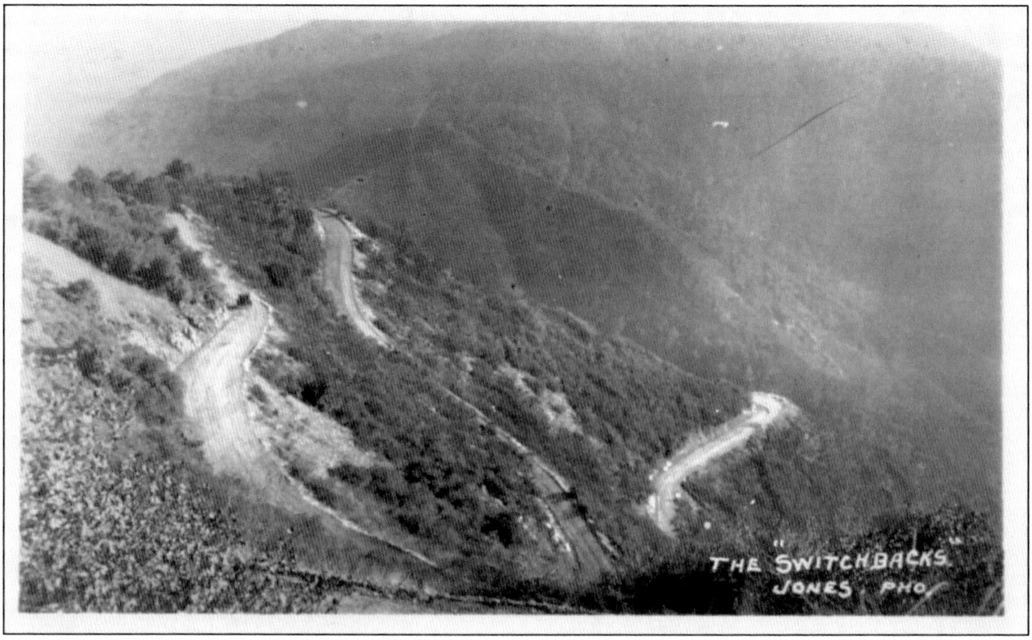

A "FIERCE" AUTOMOBILE RIDE. This writer says, "George said send this to you and ask if you remember coming down. Wasn't it fierce? I love to look at the picture though—Mums. P.S. Did we not have a good time that day." This 1928 postcard was sent to Minnesota. Once again, the switchbacks on the Rim of the World Drive inspired profound and lasting memories. (JP.)

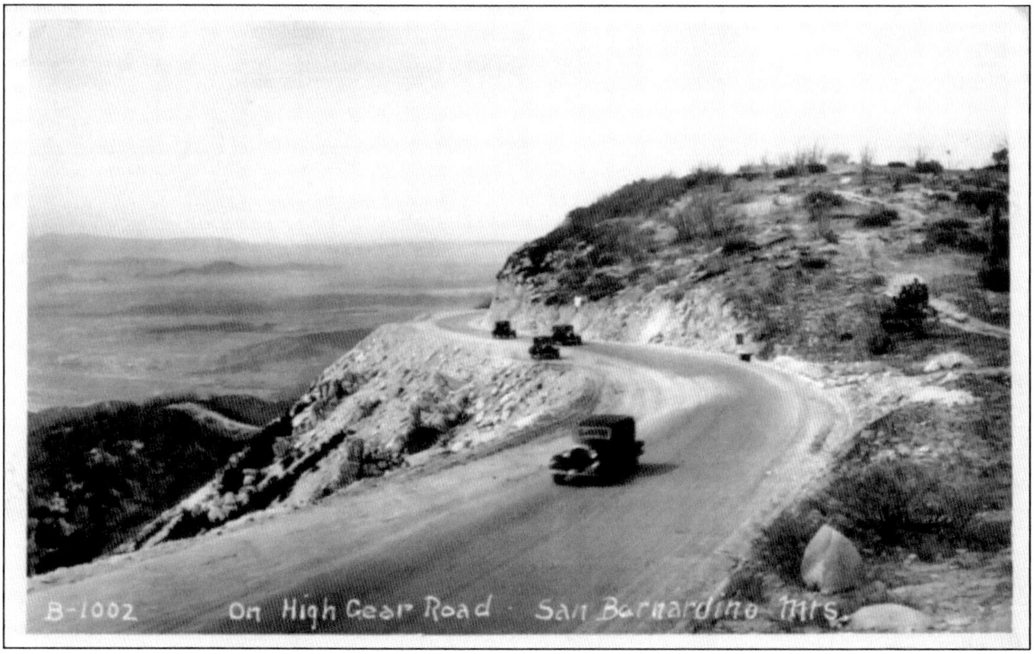

BIG DAY OUT. This visitor notes, "Thursday—We made a trip to the S. B. Mts. today past Big Bear Lake down into the Mojave desert to Victorville and over the Cajon Pass back to Riverside. Love Dad and Mother." Postmarked April 25, 1935, this card was written shortly after the new high-gear road was completed. The message underscores the speed and convenience of the new road.

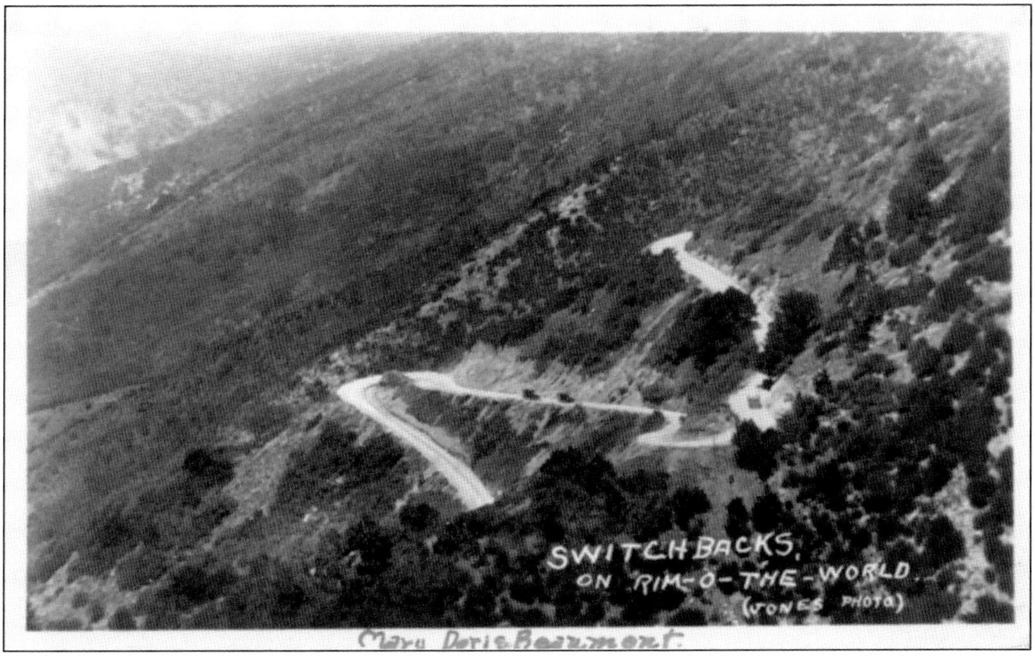

A Big Fan of the Road. "Dear Virginia, Here is a card showing the road we have to come up to get to our cabin. Some road. What a thrill it is to go up and down on it. Doris," reads the back of this card. The June 1935 postcard makes it abundantly clear how the newly opened Rim of the World Drive high-gear road made the drive a thrill rather than a terror. (JP.)

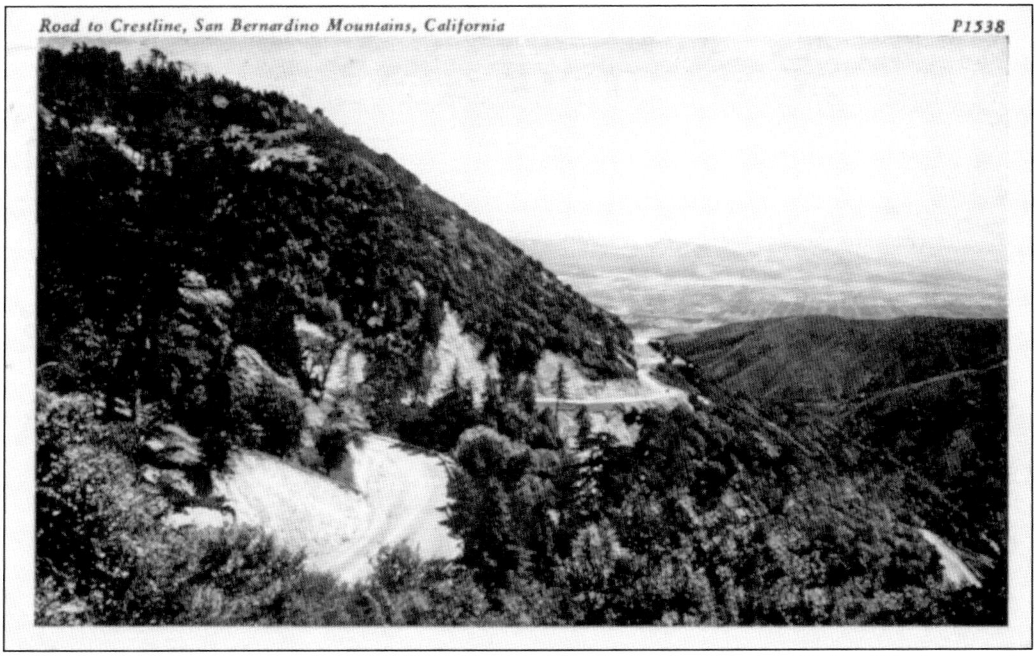

It's Surely Beautiful. A 1938 message sent to Illinois reads, "Dearest Folks: We drove right up this road going up to Crest-Line in the Mts. It's surely beautiful, and only a 15 mile drive from San Bernardino. We're down here spending the weekend. Love, Louise & Art." By 1938, a drive up the high-gear road to Crestline was only a quick side trip. (R.)

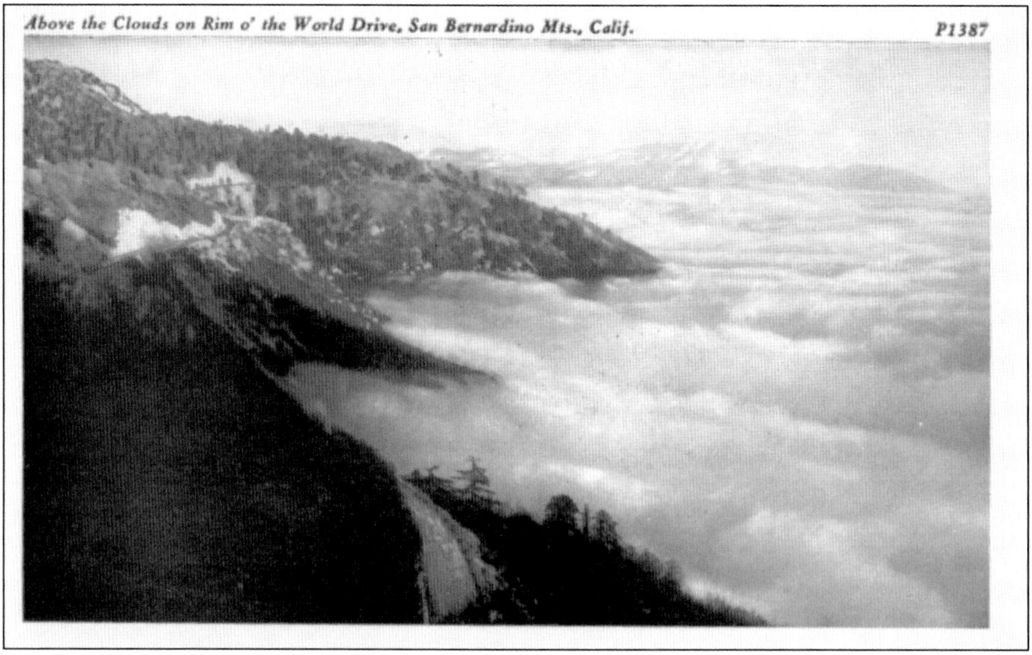

WAY UP IN THE CLOUDS. "Isn't this a beautiful drive way up in the clouds—I am glad though, I wasn't in the driver's seat. M." Dated June 12, 1939, and sent from Cedar Glen to Chicago, this message proves that despite fog-related dangers and fears, the beauty of the Rim of the World Drive could be overwhelming. (R.)

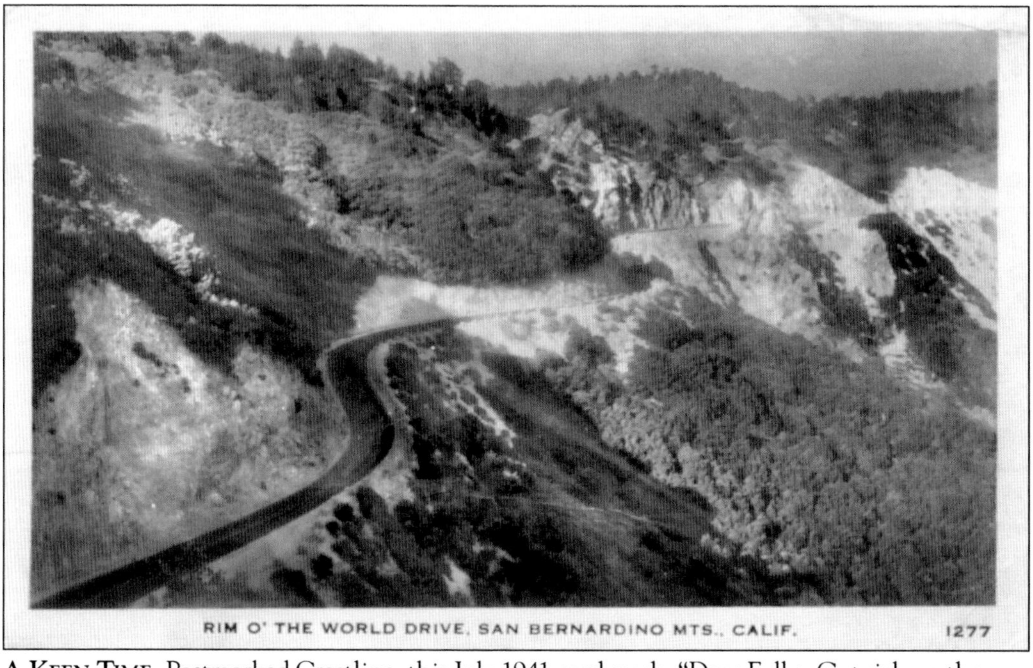

A KEEN TIME. Postmarked Crestline, this July 1941 card reads, "Dear Folks, Got sick on the way up the hill. Don't worry, camp counselors weren't mad about the bus. Said it happens a lot. Am having a keen time. Love Clint." It has always taken a fair amount of intestinal fortitude to go up, down, and along the crest of the Rim of the World Drive. (R.)

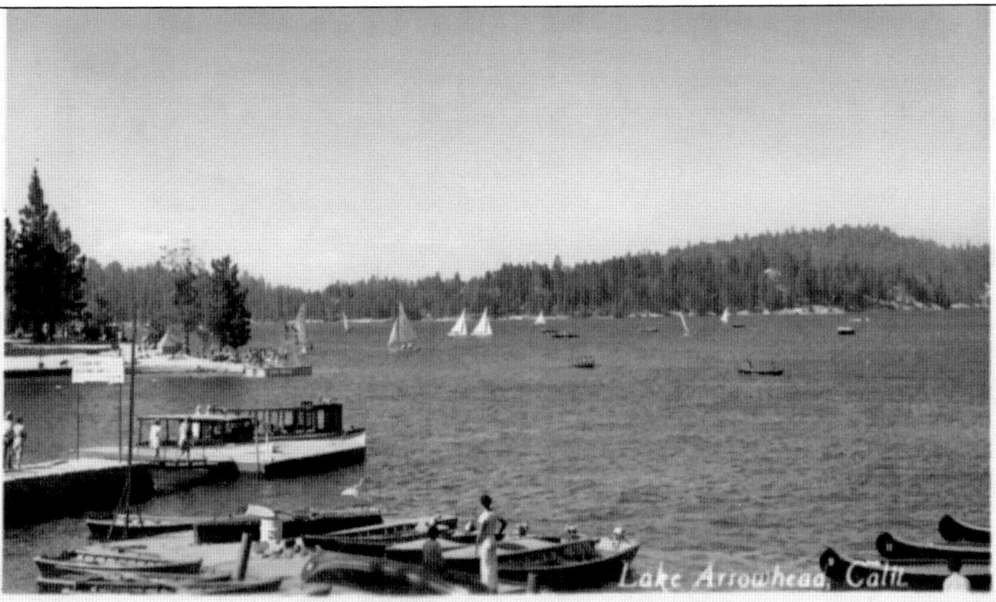

"HELLOWSKI" FROM LAKE ARROWHEAD. "What a time we are having. Good to be spending time with friends. Worth the trouble to get here," writes "Ethan." Whether the writer of this August 1943 postcard was referring to the actual road trip on the Rim of the World Drive, the wartime rationing of gasoline, or some other trouble, he was clearly glad to be spending some time with friends.

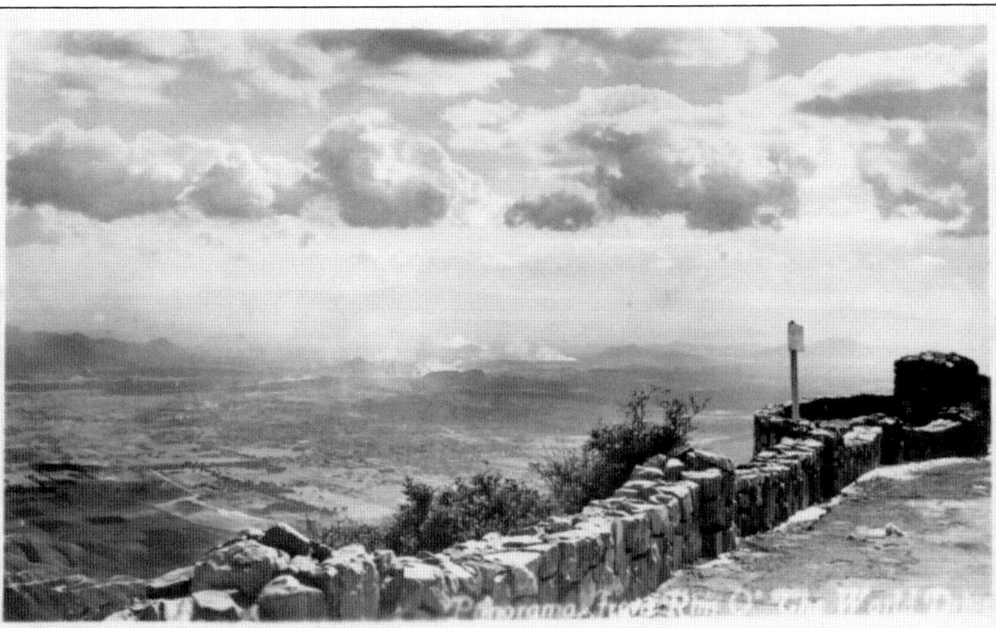

ON TOP OF THE WORLD. Sent from Lake Arrowhead to Chicago on September 20, 1946, this card reads, "Dear Al & Arlene—Up here on top of the world. Surely beautiful—like fairyland. A lovely day & beautiful drive. Love, Marie & Paul." Postwar Americans were already flocking to the San Bernardino Mountains on the Rim of the World Drive, beginning a veritable golden age of tourism.

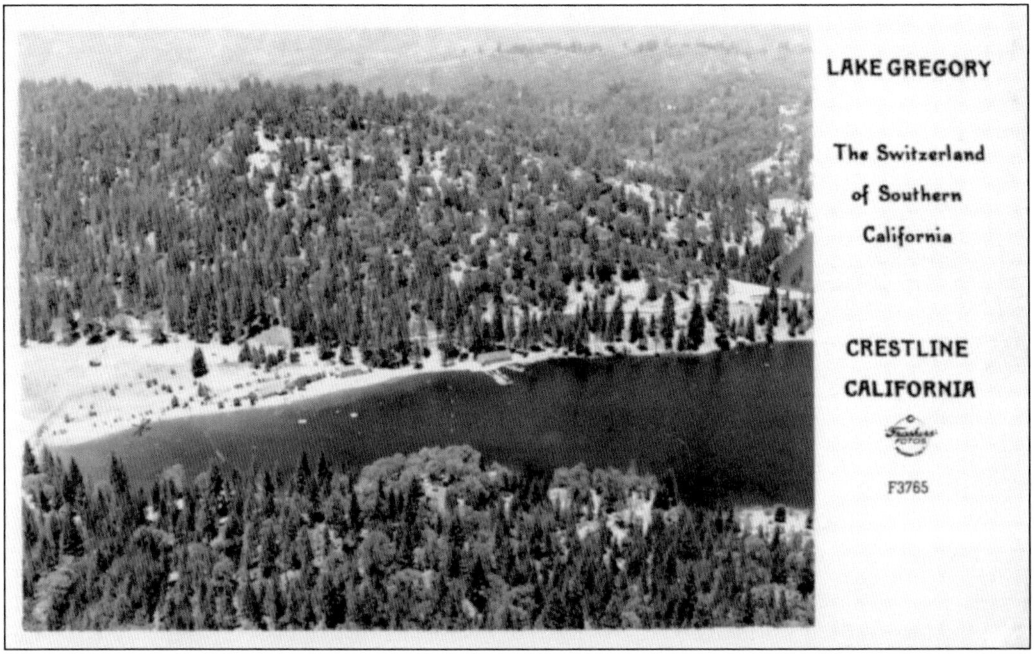

A Two-Hour Trip from Burbank. Dated June 27, 1949, this postcard reads: "Dear Mom: We've had a wonderful day here at Crestline. Left at 10:30, it's 76 miles—a 2 hour trip at least. Have met some swell kids. Love Rob." By 1949, it only took two hours to get to Crestline from Burbank. Compare this to a full day's trip by wagon from San Bernardino in 1908. (FI.)

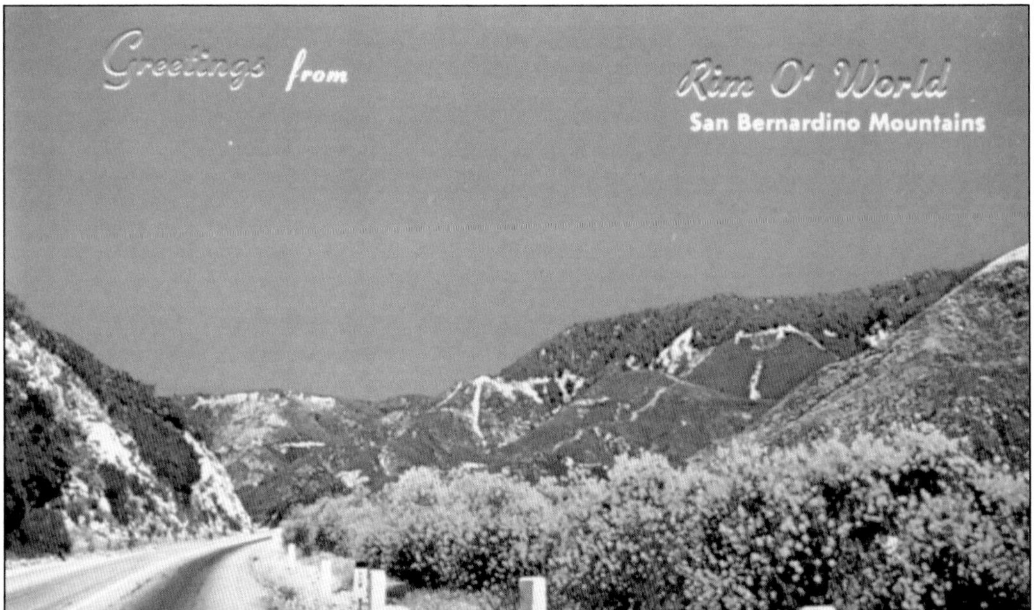

Run-in with Deer. Daisy writes to Mille on June 12, 1966: "We are here again. We almost had a wreck near the top of the road. A deer jumped up the canyon right into the front of the car and knocked us across the road. Love Daisy." Deer can still be seen today dashing across sections of the Rim of the World Drive. (WRP.)

SELECT BIBLIOGRAPHY

Beattie, George and Helen. *Heritage of the Valley*. Oakland, CA: Biobooks, 1951.

Core, Tom. *Big Bear, The First 100 Years*. Big Bear City, CA: Tom Core Trust, 2002.

Garrett, Lewis. *Place Names of the San Bernardino Mountains*. Big Bear City, CA: Big Bear Valley Historical Society, 1998.

Hatheway, Roger and Russell Keller. "Mountain Mileposts" column. *Mountain News* and *Crestline-Courier News*, 1993 to present.

Ingersoll, Luther A. *Century Annals of San Bernardino County, 1769–1904*. Los Angeles, CA: self-published, 1904.

LaFuze, Pauliena. *Saga of the San Bernardinos*. 2 vols. Colton, CA: San Bernardino County Museum, 1971.

Rider, Fremont. *Rider's California*. New York: Macmillan Company, 1925.

Robinson, John W. *The San Bernardinos*. Arcadia, CA: Santa Anita Historical Society, 1989.

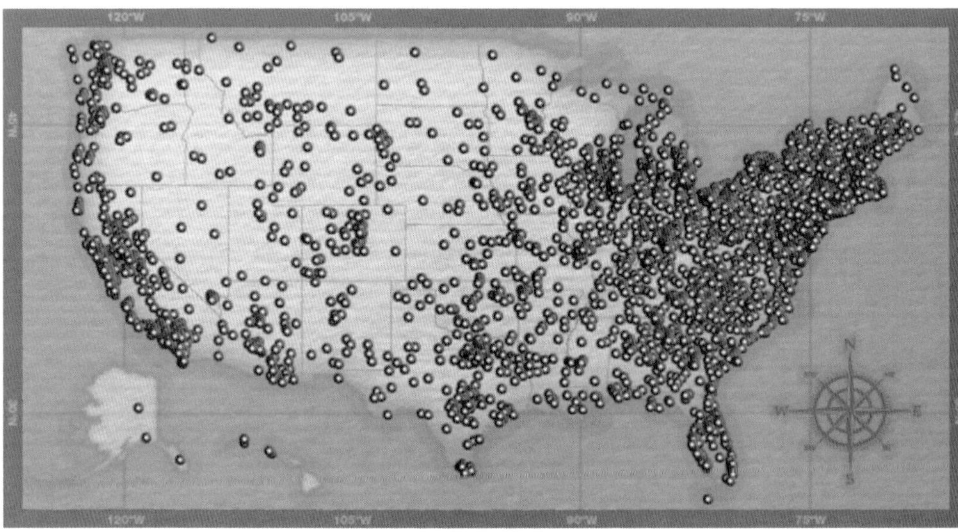

Consistent with our mission to preserve history on a local level, this book was printed in South Carolina on American-made paper and manufactured entirely in the United States. Products carrying the accredited Forest Stewardship Council (FSC) label are printed on 100 percent FSC-certified paper.

MADE IN THE USA